Contents

KT-484-187

Introduction

How to use this book

Each unit in this book contains information, investigations or practical research, suggestions for a child observation task and a list of questions. The use of **bold** (darker print) helps you build up a vocabulary of child development words.

1 Information

This explains the background topic and the facts you need to **research** (fact-find) in order to complete the unit.

2 Research

This is in the form of different investigations:

Type A sets out an **hypothesis** (an informed guess) about how children develop for you to **analyse**. The research task helps you with the analysis. From the evidence of your findings, you can **evaluate** the hypothesis and **draw conclusions** about it. In some cases, you are then asked to test your conclusions by child observation.

Type B extends the information in the unit. The research task asks you to **identify** the **needs** of children and the **resources** available to meet those needs. This involves you in **decision-making** and **problem-solving**.

Type C is a **shared activity** when more information is sought than you can get from observing one child. Your findings are **pooled** in class so that students observing a different age-group can build on their knowledge. Sensitive issues may be '**brainstormed**' first to widen your understanding of the behaviours involved.

3 Child observation

You are asked to **record** one or more **facts** about the child or children you are studying. These records can be collected together and the facts sought when you meet the child. Note the word 'facts'. Human behaviour is highly complex. There is no one 'right' way to raise a child. Parents and children are entitled to their full and total privacy. The same is true for nursery staff, playgroup leaders and other professionals working in child care. The **behaviours** to identify, analyse and draw conclusions about are **those you are asked to record**. N*ever* make guesses or give your opinion about the child (or background) you observe.

4 Questions

The first questions are usually the easiest. Work down the list as far as you can. At the end, there may be another investigation. Help on where to find the information is in the **Resources List** at the end of the book.

A practical assignment

Many of the research tasks can be the basis for your coursework. For example, the investigations on play can lead to a decision to make a toy. Whatever project you choose, follow the spider-web plan.

YOUR SPIDER-WEB PLAN

Investigate
different kinds of toys and the different age groups they relate to

Analyse
the results of your investigation and draw up lists of different toys

Assignment
DESIGN OF NEW TOY

Survey
interview people to check the usefulness of your analysis

Conclusion
write a broad outline of your assignment, describing briefly what you have done at each stage

Execution of project
plan, design and draw an idea of the toy; make a mock-up of the toy

EXAMINING
Child
D   t

D   N

Heinemann Educational Publishers
Halley Court, Jordan Hill, Oxford OX2 8EJ
A Division of Reed Educational & Professional
Publishing Ltd

OXFORD MELBOURNE AUCKLAND
JOHANNESBURG BLANTYRE GABORONE
IBADAN PORTSMOUTH (NH) USA CHICAGO

© Dorothy Baldwin, 1996

First published 1996

04 03 02 01
10 9 8 7 6

British Library Cataloguing in Publication Data

A catalogue record for this book is available from the
British Library

ISBN 0 435 42059 3

Designed and produced by Gecko Ltd, Bicester, Oxon
Illustrated by Mike Bell, Gill Hunt, Martin Sanders and
Gecko Ltd
Printed and bound in Spain by Mateu Cromo

Acknowledgements

The publishers would like to thank the following for the
use of copyright material.
British Standards Institute for the symbol on p. 30;
Central Statistical Office, the Department of Health and
the Department of Social Securiy for statistics used
throughout; Oxfordshire County Council for the council
tax information on p. 136.

The publishers would like to thank the following for
permission to use photographs:
Animal Photography p. 120; Rod Ashford/Ace Photo
Agency p. 142; Yves Baulieu/Publiphoto Diffusion/
Science Photo Library p. 181; Biophoto
Associates/Science Photo Library p. 73 (right); BSIP
Laurent/Science Photo Library p. 182; Mark
Chapke/Science Photo Library p. 106; Patricia Christie
pp. 124 (top), 130; Lupe Cunha pp. 7, 12, 24, 38, 70,
74, 75, 76, 81, 87, 177, 180, 186 (top); Pauline Cutler/
Bubbles p. 138; Sue Ford p. 117; Simon Fraser, Hexham
General/Science Photo Library p. 54; Peter Gould p.
161; Sally and Richard Greenhill pp. 6, 13 (left), 14
(bottom), 23, 43, 47, 48, 50, 52, 55, 56, 57, 59, 94
(both), 100, 107, 109, 114 (top), 115, 119, 123, 126,
131, 133, 148, 155, 178, 185, 186 (bottom); Robert
Harding Picture Library p. 143; Alan Hart Davis p. 173
(right); Mark Henley/Impact Pictures p.124 (bottom);
Pam Isherwood/Format p. 170 (left); Sandra Lousada/
Collections p. 29; Peter Menzel/Science Photo Library p.
17; Rex Morton/Bubbles p. 89; Mugshots/Ace Photo
Agency p. 125; Gary Parker/Science Photo Library p. 173
(left); Popperfoto p. 80; Betty Press/Panos Pictures
p. 146; Chris Priest/Mark Clarke/Science Photo Library
p. 183; Tim Rooke/Rex Features p. 169; Science Photo
Library pp. 13 (right), 108, 156, 172; Dr Gary
Settles/Science Photo Library p. 102; Shelter p. 140;
Anthea Sieveking/Collections pp. 14 (top), 22, 37, 39,
73 (left), 98, 114 (bottom), 121, 122, 127, 184, 189;
Sipa/Rex Features pp. 15, 170 (right); Loisjoy
Thurston/Bubbles p. 179; Alexandra Tstarus/Science
Photo Library p. 42; J. Woodcock/Bubbles p. 151.

The publishers would also like to thank the following:
Silvercross Ltd for the photograph of a pram on p. 33
(top); Mothercare for the photograph of a buggy on p. 33
(bottom); the National Deaf Children's Society for their
kind permission to use the photograph on p. 96; Martha
Christie and Zoe Jordan for the drawings on p. 83.

The cartoons on pp. 166 and 167 are based on
illustrations in a leaflet published by the Health
Education Authority, 1992.

The publishers would like to thank Sally and Richard
Greenhill for permission to reproduce the cover
photograph.

The publishers have made every effort to trace
copyright holders. However, if any material has been
incorrectly acknowledged, we would be pleased to
correct this at the earliest opportunity.

Stages to work through

A Assignment:
design a toy for a child of a particular age

B Investigation:
find out all the different kinds of toys and the different age groups they relate to

C Analysis:
- list toys according to age group
- list toys according to purpose
- list toys according to developmental stage
- list toys according to educational factors
- list toys according to materials they are made of

* Short-list several kinds of toys you might consider developing for the child, which relate to its age, skills and interests.

D Survey:
visit several friends, neighbours and playgroups and ask them (i) what toys their children have (ii) why they chose those toys (iii) any special toys they favour for their children (iv) their opinion of the toys you have short-listed to develop

* Check the results of your survey against your analysis.

E Execution of the project:
- **a** Select one of the short-listed toys in the light of the survey and your knowledge of the particular child.
- **b** Prepare a design of your own, using the short-listed toy as a guide.
- **c** Give your reasons for choosing this particular design and for developing it.
- **d** Draw the design of your new toy.
- **e** Test the design to see if it works and by asking the teacher to evaluate it.
- **f** Make a model of the toy.

F Conclusion:
write a broad outline of each stage you have gone through (A, B, C, D and E)

Notes for your coursework

1 Give the child's age and stage of development. Identify the child's needs. Decide how to record your findings: photographs, writings, maps, sketches, drawings, flow charts, tape and video recordings. Write about each decision you make and any changes or adaptations to your task as you go along, giving the reasons why.

2 Factors to consider include: the frustration of certain toys; their aesthetic appeal, is the design attractive? is it durable, tough, hardwearing? is it versatile, with a number of uses? does it have multi-cultural appeal? has it a gender-bias? is it safe, easy to clean and maintain? is it value for money? what play and storage space does it require?

3 Describe the limitations on your choice: time, money, skills, resources, facilities to use, outside help you can seek. Visit a toy shop, toy library and playgroup to look at the range of toys. Send for toy catalogues from manufacturers such as GALT and Early Learning Centre. Write how these factors affect your choice. Check through the investigations in Section 5 which deal with toys.

4 Produce a clear design, which can be a drawing, plan or model. Select the materials, tools and the equipment you need. Cost the design, and compare it with a manufactured item. Set your budget. List the tasks involved, order of work and set your deadlines. Think of ways you may be able to extend or add to the toy as the child develops. Make any patterns necessary.

The spider-web plan can be adapted to whatever project you choose. It may not seem clear to you now but it will become so as you work through your first investigations.

Information for your research

The Resources List at the end of the book is for outside help with your research. It contains suggestions for speakers, videos, leaflets, and so on. Tracking down free information is a skill in itself. *Apply to your local agencies first.* If you send for information by post: **a** give the name of the leaflet and **b** enclose a stamped and self-addressed envelope. If more than one student seeks the same information, send one request.

A child's needs

All humans have needs. Some are for basic survival: air, food and water. Others improve the quality of life: clean air, fresh food and unpolluted water.

Physical needs concern the health of the body: clothing, housing, heating, hygiene, nutrition, sleep, exercise.

Intellectual needs concern the growth of the mind: information, recreation, entertainment, stimulation.

Emotional needs concern the balance of the feelings: love, fear; satisfaction, frustration; pleasure, pain.

Social needs include community help, consumer concerns, safety and protection, family and home management.

Each one of these four needs *depends* upon the other ones. For example, a hungry baby is too upset to learn about its world. It cries for food and cannot calm down until the pain of hunger is removed. A well-fed baby is relaxed and keen to learn.

A **resource** is any person or thing which meets a need. Babies lack the resources to meet their own needs. They can breathe but they cannot get their own food and water. Parents are the first resource to meet a baby's needs. Other **carers** include the family, friends, nursery nurses, midwives, health visitors, doctors, playgroup leaders, social workers, teachers.

At a wider level, governments, international charities and world organizations are a further resource. Babies and children have special needs which adults do not have. One way to identify these needs is to study the rights of children.

On 20 November 1959, the United Nations (UN) declared that each child has rights to:
- a name and nationality
- love, understanding and protection
- adequate nutrition, housing and medical services
- education, play and recreation
- special care, if handicapped
- develop physically and mentally in a healthy manner
- protection against neglect, cruelty and exploitation
- be among the first to receive relief in times of disaster
- equality of race, colour, sex, religion, national or social origin
- be brought up in a spirit of tolerance, peace and universal brotherhood.

A **priority** is any person or thing with a first claim on your resources. The UN declaration places the well-being of children as a priority in times of disaster. But when a baby is hungry or cold this feels like disaster! Parents might say that the needs of their baby have first priority on their resources.

Identity

A name and nationality help babies develop a sense of **identity**. At birth, they have no idea who they are nor where they are. Identity tags are clipped around their wrists and ankles during their stay in the maternity ward. The kind of identity a baby develops is extremely important.

Babies have **family** names: Smith, Patel, O'Connor. In general, the baby takes the name of the father's family. First names are **given** names and parents can choose one or many for their baby. Given names can be from either side of the family. Some are **gender-specific**, given to one gender only. Fiona and James are gender-specific names. They help a baby develop a sense of her or his gender identity.

It is not always easy to choose a given name for a baby that will be acceptable to an older child. 'I wish you'd called me something else', children

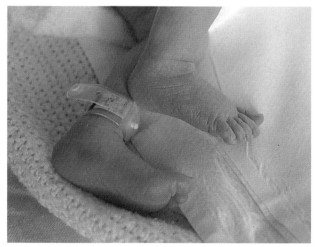

■ The new baby's identity tag

may say, and make up a new name for a while. Given names go in and out of fashion. Newspapers list the most popular ones each year. Books of given names can help parents in their choice.

The health of Britain's children

The health of our children has improved greatly in the last 20 years. They are taller, heavier and suffer fewer infectious diseases. But there are signs that they are less happy. Though the *physical* health of children has improved, their emotional, intellectual and social skills have not.

A **self-image** is the picture you build in your mind of what you are like and how you think other people see you. A self-image is **positive** when you feel 'good' about yourself. It is **negative** when you feel 'bad' about yourself. These feelings can change as you grow and when you gain new experiences in life.

Babies cannot build their own self-image. They are not aware of other people as separate from themselves. As they grow, they develop a positive or negative self-image from the people around them: parents, other family members and carers, school friends and the community. Children who develop a positive self-image learn to value themselves. We say their **self-esteem** is high. Children with a negative self-image learn to devalue themselves. They feel worthless and unhappy. They have low self-esteem.

■ Choose a name for this baby, with reasons for your choice

The importance of helping babies develop a positive self-image is one of the aims of the Children Act (1989). The Act considers the emotional needs of children, including respect for their feelings. Children whose feelings are respected usually develop a positive self-image. They value themselves and they value their ability to learn and make friends.

— Child observation

Record the given names of the child you are studying. Write the age in years and months e.g. 3 years and 7 months. When making observations, remember to record the age of the child at that particular stage.

— Questions

1 What are the four areas of human needs? Explain why you might be less keen to learn when you feel
   a hungry
   b bored
   c cross.

2 List your favourite given names. Which gender is more likely to be named after
   a flowers
   b jewels
   c months of the year?
   Why is it more usual for American than British boys to be given names like Prince, Earl, Duke, Lord?

3 What is meant by a priority? Suggest two reasons why parents might say their baby has first priority on their resources.

4 Suggest, with reasons, one other group of people to be given priority in times of disaster.

5 The words identity, self-image and self-esteem mean nearly the same things. Complete the following sentences to help you separate their meanings. My self-image is the picture ... A child with low self-esteem feels ... My gender-identity is ...

6 Copy the rights of children into your folder. State which of these rights you might be most interested in, and why.

THE DAILY POST

Situations Vacant: Responsible adults sought for a 20-year project. No previous experience required but candidates need a knowledge of human growth and development. Also nutrition, textiles, heating, housing, hygiene, home management, budgeting choices, consumer issues, state welfare benefits, medical and educational systems.

Personal qualities: high motivation, sense of humour, energy, patience, compassion, ability to act without supervision. Hours of work vary and can be up to 24 hours daily, including weekends. Salary nil, but rewarding post for the right candidate.

Child-care tasks

The table below shows a record of the time spent on child-care tasks by a small group of families with young children. **Factors** such as the distance between home, playgroups and shops, and the use of public or private transport, were not included in the study. But the findings are interesting as an *average* of the time parents spend in child-care tasks during 24 hours.

Seven-eighths of the time was given by mothers. Two-thirds of the mothers said that, in one week, they had no spare time lasting one hour or more which was free of child-care responsibilities. Nine-tenths said child care was tiring. Many added that it was harder work than being economically active (in a paid job).

Busy mothers may need more human resources, more help from family members or other carers. They may need more material resources: more food for more energy, more money to buy a washing machine for more free time, and so on. The needs of parents vary.

Average time in minutes spent on child-care tasks during 24 hours	
Task	Time in minutes
Waking up and getting dressed	38
Nappy changes and/or toilet	40
Escorting to and from playgroup	35
Special shopping needs	29
Food preparation and feeding	119
Washing, bathtime	43
Preparing for bed	38
Special laundry needs	34
Tidying up and clearing toys	48

Aesthetic needs

'What is life if, full of care,
We have no time to stand and stare.'

W H Davies

Music appeals directly to the human spirit. It tugs at the heart. It stirs the emotions and can move people to tears of longing or delight. This is our **aesthetic** sense, the ability to appreciate beauty in all its forms, not just music.

Beauty can be found anywhere, from the wider appeal of nature to the homely appeal of delicious tastes, sweet smells, clean clothes, warm rooms. These homely appeals add to the **quality of life**. They enrich the human spirit, bringing joy, pleasure, comfort, peace.

■ Choose which of these kitchens you find more appealing, giving reasons for your choice

To be *effective*, a home requires planning, good organization and attention to detail. A **prototype** is a model or 'mock-up' to test out an idea before making the real thing. If the test involves practical work, the task is often named a 'dry run'.

Child observation

It may be possible to identify the time spent in preparing or feeding the child at home or a playgroup.

Investigation

Check your planning and organization skills.

a Identify the resources required to produce a cup of tea.

b Record or collect the resources.

c Do a practice 'dry run' to check your list.

d You may wish to show your practical skills and aesthetic sense by making and serving the tea.

e Evaluate your skills, identifying any areas which could be improved and describe how you would make these improvements.

Questions

1 From the information in the table opposite, state
  a the total time for child-care tasks in 24 hours
  b the time left for the carer
  c other likely demands on this time.

2 How much time is used for meeting
  a the nutritional needs of children
  b their special laundry needs
  c tidying after them?

3 Which did the busy mothers find more tiring, paid or non-paid employment? Try to think of some reasons for your answer.

4 Explain, with two examples of your own, what you understand by the words 'quality of life'.

5 What personal qualities does a parent need? List them in order of priority, putting the ones you think are most important first.

6 Think about the working conditions of parents: hours, salary, range of tasks. How do these fit in with their aesthetic needs?

7 Jane and Peter like fresh flowers in their home, but they cannot afford them with the new baby. Suggest one item they can buy or make which will last longer than cut flowers. You can extend your answer by researching options from a home-decorating magazine.

Family needs

The **family** is a social group of parents and children. It provides **care** and **support** for its members and meets the **intimacy** needs of the group. Intimacy is a close loving relationship with at least one other person, a sense of belonging, identity and warmth.

Most people belong to at least two families in their life: the one they are born into, and the one they create when they have children of their own. Children are **dependant** people under age sixteen, or age sixteen to eighteen and in full-time education. The family group includes children who are **fostered** and **adopted**.

A **spouse** is a married partner.

A **cohabitee** is an unmarried partner.

A **lone parent** may be divorced, widowed or never-married.

A **sibling** is a person's sister or brother; they have the same parents.

A **half-sibling** is a sibling of one parent in the family.

A **step**-family can be **half-** or **step**-parents and siblings.

A **nuclear** family is two parents and one or more of their children sharing a home.

An **extended** family includes all the **kin** who may live together or in separate homes.

In the 17th century, when many women died in childbirth, it was normal for children to be raised in blended families. Remarriage for the third or fourth time was not unusual. Children had step-parents and half-siblings and grandparents, some of whom they hardly knew. Today, families are becoming more like those in the 17th century. This is partly the result of the trend towards more divorce and remarriage.

Although in the UK only 40 per cent of families are nuclear, more people live in them than in other types (1992, the latest **data**). The trend is towards more lone parents. Of all families with dependant children, 17 per cent are headed by a lone mother and 1 per cent by a lone father. In 1995, there were 1.2 million lone parent families with 3.3 million dependant children.

Needs outside the home

Family life happens in step-by-step stages: the infant, the child, the teenager, the parent, the grandparent. Each family member takes turn at being dependent and **independent**.

People are independent when they can meet their own needs. Yet everyone has needs outside the home. For example, parents cannot stop other people from polluting the child's air, food or water. Just as babies depend upon parents to meet their needs, so parents depend upon government to control the **pollution** of the **environment**. In turn, government depends upon the finances of parents to pay for the **public health services**. We say that the needs of parents and government are **interdependent**, each depends upon the other to meet a wide range of needs.

━ Child observation ━

Record the number of siblings of the child you are studying.

■ Family life happens in step-by-step stages: the infant, the child, the teenager, the parent, the grandparent

Investigation

Investigate different ways to present information (data).

Some students did a class survey to collect data on the number of their grandparents still living. They asked how many had:

A no grandparents

B one grandparent

C two grandparents

D three grandparents (include step-grandparents)

E four or more grandparents

F don't know?

There were 30 students in the class. The answers they gave were:

C	F	D	D	E	B
E	A	E	A	B	C
D	D	C	E	A	D
D	C	D	E	D	E
E	D	E	D	C	D

They presented their findings as follows:

Number of grandparents	A	B	C	D	E	F
Number of students	3	2	?	?	?	?

Copy and complete this table.

They could have presented their findings as follows:

3 students have no grandparents still living

2 students have ? grandparent still living

? students have ? grandparents still living

Copy and complete this table.

Which of the above two methods for presenting data would you choose? Why?

The same data can be presented as a **pie chart** and a **bar chart** (histogram). They would look like this:

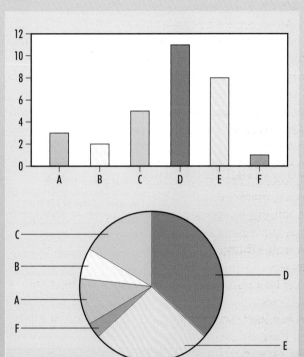

Do a survey of your class on the numbers of grandparents still living. The increase in divorce and re-marriage means that family members can lose touch. There are always 'don't knows' in surveys. When doing any survey, avoid pressing for answers from the 'don't knows'. Be sensitive. Be polite. Avoid wasting people's time.

Present the class data you have collected in two different ways.

Questions

1 At which stages in life do you think people are
   a the most dependent
   b provide the most support?

2 People now live much longer than in the 17th century, and many families have great grandparents still living. Test your skills at presenting data by doing a class survey of great grandparents.

3 Consider a situation where the air in a street is heavily polluted by exhaust fumes from traffic. Which government department controls this?

4 'Partners are sometimes called **mutual dependants**.' What does this statement mean?

5 To some extent, everyone is dependent. Discuss.

11

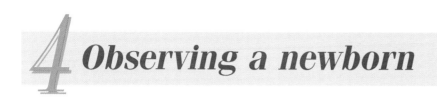

To **observe** is to pay special attention to a person or thing. It is much more than the usual quick glance, or the sound which is only half-heard and vaguely remembered. When you observe you watch closely, listen carefully, gather information from all your senses and then come to some conclusions.

Experts in child development observe newborns closely. They:

- **identify** new information
- **analyse** (examine, work out) the reasons for it
- draw **conclusions** (theories) from their analysis
- **record** their conclusions and test them out.

Observing baby shape

The head of a newborn is large compared to its body size. The abdomen (stomach area) appears swollen. The legs are short. Most babies have sweetly plump cheeks and a general roundness to their body. The observers learned that the chubby look of babies is due to a layer of fat under the skin. They concluded that this helps a baby in the first days of life when it does not take much milk.

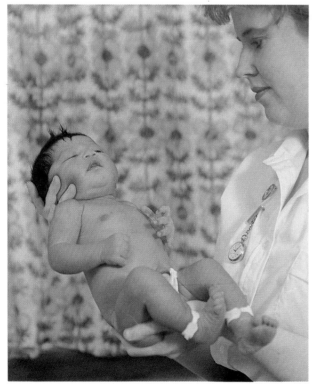

■ A chubby newborn

Observing baby appearance

A newborn has spent nine months surrounded by water. Its skin may be wrinkled or covered with **vernix**, a whitish cream which acts as a protective body oil. Some babies have thick dark hair which falls out in the first weeks. The new hair which grows may be lighter in colour and thinner in texture. The blue eyes of some newborns change colour by about two months old.

When lying on its back, a newborn's head rolls to one side. Babies like to look at their world and cannot see much from one side. The observers concluded that (i) newborns cannot hold their head upright (ii) they need firm support for their neck when they are picked up. (Of course we can tell this just by picking up a baby. But that would hurt the infant and make it feel very insecure.)

At birth, the brain and nervous system are undeveloped. In the first three months of life, infants have almost no control over their movements. They gaze at their world with solemn eyes, but only for short periods of time. They shiver, yawn, blink, sneeze, stretch and wave their arms and legs. But these are jerky movements, and not under their control. Human babies have a much longer period of **helplessness** than any other animal.

Observing baby size

The baby's measurements are taken soon after birth and used as a **baseline** to check its future growth.

A **fontanelle** is a soft area on the baby's head where the skull bones have not joined. Sometimes a **pulse** can be seen beating under the skin at the top of the head. This pulse is from the blood supply to the brain. There is no need to worry when washing a baby's head. The delicate brain underneath is protected by tough membranes. The fontanelles close by eighteen months after birth.

Before birth, the baby receives nourishment from its mother through the **umbilical cord**. This cord is cut at birth and the stump is left to dry out, and drops off in seven to ten days.

Birth marks, sometimes called 'stork bites', are blotches of red which soon fade. Dark-skinned

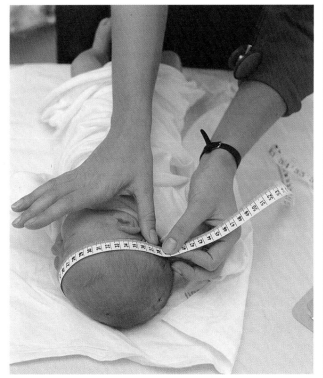

■ The average **head circumference** of a newborn is 35 cm
The average **length** of a newborn is 52 cm
The average **weight** of a newborn is 3.5 kg

■ The weight of this newborn will be recorded on a progress chart

babies can have blue–black blotches. Birth marks, which are larger and form raised patches, tend to fade by school age. If they remain and cause the child embarrassment, many can be removed by new laser technology.

Jaundice is a liver condition which colours the skin and the whites of the eyes yellow. It clears up in a baby's first week.

Recording observations

Parents can worry about any of the above conditions. The fact that they have been observed in hundreds of newborns reassures the parents that all is well. One value of **recording** observations is that human memory is faulty. We may think we remember clearly but studies show just as clearly that this is not always so.

— Child observation

If possible, ask the parents of the child what they remember of the appearance and measurements of the baby. They may keep an album of the child's progress, vaccinations, first tooth, and so on.

— Questions

1 Draw or collect pictures of a newborn and describe its shape.
2 State the average weight and length of a newborn and describe five actions which a baby shows.
3 What is the value of observation? State four ways to develop your powers of child observation.

Parents have a sense of magic and awe at their new baby. They feel as if they have created the most enchanting infant ever! Yet do all parents feel this way? In 1859, Queen Victoria wrote in her diary: 'An ugly baby is a very nasty object. And the prettiest is frightful when undressed – till about 4 months, which is as long as they have their big body and little limbs and that terrible frog-like action.'

A **reflex movement** is an automatic response to meet some need we may not even be aware of. For example, the eyes need to be kept clean and damp. When they are dry, we blink to moisten them without thinking. Blinking also cleans the eyes by sweeping dust into the corners. The eye-blink reflex keeps the eyes clean and damp automatically, without us having to think. A reflex response is a protective movement for healthy survival.

Babies are born with **special reflexes** to meet their survival needs. If the top lip is stroked, the mouth opens automatically. If an object is put in the mouth, sucking begins. If one cheek is patted, the head turns to that side as if searching for food. These are called the **rooting** and **sucking** reflexes. They meet the baby's survival needs for nourishment. At birth, they are tested to check that the baby's sense of touch is working and that its nervous system is developing.

Other reflexes may have been useful at an early stage in human evolution. If the baby's palm is

■ The grasp reflex

stroked, the hand clenches in the **grasp** reflex. This may have been to enable the baby to grasp its mother's fur. If the head is unsupported, the arms are flung wide in the falling reflex. In sudden bright light or loud noise, the head jerks in the startle reflex.

Until three months, a baby's movements are largely spontaneous. By between twelve and fourteen weeks, their special reflexes disappear. Other reflexes such as the eye-blink remain for life. When Queen Victoria wrote of 'that terrible frog-like action' of babies, she may have been describing the falling or startle reflex.

Facts and opinions

Facts are ideas which can be proved correct. **Opinions** are ideas which can be proved correct or incorrect. Part of your child development course is to **analyse** the theories and decide if they are facts or opinions.

Two of the following statements are facts. Two are opinions.
- A baby needs firm support for its head and shoulders.
- A baby needs protection against accidents and ill-health.
- A baby needs a toy telephone to play with.
- A baby needs woollen garments to keep it warm.

Before you decide which is which, consider the lifestyle of the children in the photograph on the opposite page.

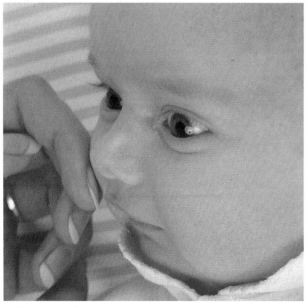

■ The rooting reflex

■ Sufi enjoying a family meal

Lifestyle

A lifestyle is a certain way of organizing the choices in your life. In general, lifestyles are based upon the climate and geography of the area where you live. The history of the peoples and their material resources are also involved in this choice. Sufi would over-heat in woollen garments and become very ill. There is no electricity in the village. Each culture develops its own lifestyle. Winter clothing and toy telephones have no place in Sufi's lifestyle. The needs of babies are related to their lifestyle.

Within each culture, different families develop different lifestyles. For example, Sufi's family chooses foods which are highly-spiced. Mo's family prefers more bland-tasting foods. Both choices of taste are equally valid. One is not 'better' nor 'worse' than the other. Each is an 'opinion' of taste.

▬ *Child observation* ▬

Try to watch a new baby being fed. Record any actions the mother makes to start the infant feeding.

▬ *Questions* ▬

1 Describe two things you can do to start a baby feeding.
2 Draw a diagram of a newborn responding by reflex. Add labels to explain what is happening.
3 Why do newborns have special reflexes?
4 At what age do the special reflexes fade?
5 Which are more helpful to parents, facts or opinions? Why?
6 The needs of babies are related to their lifestyle. Discuss.
7 Find out the number of children Queen Victoria had. Comment on what she wrote in her diary.

6 Growth and development

Growth

Growth is an increase in body size (mass). A baby's measurements are matched against charts which are averaged on thousands of other newborns. At each stage of growth, the increase in height and weight are marked on the infant's chart. In this way, each baby's healthy growth can be **predicted**.

The following figures represent the average human weight from conception to four months after birth.

Age from conception in months	0	1	3	5	9	11	13
Mass in grams	0	100	300	750	3500	5200	7000

Development

If a newborn grew only in size it would become a soft helpless adult. Development is an increase in complexity. It is progress in all human functions; physical, intellectual, emotional and social. Though growth and development are different, they happen together and are checked and recorded together.

Milestones

The stages of growth and development are milestones in a child's life. These milestones have been studied worldwide and recorded. The observers found a remarkable sameness in milestones regardless of where a baby is raised. For example, at eighteen months, the average toddler walks without support.

Infants inherit different **genes** from each parent. Genes carry the instructions for family likeness (characteristics). These include the colour of skin, hair and eyes; the face and body shape; the presence of dimples, freckles or moles; the chance of certain diseases and **life expectancy** (how long a person is expected to live).

But genes are not the whole story. Many other factors affect growth and development. If a baby's progress falls too far below its predicted increase, this is named **failure to thrive**. One reason may be a lack of the **growth hormone**. Other reasons may be **environmental**. One or more factors in the baby's surroundings is not suitable for healthy development.

Failure to thrive is always serious because each new stage of development is built on an earlier stage. Lack of progress at one stage can lead to an **impairment** of the next. A baby who falls well below its predicted rate of growth needs medical attention to identify the cause.

Low birthweight

Low birthweight is 2500 grams or less. A **full-term** baby is one who has spent 40 weeks in the uterus (womb). A **premature** baby is one born before it has completed at least 36 weeks in the uterus. Infants with low birthweight can be premature or they can be full term and have other health problems.

One major problem for low birthweight babies is **respiratory distress**. The lungs have not developed enough to breathe normally. The infant is placed in a heated **incubator** and admitted to the Special Care Baby Unit.

A **ventilator** is a **life support** machine that puffs oxygen-rich air into the lungs. Other machines monitor the baby's heart rate and analyse the blood for the right balance of nutrients. Babies too weak to suck are fed by tube through the nose into the stomach. The food is either the mother's milk or a mixture of special sugars and minerals to build up body weight. Each baby's progress is carefully **monitored** and any therapy needed is provided by skilled nurses.

Babies born up to eight weeks premature have an excellent chance of survival. At twelve weeks premature, they have a 70 per cent chance though this is increasing all the time. Low birthweight babies stay in the incubator until they are strong enough to survive in the outside world. They can usually go home by the time they would have developed to full term.

Personal growth

Each newborn is different, a complete individual. Milestones are **guidelines** of what children can be expected to do at certain ages, not what they must do. A happy child is a healthy child, whether

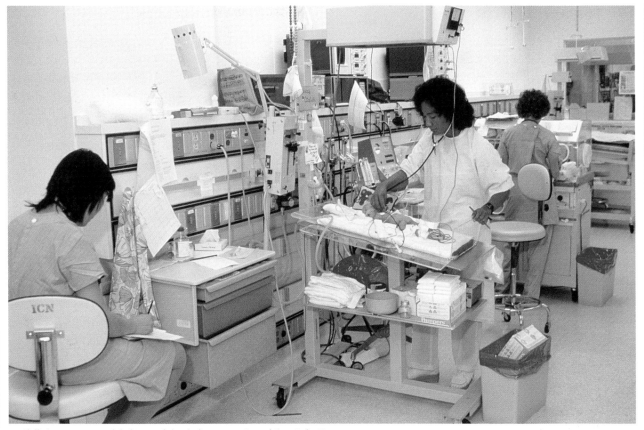

■ Skilled nurses give each baby round the clock care in a Special Care Baby Unit

or not it is slightly above or below its predicted rate of progress. Growth stops in the teens but development continues. Social skills, work skills, parenting skills; these and many other skills have to be learned. Development is a lifelong process. After childhood, it is named **personal growth**.

▬ *Child observation* ▬

Ask the parents what they think the child may have inherited. Do the parents seem pleased about this? If so, what do you think their pleasure suggests?

▬ *Questions* ▬

1 Using the figures on the opposite page
  a give the weight in kilograms of a newborn baby
  b give the weight in kilograms of a four-month-old baby.
2 Give the meanings of
  a full-term
  b premature.
3 Kim's daughter is happy and healthy but slightly below her milestone for height. Explain why Kim need not worry over this.

4 What does failure to thrive mean and why is it always serious?
5 Explain the difference between growth and development.
6 Name the life-support systems for a low birthweight baby.
7 Which statement in the rights of children on page 6 suggests that each baby has a right to healthy growth and development?

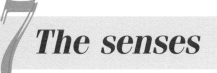

7 The senses

The sensory system

The senses of sight, hearing, smell, taste and touch make up the sensory system. Each sense is working at birth, although some are less well developed than others. As the baby grows, its senses become stronger, clearer and more refined. The sensory system helps the baby survive.

The skin is the organ of touch. It has nerve receptors for pressure, pain and temperature (heat and cold). Newborns are more sensitive to cold than heat, perhaps because they have just left the warm environment of their mother's uterus.

Newborns soon learn the smell of their mother. A two-day-old baby turns its head in the direction of a cloth which holds the smell of her milk.

Newborns screw up their eyes in very bright light. If asleep, the eyelids and lips close more tightly. If the light persists, the head is moved restlessly from side to side, or thrown back from the source of light. Sudden high-pitched sounds upset babies. Soft low voices are more effective at soothing a crying newborn. From these observations, we can conclude that the senses of smell, sight and hearing are working at birth.

The sense of taste

To find out if newborns have a sense of taste, 192 babies between 1 and 4 days old were given drinks of sugared and plain water. The sweeter the water, the more the newborns drank. The study concluded that babies are born with a 'sweet tooth'.

The researchers then analysed the sweetness in human and cow's milk. They concluded that a baby's 'sweet tooth' is inborn. **Pre-natal** means before birth. **Post-natal** means after birth. An ability which is present at birth is **innate** (inborn).

The sugar in human and cow's milk is **lactose**. Lactose has the least sweet taste of all sugars. It is formed from glucose and galactose. The most common sugar is **sucrose**. This is more usually called table sugar. It comes from beet and cane plants and is formed from glucose and fructose. Sucrose is the strongest tasting and sweetest of all dietary sugars.

Child growth surveys

The data shown in the charts above are from the Pre-School Child Growth Surveys by the Department of Human Nutrition of the London School of Hygiene and Tropical Medicine. A total of 12,271 children were measured in four surveys between 1973 and 1982. All measurements were taken within one week of the age point given in the charts.

▬ Child observation ▬

Measure the height, and weight if possible, of the child. Record the measurements and compare them with the average predicted rate. *First*, practise your measuring skills with a partner in class and ask your teacher to evaluate them.

▬ Investigation ▬

Identify the sweet taste in cow's milk.
You will need:
milk, table sugar, teaspoon, glass, water.

a Swirl a sip of milk around your mouth before spitting it out. Record the sweetness on a scale of 1 to 10, 1 being least sweet.

b Swirl a teaspoon of sugared water around your mouth and spit it out. On the 1 to 10 scale, record how much sweeter it tastes.

c Clean your taste buds thoroughly with plain water.

d Swirl a second teaspoon of milk around your mouth. On the same scale, record how much sweeter it now tastes.

e What conclusion can you draw of the sweetness in cows' milk?

f Explain the reason for **c**.

g You can extend your study by testing a variety of fresh fruits and vegetables for sweetness.

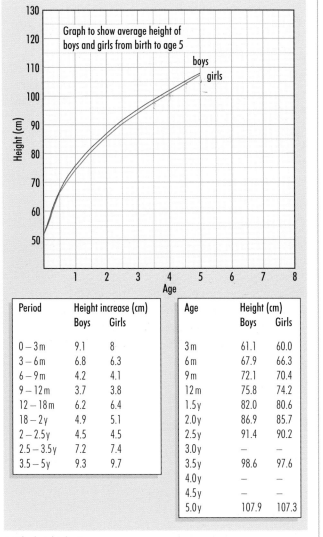

Period	Height increase (cm)		Age	Height (cm)	
	Boys	Girls		Boys	Girls
0 – 3 m	9.1	8	3 m	61.1	60.0
3 – 6 m	6.8	6.3	6 m	67.9	66.3
6 – 9 m	4.2	4.1	9 m	72.1	70.4
9 – 12 m	3.7	3.8	12 m	75.8	74.2
12 – 18 m	6.2	6.4	1.5 y	82.0	80.6
18 – 2 y	4.9	5.1	2.0 y	86.9	85.7
2 – 2.5 y	4.5	4.5	2.5 y	91.4	90.2
2.5 – 3.5 y	7.2	7.4	3.0 y	–	–
3.5 – 5 y	9.3	9.7	3.5 y	98.6	97.6
			4.0 y	–	–
			4.5 y	–	–
			5.0 y	107.9	107.3

■ The height chart

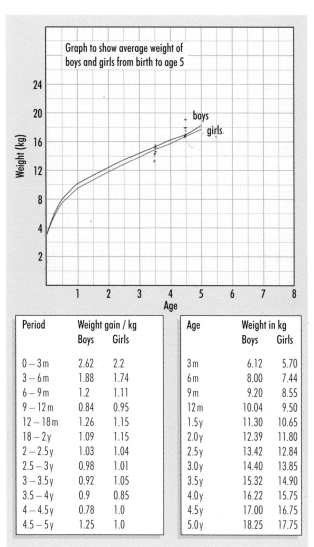

Period	Weight gain / kg		Age	Weight in kg	
	Boys	Girls		Boys	Girls
0 – 3 m	2.62	2.2	3 m	6.12	5.70
3 – 6 m	1.88	1.74	6 m	8.00	7.44
6 – 9 m	1.2	1.11	9 m	9.20	8.55
9 – 12 m	0.84	0.95	12 m	10.04	9.50
12 – 18 m	1.26	1.15	1.5 y	11.30	10.65
18 – 2 y	1.09	1.15	2.0 y	12.39	11.80
2 – 2.5 y	1.03	1.04	2.5 y	13.42	12.84
2.5 – 3 y	0.98	1.01	3.0 y	14.40	13.85
3 – 3.5 y	0.92	1.05	3.5 y	15.32	14.90
3.5 – 4 y	0.9	0.85	4.0 y	16.22	15.75
4 – 4.5 y	0.78	1.0	4.5 y	17.00	16.75
4.5 – 5 y	1.25	1.0	5.0 y	18.25	17.75

■ The weight chart

Questions

1 Name the senses which are working at birth. Refer to page 14 and explain how you know a baby's sense of touch is working at birth.

2 'A baby prefers soft lights and gentle sounds.' Explain, with reasons, whether this statement is a fact or an opinion.

3 Give the meanings of
   a sensory system
   b pre-natal
   c post-natal
   d innate.

4 From the graphs above, which gender is
   a taller
   b heavier?

   'Between the ages eleven and fourteen, most girls are taller and weigh more than most boys.' Suggest ways in which you could test this statement.

5 Name the sugar in human and cow's milk. Is it more or less strong than table sugar?

6 Suggest ways in which each of the five senses can help an older child to survive.

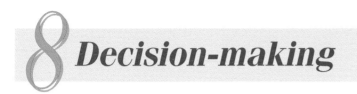

8 Decision-making

Decision-making includes solving problems. During child development, there may not be one 'perfect' way to solve a problem. Each baby and each family are different. Your task in decision-making is to *choose* which solution is most likely to meet a baby's needs.

Choices

'I haven't time to prepare for my job interview.'
'I can't decide what to wear for it.'

Which two limits on resources does the speaker refer to?

Limited resources create the need for choices.

Options

In order to make choices, there must be options (alternatives). Joanna's options are a patterned sweater, a plain blouse, an old T-shirt under a jacket. Where is she going? At what time of year? What is the impression she wishes to make? What other garments or accessories might affect her choice? List other factors Joanna might check before making her final decision.

Information about options is needed to make effective choices.

Choices have consequences

Busy parents are constantly making choices. When buying a baby garment, what might be the consequences if they choose a material without checking the label for fire risk factors?

Joanna's priority is to avoid wearing a coat. She chooses the sweater, though the pattern clashes with her kilt. On her way to the interview, it pours with rain. She arrives unprepared and wet through. Joanna chose to put her priority before her goal. What was her goal? What are the likely consequences of her choice not to wear a coat?

Goals

A goal is an objective you aim to reach. It needs thought, effort and ambition. It needs careful planning and then working step-by-step through the plan. Goals can be long term or short term. Which of the following long-term goals would you like to reach within the next year:
◆ increase your energy level
◆ improve your learning power
◆ develop your social skills
◆ pass your examinations
◆ go to college
◆ open a bank account
◆ become more healthy
◆ become more happy
◆ generally become a more *effective* person?

To reach a goal, you must **commit** to it fully. This does not mean neglecting the other sides of your life. But a goal is not a goal unless you are committed to reaching it. It stays a vague wish, a dreamy hope, an unfocused longing which gets you nowhere.

Goals are very important in decision-making. They keep your focus on what you intend to achieve. For your practical assignment, choose a goal which is realistic, one you can reach.

Practical assignment

When deciding on your individual task, focus on your goal. This is to produce an **effective** piece of work, one which meets the needs of a child (and helps you pass the practical examination).

Examine your options. The task can be a toy, garment, design for nursery curtains, picture/number/story book, safety catch for windows, preparing a bottle-feed or party food, researching state benefits for disabled children, surveying parents' attitudes to pre-school education, and so on. Which option is most likely to meet your resources of time, energy, funds, skills? Which is most likely to meet your priorities? – these may be to learn a new practical skill or improve one you already have. Before arriving at your final decision, examine the consequences of your choice in relation to your goal.

Goals can be short term or long term. The short-term goals of parents are to meet the child's immediate needs. The physical care of newborns is the major priority. But, and at the same time, the emotional, intellectual and social care of the infant

■ Some suggestions for your practical assignment and some resources for your research work

remain priorities. Parents (and carers) who forget some of a baby's needs have forgotten to focus on their long-term goal.

The long-term goal of parenting is to raise a happy and healthy adult. Many studies show that happy babies develop more quickly and suffer less ill health than sad ones. Even toddlers can become **depressed** if some of their needs are not met.

Parents and carers do not have unlimited resources of time, funds or energy. When studying all the factors in decision-making for your Child Development course, take into account the limited resources of busy parents.

Child observation

Watch the child engaged in play. Does the play seem to have any goals? Describe any behaviours of the child which might suggest that children do have goals when they play.

Questions

1 Describe a typical newborn baby, including
   a average weight in kg
   b general appearance
   c reflex actions.

2 List the basic needs of a newborn and the likely consequences if these needs are not met. Using a dictionary, learn the meanings of **morals** and **ethics**. Explain why the survival needs of babies are not tested.

3 Give the meanings of
   a choices
   b options
   c consequences.

4 Choose one of the goals listed on the opposite page. Suggest some ways in which you could commit to attaining it. Describe some likely consequences of failing to commit to it. Explain the value of goals in your decision-making.

9 *Bonding*

Bonding means forming a very strong and close attachment to another person. At birth, it is the miracle of love which parents feel for their baby. They adore the infant, no matter what it is like. They will care for the newborn, whether it is a girl or a boy, full term or premature, smooth skinned or wrinkled, the first or the last born. Bonding to another person without any conditions is named **unconditional love**.

Bonding can happen when a mother first sees her baby, or it can take some while. People are different, and mothers are people too. But the process can happen more quickly when parents get to know their babies immediately after the birth.

An American study found that most mothers who spent an hour with their babies after the birth could choose their child out of three sleeping infants. During that first hour, the mothers played with their babies, cuddled them and admired their little bodies. They put the infants to the breast, talking to them at the same time.

The babies were then taken to the hospital nursery while the mothers had a rest. Later, the mothers were asked to take part in a bonding study. They agreed to be blindfolded and then given three babies to hold. In 70 per cent of cases, the mothers identified their own child by just feeling the backs of the infants' hands.

Zoe had a difficult birth and was too ill to see her baby for ten days. When he was placed in her arms, she bonded with him immediately. Other mothers require a longer time.

Human emotions

Not all mothers bond immediately. There are many factors which can slow down the bonding process. For example, Laura had a difficult birth and turned away from her new baby. She said:

'I blamed him for the pain he caused me. As if it was his fault, poor lamb! It took weeks before I felt this over-powering love. Mind you, I nurtured him just the same as if I had bonded with him during that time.'

Human emotions are complex. No parent should feel guilty if they do not bond with their baby immediately. Before the birth, they have formed a mental picture of what their child will look like. When it looks quite different (as it always

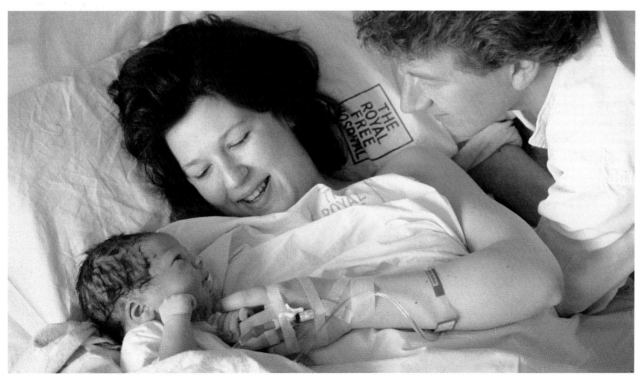

does!), they require time to adjust. Other factors which can slow the bonding process include poor health, stress at home, money worries, work problems and the awesome responsibility of being a parent. (The depression which some mothers suffer is discussed on page 187.) Both parents need time to relax and open themselves to love.

Fathers

It is thought that fathers bond more quickly if they witness the birth. Some studies have proved this, others have not. The focus today is for men to have a more active role in family life. Fathers are encouraged to share in the child-care tasks and be supportive in their parenting role.

Continuity of care

Continuity of care means getting the same type of nurture from the same type of people in the same kind of environment. Babies need **familiar nurture**, loving comfort from the same carers in the same surroundings. Babies need food, clothes, warmth, safety and shelter. They need these things from carers who are always ready to nurture them, whether it is in the middle of the night or not.

The surge of love which happens at bonding contains powerful feelings of **protection**. The parents have a passionate belief that they are responsible for whatever happens to the baby. This helps to make sure that the infant will receive the nurture it needs.

It is easy to think of bonding as great value to the infant. But it is of immense value to the parents as well. Other studies have found that the closer the bonding, the more ready a parent is to meet the baby's needs. And that the sooner a baby's needs are met, the sooner it settles into a **relaxed routine**.

Bonding can be seen as the baby's lifeline for survival, rather like the umbilical cord. Since a newborn cannot meet its own needs, there must be at least one adult ready to sacrifice a large part of her/his own life to nurture it. As the famous child psychologist Bruno Bronfenbrenner said, 'Somebody's gotta be crazy about that kid!'

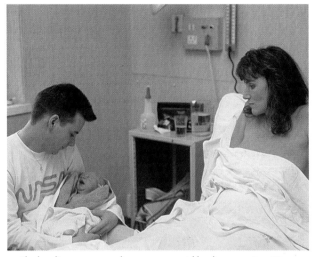

■ The bonding process can happen more quickly when parents get to know their babies immediately after the birth

— *Child observation* —

Visit a maternity ward and watch the ways parents behave with their new babies. The parents of the child you are studying may describe their feelings when they first saw their baby.

— *Questions* —

1 Explain the value of bonding for an infant's development.

2 Sam and Sarah are dismayed to find that they do not bond with their baby immediately. Explain why they should not feel guilty.

3 'The sooner a baby's needs are met, the sooner it settles into a relaxed routine.' In what ways can bonding be a great benefit to parents as well as to babies in family life?

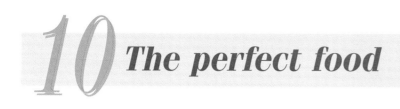

10 The perfect food

Milk is a highly nutritious food. It is rich in proteins, carbohydrates, fats, vitamins and minerals. Human milk contains all the nutrients an infant needs in the first sixteen weeks of life. It is our first source of nourishment and many adults drink milk throughout their lives. Depending on where they live, they enjoy a glass of goats' or cows' or sheep's or buffalo milk every day.

A baby's sucking reflex reaches a peak half an hour after birth. If it is given the breast, it sucks automatically. The first liquid from the breast is called **colostrum** and has a high protein content. For the next three to five days the baby mainly sleeps, perhaps to recover from the stress of birth. During this time, colostrum is replaced by breast milk, which has a different balance of nutrients and more water – good for a thirsty baby.

The breasts

Breast tissue contains blood vessels, lymph glands, fat cells and milk glands. A **gland** is a structure which produces fluids. Milk is brought by ducts to the **nipples**, which have about 20 small openings. The bumpy area around each nipple is the **areola**. During pregnancy, the areola and nipple darken, perhaps to help the baby more easily find the breast.

One of the first signs of pregnancy is a tingling in the breasts as they begin to swell. A pattern of delicate blue veins can appear on the skin. Over the next few months, the breasts increase greatly in size. A few women find this uncomfortable but others delight in their new shape. Because breast tissue has no muscle, many mothers-to-be need the support of a well-fitting bra. After the birth, mothers can use a nursing bra, which opens at the front, to make feeding the baby easier.

The balance of nutrients

The balance of nutrients in human milk changes during each feed to meet the baby's changing needs. At the beginning, the **fore milk** contains lactose and is thirst quenching. This means the baby gets a slightly sweet drink first. The fore milk is followed by the richer **hind milk**, which contains the nutrients the baby needs.

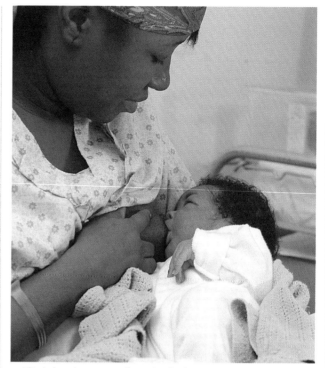

■ This baby is being given the perfect food

Infants used to be moved from one breast to the other after ten minutes to reduce the risk of the nipples getting sore. But this upsets the very clever balance of the feed. Too much lactose can cause colicky pains. Not enough of the richer milk can cause hunger pains soon after the feed.

How can a mother tell if her baby is getting enough milk? One good sign is at least 6 wet nappies every 24 hours without any other drinks. Another sign is an infant who settles soon after the feed and stays asleep for about four hours. The midwife or health visitor will check the baby's weight (see page 183).

Human milk is the perfect food for human babies.
- It has the right balance of all the food substances.
- It is easier for the baby to digest and absorb.
- It changes the balance of food substances to meet the changing needs of the growing baby.
- It contains **antibodies**, white cells and special proteins to help fight germs.
- It is at the right temperature, not too hot nor too cold.

◆ It is clean and free from germs.

◆ It is free and available when needed.

◆ Sucking from the breast requires more energy and there is less risk of the baby becoming overweight. The infant feels healthily tired, and settles sooner to sleep.

Difficulties in feeding

Newborns suck in very short bursts which lack the pressure to draw in milk. They must learn to co-ordinate their sucking and swallowing reflexes. A few infants squeeze without sucking or suck without swallowing. Others keep their mouths open so that air is sucked in while the milk dribbles out. It can take hours or days of practice before an infant learns to breast-feed happily. The midwife helps the mother and baby during this time.

A few women develop sore nipples. Sore nipples may be due to **thrush**, a fungus infection which clears up quickly with creams from the health visitor or doctor. Washing the breasts carefully before and after the feed avoids the risk of thrush.

▬ *Investigation* ▬

A few babies have difficulty learning to feed.

You will need:

drinking straws, glasses of water.

a Place a straw in a glass of water.

b Suck in very short sips. (Spit out after a few sips.)

c Record your mouth movements and how this sucking felt.

d Again, suck in very short bursts and swallow the water.

e Record how many mouth movements this takes.

f Comment on the sucking and swallowing skills involved.

▬ *Child observation* ▬

Find out if the child was breast-fed. If so, record for how long and if there were any learning difficulties.

▬ *Questions* ▬

1 Most babies lose weight and then exceed their birthweight by the end of the second week. Explain the function of the layer of fat which gives the newborn its plump, chubby look.

2 A friend tells Lisa to move the baby from one breast to the other during the feed. Describe how you would explain to Lisa the likely consequences of this old-fashioned advice.

3 Mary blames her sore nipples on breast-feeding and gives her baby formula milk. But the soreness remains. What mistake has Mary made? List the health advantages that her baby now lacks.

4 'I can't see how much milk my baby gets,' Amanda worries. 'Perhaps it's not enough.' Describe the two signs which mothers can rely on to know that their baby is well-fed.

5 When a cold virus rampaged through one maternity ward, the only baby to catch it was the only baby who was not breast-fed. Suggest one reason for this.

Lactation means producing milk. Lactation is controlled by a hormone named **prolactin** (for milk). Milk is produced as a reflex response to sucking. The more a baby sucks, the more milk is produced, the more prolactin is released. Giving a 'top-up' of **infant formula milk** upsets this natural balance. It can reduce the mother's milk supply and the baby's sucking skills.

Prolactin is linked with the birth hormone, **oxytocin**. Oxytocin is one of the 'feel good' hormones. It promotes a sense of well being, of fondness and caring for other people. This is named **nurturing** behaviour. These 'feel good' hormones show in many ways: stroking, kissing, cuddling and touching. Breast-feeding is thought to increase nurturing behaviour in women. It is also thought to help in the bonding process.

Breast-feeding benefits the mother's health in other ways too.

◆ Some of the weight she gains in pregnancy is specially for lactation. About 4 kg of this weight is used in breast-feeding.

◆ Sucking on the breast helps her uterus contract. This reduces the risk of bleeding (haemorrhage) after the birth and helps the uterus return to its normal size more quickly.

◆ The mother cares for her diet (page 178) in order to satisfy her baby and this helps regain her strength more quickly.

◆ A baby nursing contentedly on the breast gives a tremendous boost to the mother's confidence in her parenting role.

◆ The more confident the mother, the more contented the baby, the sooner both parent and child settle into a relaxed routine.

Infant **formula** is made from cows' milk. The manufacturers try to design it to be as near human milk as possible, but cannot quite.

◆ It has a different balance of food substances.

◆ It has different types of proteins and carbohydrates.

◆ It lacks certain hormones and essential fats.

◆ It can be less easy for the baby to digest and absorb.

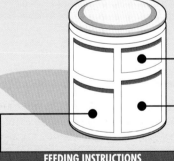

INGREDIENTS

Skimmed Milk, Whey Powder, Demineralized Whey Powder, Lactose, Vegetable Oils (Palm, Coconut, Soya), Lecithin (Soya), Magnesium Chloride, Copper Sulphate, Potassium Iodide, Ferrous Lactate, Zinc Sulphate, Vitamin A, Thiamin, Vitamin B6, Vitamin B12, Biotin, Folic Acid, Niacin, Pantothenic Acid, Vitamin C, Vitamin D3, Vitamin E, Vitamin K, Tourine.

FEEDING INSTRUCTIONS

Good dental hygiene is as important for babies and toddlers as it is for older children and adults. Prolonged or frequent contact of drinks or feeds with the teeth, e.g. from using bottles or beakers as comforters, increases the risk of tooth decay. In accordance with normal dental hygiene your baby's teeth should be cleaned after the last feed at night. Ask your health professional or dentist for advice. Never leave your baby alone during feeding.

• **Mix** 1 scoop of formula to 1 fl oz (28ml) of water.
• **Do not** use artificially softened water.
• **Mixed feeds** can be refrigerated. Use within 24 hours.
• **Discard** unfinished feeds.
• **Do not** heat feeds in a microwave oven.
• **Do not** add sugar or cereal to bottle feeds.

FEEDING GUIDE

Age	Approximate weight		Feeds per 24 hours	Level scoops of powder per feed	Quantity of warm (previously boiled) water	
	kg	lb			ml	fl oz
0–1 weeks	3.0	7	6	3	85	3
1–4 weeks	3.5	8	5	4	115	4
1–2 months	4.5	10	5	5	140	5
3 months	5.5	12	5	6	170	6
4 months	6.5	14	5	7	200	7
5–6 months	7–8	15–18	5	8	225	8
6 months +	8 +	18 +	4	8	225	8

■ Are the ingredients of formula milk easy to understand?

◆ It lacks antibodies to protect against germs so the bottle-fed infant is more vulnerable to infections.
◆ It is not free, but must be bought and prepared before a feed.
◆ The balance of nutrients does not change during the feed to meet the changing needs of the baby.
◆ Because less energy is required to suck from a bottle than the breast, there is a higher chance of the baby becoming overweight.

Human milk has special values that formula milk lacks. Some of these are not understood, even by the Department of Health. The 1991 report *Dietary Reference Values for Food Energy and Nutrients for the United Kingdom* refers to the 'poorly understood special properties and qualities of breast milk' (see unit 31).

Human milk contains essential long-chain fats and hormones not found in formula milk. Scientists think these fats and hormones may help the developing brain of the baby and increase its intelligence. They studied 300 premature babies who were fed by tube. In group A, 210 mothers chose to provide their milk, (though some could not). The 90 mothers in group B chose not to provide their milk.

When the babies were eight years old, their intelligence was measured by a range of tests. The group A children scored an average of eight points higher than the group B children. Since both groups were fed by tube, the effects of bonding at breast-feeding were ruled out.

Mothers who breast-feed tend to be better educated and come from higher-income families. The study (by Lucas et al, 1992) ruled out this factor. The children whose mothers wanted to provide milk but could not did no better on the intelligence tests than the children in group B.

The low fat content of formula milk may interfere with the baby's developing senses. Another study found that a breast-fed infant's vision at four and at six months was better than babies of the same age who were formula fed. If polyunsaturated fats were added to the formula, the bottle-fed baby's vision was similar.

Human error

Making up a formula feed requires strict hygiene and attention to the instructions. But accidents do happen. In 1962, three babies in a hospital nursery were given formula milk which had been accidentally mixed with salt. Though newborns have a sense of taste, it does not always protect them from harm. The babies drank the salt mixture contentedly until they literally drank themselves to death.

These factors plus the lack of antibodies may be the reasons why bottle-fed babies are more likely to suffer from:
◆ **allergies**: especially to cow's milk, cheese and yoghurt
◆ **eczema**: an itchy, often painful, skin condition
◆ **gastroenteritis**: upset stomach and bowels due to food poisoning
◆ **nappy rash**: an outbreak of spots and raw skin on the bottom
◆ **constipation**: hard, dry stools which are painful to pass
◆ **respiratory problems**: wheezing breath, fits of coughing.

▬ *Questions* ▬

1 Give the meanings of
  a lactation
  b formula milk
  c nurturing behaviour
  d human error
  e eczema.

2 Explain why a baby fed on formula milk is at greater risk of
  a becoming overweight
  b becoming constipated.

3 'It's a difficult decision, to breast-feed or not,' Rebecca sighs. Describe in detail how you would help Rebecca in her decision-making, beginning with the advantages to her own health.

12 Formula feeding

A few mothers are unable to breast-feed. They learn how to plan, prepare and manage bottle-feeding. This involves paying attention to hygiene and to the skills of consumer awareness: checking the nutritional content of the feed, the 'best before' dates, the feeding and sterilizing equipment, its safe storage and cost.

A feeding bottle should be designed:

◆ with a wide neck for easy pouring and cleaning
◆ in clear material to check it is clean inside
◆ with clear markings for measurements on the side
◆ with a special cap to keep the teat clean
◆ with a rim to store the teat hygienically inside the bottle.

Attitudes to feeding

There is a family pattern in feeding. One study found that 75 per cent of women who were breast-fed chose this course. Of the women who were bottle-fed as babies, only 48 per cent chose to breast-feed.

— Investigation

Practise cleaning used feeding equipment.
You will need:

bottles and teats, bottle brush, soap, detergent, kitchen cloth, kettle, sterilizing equipment.

Strict hygiene is essential. Germs can be passed from your hands, the feeding equipment or the work surface. Wash your hands and the work surface. Then wash all the equipment with a bottle brush in warm water with detergent. Rinse with boiled water. Tap water is not sterile and must be freshly boiled.

To sterilize the equipment, choose one of the following methods:

a boil everything in a covered saucepan for ten minutes, making sure the bottles, teats and caps are fully immersed

b add sterilizing tablets or fluid to a cold water tank

c use a special steamer

d use a microwave steam-sterilizer.

— Investigation

Practise your handling and measuring skills.
You will need:
a tin of infant formula, the scoop in the tin, a kettle, a sterilized plastic knife.

a Read the feeding guide on the tin for a baby weighing 4.5 kg.

b Boil fresh water and allow to cool to about 50°C.

c Pour the exact required volume into the bottle.

d Wash your hands.

e Level off each scoop of powdered milk, using the back of a sterilized plastic knife. Do not press the powder down. Tip each scoop carefully into the bottle. Seal, and shake well.

f If any part of the equipment is dropped, or becomes unsterile for any reason, the formula must be thrown away and all the equipment re-sterilized.

g Evaluate your task. Identify any problem areas which need more planning or practice. Record the total time required to prepare a baby's feed.

The baby is hungry. The milk is not at the correct temperature. Identify and rehearse ways to
a heat b cool the feed.

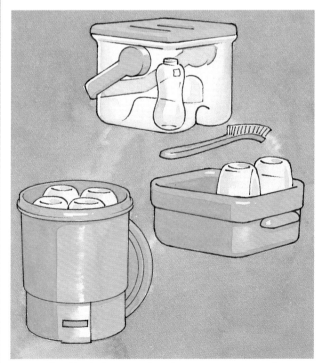

■ Examples of bottle cleaning and sterilizing equipment

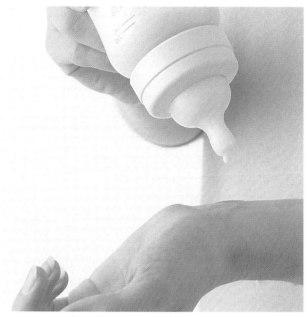

■ The milk should feel warm, not hot

— *Individual task* —

Prepare a feed for a baby weighing 4.5 kg.

To complete this task as an assignment, you will need to survey the opinions of parents and health visitors on breast- or bottle-feeding. This is a sensitive issue and you must check your survey questions with your teacher first.

— *Further investigations* —

♦ The baby has an intolerance to the protein or carbohydrate in cows' milk (unit 36). Investigate soy-based formula milk.

♦ The parents are travelling abroad. Investigate pre-prepared and pre-bottled formula.

♦ The baby is cared for by a lazy carer. Investigate prop-feeding and its hazards.

♦ The baby is ill and can only be fed human milk. Investigate human milk banks.

In Western culture, breasts have become a sexual focus rather than a source of nourishment. Nipples are very sensitive and can become erect when touched. Women can have a natural modesty about exposing their breasts. They can feel it

might be unpleasant to feel a baby sucking at the nipple. Some breasts develop lumps which, though harmless, feel tender. Women can express their milk and store it under hygienic conditions to be used later in bottles. This allows a woman to be away from her baby for a few hours.

Because 'breast is best', women who cannot or choose not to breast-feed are made to feel 'bad' by the attitudes of others. This insensitive approach is not new. In ancient Greece, the philosopher Aristotle scolded such people. No woman should be made to feel a 'failure' or 'bad', whatever her decision. The consequences of such an insensitive attitude can seriously affect her sense of well-being and that of her baby.

— *Questions* —

1 List all the equipment necessary to bottle-feed a baby.
2 Choose one method of cleaning the equipment and describe
  a how
  b when
  c why it should be cleaned.
3 Suggest, with reasons, a safe and hygienic storage place for the formula and equipment in a busy family kitchen.
4 Identify the correct temperature at which infant formula can be stored in the refrigerator and for how long.
5 Cost the price of feeding the baby based on the estimated number of days' use of the formula.
6 The minimum equipment is two bottles, six teats, one jug, one spoon set, one sterilization unit and packet of tablets, one cup. Cost the total outlay on all the equipment needed to bottle-feed a baby.
7 Estimate the total time for preparing the feed, sterilizing the equipment and storing it safely afterwards.
8 Collect advertisements for different brands of formula milk and feeding and sterilizing equipment. Comment on their appeal.
9 Discuss possible reasons why some mothers prefer to bottle-feed rather than breast-feed their babies.

13 Heating

Newborns cannot control their body temperature as adults can. Even small changes in the air temperature can make them very ill, very quickly. Children develop a well-regulated system to control their body temperature, rather like the thermostat on a central heating system.

When 50 warmed babies were placed naked in incubators heated to 29.4°C, most of them slept or rested quietly. When the heating was lowered to 25°C, most of them moved restlessly or cried. When the heating was raised to 38°C, they all moved and cried non-stop.

Shivering is the body's reflex response to protect against cold. Tiny muscles under the skin move in jerky spasms to produce heat. Adults can warm up by hot food and exercise; babies cannot. Warm clothing and warm rooms meet the heating needs of babies in cold weather.

Sweating is the body's reflex response to protect against over-heating. As the temperature rises, tiny sweat glands in the skin pour out water and salts. As the water evaporates, it cools the skin. Adults can cool down in other ways. Babies cannot. Cool clothing and cool rooms meet the temperature needs of babies in hot weather.

The UK recommended room temperature for sleeping infants is 18°C. This takes into account a warm and well-fed infant in a 'baby-gro' (or stretch suit) and covered with light blankets. Nowadays, most homes have central heating and a baby is more at risk of over-heating than chilling.

Fabrics and body heat

Thermal comfort is when your skin is about 34°C. Without clothes, the air temperature needs to be 28–30°C. The flow of heat through a fabric is measured in **togs**. Tests on adult underwear show that it is the thickness of the fabric rather than the fibre or the weave which conserves (keeps in) body heat.

Clothes/covering	Togs
Naked	0.00
Summer dress	0.75
Light trousers and top	0.90
Skirt, blouse, cardigan	1.20
Trousers, shirt, jumper	1.20
Suit and overcoat	2.25
Anorak	7.00
Good quality duvet	11.00

A fabric which is **absorbent** prevents sweat from building up on the skin. This type of fabric is said to 'breathe', in warm weather the wearer feels cool. A garment can be low in togs yet if it is non-absorbent the skin feels clammy and the person remains uncomfortably hot.

Wool, cotton, linen and muslin are natural fabrics. They allow the skin to breathe. Synthetic fabrics include polyester which is crease-resistant, acrylic which is lightweight, crease-resistant and non-irritating to the skin, and viscose which is absorbent. Many baby garments and bed linen are made of mixes of natural and synthetic fabrics, and the advantages of each type are combined.

■ A modern thermostat

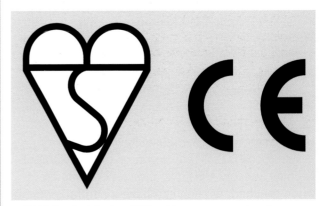

■ British Standards Institute (BSI) and European approval marks

Hyperthermia is a near-death condition when a baby's temperature is dangerously above body heat. An overheated baby loses precious fluids in sweating. Body fluids are essential because water is the element in which cells survive. A sweating baby is at risk of **dehydration**. The skin over the fontanelle may look shrunken and tight.

Hypothermia is dangerously low body temperature. A chilled baby loses precious energy in shivering. Energy is essential not only for growth and development but for all chemical changes, for fighting infection, for movement, even for sleep.

Sweating or shivering are danger signs in a baby.

As babies grow, the control of their body temperature improves. They become aware when they are over-heated. They pluck at their clothing and say 'hot' and 'off'. But they remain less aware when they are chilled. Some toddlers have rosy cheeks in cold weather, and parents can mistake this flush for over-heating. If they feel the skin of the neck, they can check whether the child is warm.

Many children (and adults) remain unaware of the feelings of dehydration. Toddlers may ask for food when what they really need is a drink. It is easy to understand why small children associate food with the dry feeling in their mouth. Parents can check that the child is not thirsty before offering food (see unit 35).

Investigation

Identify the speed at which different fabrics (i) absorb and (ii) release moisture.

You will need:

small squares of cotton, wool, linen, silk and synthetic mixes, a basin of water, a drying line, a clock.

a Float each square on the water.

b Record the time it took for each square to become soaked.

c Describe what happened when each became thoroughly soaked.

d Take each square directly from the water and hang it to dry.

e Record the time it took for each square to dry.

f From the evidence of your findings, choose a suitable fabric to make a garment for (i) a summer baby and (ii) a winter baby, giving reasons for each choice.

Child observation

Record the type of heating used in the child's home or playgroup. Describe the type of safety guards used.

Questions

1 Identify two ways to increase body heat when you are chilled. Explain why a baby cannot employ these methods.

2 Explain what is meant by dehydration and why this condition is especially serious for babies.

3 Review the information in this unit. What temperature do you think an incubator should be set at?

4 Copy the BSI and European labels into your folder.

5 'Thirty years ago babies froze slowly to death while being nursed tenderly in a room heated to 16°C. Thirty years ago draughty British homes were heated by coal fires. By 1992, 82 per cent of homes had central heating.' Explain why today's parents need to be more on guard against over-heating and dehydration than hypothermia.

14 Clothing

The layette

A baby's first wardrobe is named a **layette**. Some parents choose the layette as soon as the pregnancy is confirmed. Others wait until the final month. Grandparents may knit or sew garments. Friends may buy cute bonnets or shawls that they simply cannot resist! The clothing needs of a new baby can be fun to meet.

The fabrics for baby clothes should be soft, absorbent, washable, quick-drying and light in weight. Clothing should fit yet be roomy and comfortable. Cotton and cotton mix fabrics are cooler for summer. Washable and non-scratch wool mixes are warmer for winter. Babies dislike anything pulled over the face so vests and tops should be wrap-overs or wide enough at the neck to slip easily over the head. All-in-one baby gros and stretch suits keep the feet warm at night. Lacy garments can trap a baby's fingers. Ribbons and ties can become stuck in the mouth, are fiddly for carers to tie and untie, and can tangle into knots.

Factors to consider when choosing a layette.
- The poor temperature control of babies.
- Their ability to dirty everything quickly.
- Their fear of anything pulled over the face.
- Their sensitive skin to irritants in artificial fibres.
- The need for easy access to change a nappy.
- The fire-resistant safety factors of the fabric.
- The care labels and laundry arrangements in the home.
- The budget resources of the parents.
- The priorities of the family.
- The aesthetic appeal of the clothing.
- A newborn grows more quickly than at any other age.

Bedding

Cot-sheets should be soft as they are in contact with the baby's skin. Layers of lightweight blankets are warmer and more comfortable than one heavy bulky covering. Pillows must *never* be used to avoid the risk of smothering. Satin or shiny quilts, no matter how pretty, should also never be used. Their shiny surfaces permit them to travel up the cot and cover the baby's head.

These safety features should be checked in a cot:
- The bars must be no more than 7 cm apart to protect against the risk of the baby's head being caught between them.
- The mattress must be close fitting to the edges of the cot to protect against the risk of the baby's head or limbs becoming stuck between them.

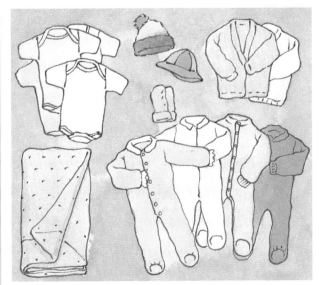

■ A minimum layette includes four stretch suits, four vests or bodysuits, two cardigans and a shawl or blanket, plus a sun hat for a summer baby or a woolly hat and one pair of mittens for a winter baby

■ Bedding includes one standard cot and mattress, three blankets and four sheets. The cost at 1995 prices was about £180

◆ Cots with a drop-side must have a catch for holding it up. This catch must be too difficult to unlock by the baby or an older sibling.

◆ Many items of baby equipment can be second-hand, but the mattress should be new. This avoids the risk of older chemicals used as fire-retardants which may have given off toxic fumes.

The Moses basket or carry-cot are options until the baby becomes too active or too large to be safely left alone. They are portable and can be carried from room to room, taken on a bus or in the back of a car. With wheel attachments and a hood, carry cots have the further advantage of being both a bed and a pram.

Prams – facts or opinions?

The following findings are from surveys into two types of prams.

'Today's parents dislike the old carriage-built pram with its toddler seat and shopping tray. They say these prams are too large, heavy, gloomy, lacking in fun and style. They do not fold up to fit in the car or bus. They are difficult to clean, steer and park in small hallways.'

'Today's parents delight in the carriage-built pram. They fear the new lightweight, flimsily-made, gimmicky buggy. It can be easily tipped up and the wheels, brakes and restraining straps may not be safe. Baby fingers can get at the metal parts and become trapped.'

■ A modern carriage-built pram (top) and a modern buggy

— Child observation

Record the type of cot or pram chosen for the child. If possible, relate this choice to the parents' lifestyle.

— Questions

1 From catalogues or a visit to the shops, identify the total costs of a layette, a cot with mattress and bedding and a pram. Suggest, with reasons, various ways for parents on a tight budget to reduce these costs.

2 Choose, with reasons, a suitable pram for the following:
   a Florence and Gary live in a tiny flat while saving for a home
   b Annie and Bob are fashion conscious and live in a large home
   c Tina is unmarried, lives at home and must walk everywhere.

3 Investigate the choice of high chairs for one of the above families. Identify the factors to analyse: safety features, cost, expected length of use, ease of cleaning, space requirements, toy attachments, removable tray, slot for baby cup, aesthetic appeal, ease of carrying, other. Choose, with reasons, a high chair for one of the above families that will enable the baby to take part in family meals.

4 List four fabrics which are suitable for baby clothes and in each case give a reason for your choice.

Hygiene is a set of rules to promote health. These rules protect against **insanitary** conditions which encourage germs to breed. Rules for a carer include: wash the hands before giving a feed and after changing a nappy. Place soiled nappies in a bucket with a lid. Wash baby clothes and clean all nursery equipment and toys regularly. Avoid coughing or sneezing near a baby.

Metabolism

The body transforms (changes) the nutrients in food into living matter, the process is called **metabolism**. Oxygen acts on the digested food, freeing the stored energy. This is also named **caloric burn**. It releases energy and produces heat and waste: carbon dioxide, sweat, urine and stools. Parents and carers need to apply the rules of hygiene when removing the baby's waste products.

Ventilation

Opening the bedroom window allows the carbon dioxide which can build up in a room overnight to disperse. This is called **ventilation**. Fresh air removes germs which are breathed out. Sunlight can destroy some of these germs. Babies may sleep by their parents' bed, share a room with siblings or have a nursery of their own. All rooms should be ventilated each day.

Nappies – facts and opinions

The choice between disposable and washable nappies include *comfort* for the baby and *cost* for the parents. Another factor is the cost to the environment. Disposables create much more solid waste but washing and drying cotton nappies uses a great deal of electricity, water and soap powder.

These add to the pollution of the environment and use precious resources.

Which?, the independent consumer guide, reported its findings on nappies in November 1994. The parents of 180 babies tested 12 disposable brands for one week. They noted *absorbency*: was the nappy effective at keeping the baby's skin dry? were there any leaks? *Shape*: did the nappy fit comfortably at the legs and the waist? were the larger sizes for a toddler too bulky? *Fastenings*: these were tested for a tendency to rip.

Which? asked its members' opinions on washable nappies: 'We had a large, enthusiastic response.' After the initial cost of cloth nappies, they can work out cheaper than disposables. The problems of sharp pins to fasten the nappies can be solved with a new plastic device called a 'Nappi Nippa' which grips the square in three places and is easier to use.

Which? also reported its readers' comments on **nappy services**. These deliver clean nappies and pick up soiled washables once a week. Members were pleased with the service and found the over-all cost of £6 to £7 a week no more than the top-selling disposables. *Which?* commented: 'Because nappy services wash loads of nappies at a time, in terms of water and energy usage, they are probably more environmentally friendly than washing one baby's nappies at home.'

Bathing

Bathing a baby removes the sweat and traces of urine and stools. Bath water cleans and refreshes the skin. Babies get surprisingly grubby: fluff between the fingers, grime under the nails, grease on the scalp, crusts in the eyes and nose. Some babies are terrified of being lowered into water. Others relax and enjoy the experience. A wet soapy baby is very slippery to hold.

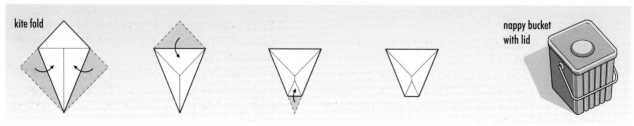

kite fold

nappy bucket with lid

■ This is one way of folding a cotton nappy

■ Stages in bathing a baby

Investigation

Role-play bathing a baby (using a life-size doll).

a Identify all the material resources required before you start.

b Plan your seating with the resources close at hand.

c Check the temperature of the room and bath water.

d Undress the 'baby' and wrap it in a towel.

e Dispose of the nappy hygienically.

f Practise safety holds to make sure the baby is secure.

g Follow each stage of cleaning and rinsing the skin.

h Lift the baby out and wrap warmly in a towel.

i Dry and dress the baby.

h Record and evaluate your baby-bathing skills.

When bathing a baby, test the temperature of the bath water with your elbow. Have ready cotton wool, soap, shampoo, a jug and two towels. Undress the baby. Clean the baby's face gently with wet cotton wool. Pat dry. Wipe the eyes from the inner corners outwards, using fresh cotton wool for each eye. Clean wax from the ear lobe. *Never* put a cotton bud in the ear as this can damage the ear drum. Use a mild shampoo for the scalp. Rinse the hair thoroughly with a jug of clean warm water. Dry the head.

Soap the body all over. Lower the baby into the water and rinse off the soap. If bath-time is enjoyable, allow time for a splash. Lift the baby out onto a towel. Dry the skin with gentle pats, making sure all the creases are dry. A cream like zinc and castor oil on the bottom helps protect against nappy rash. Dress the baby, putting on the nappy first.

Child observation

Which type of nappy did the child use? Record any opinions on this choice that the parent may wish to make.

Questions

1 Suggest, with reasons
  a the time of day you would air a baby's room
  b a suitable room temperature for bath-time.

2 Collect advertisements for a variety of nappies and identify the messages they are trying to give. Explain whether or not you think these messages are successful, and why.

3 A young baby needs nappy changes six times a day. If disposables cost 16p each, work out the total cost for
  a one day   **b** one week   **c** one year.

4 Decide on one safety rule when using a sharp nappy pin. Name one device that can avoid this problem.

Newborns cannot sleep through the night. They do not understand the adult world of clocks. They wake when their energy supply is low and cry in response to their need for food. On average, they sleep in 4 hour cycles, whatever the time. By sixteen weeks, this begins to change. They stay awake longer during the day, and sleep longer at night.

Infants have two main types of sleep patterns. **Active sleep** is lighter and more shallow. During active sleep, babies grunt, snuffle, twitch and move their limbs. Older children may cry out, talk and even walk. Active sleep is dream time. Infants dream a great deal more than adults. They have a whole new world to learn about and need more dream time to sort it out.

Quiet sleep is deep, dreamless sleep. During quiet sleep, we all lie completely still, 'like a log'. Babies cannot lift their heads or turn over if their airways are blocked. They must be placed on their backs to sleep (page 100).

On average, newborns sleep 16 hours out of every 24. The simple rule for new parents is to sleep when the baby sleeps. But not all parents can manage this. Some mothers become exhausted and wonder what conditions, if any, help their baby to become less active at night.

The sleep patterns of two groups of newborns were observed. The babies in Group A slept in hospital cots by their mothers' beds. They were fed **on demand** – given milk whenever they woke and cried. The ward lights were switched off at night.

Group B slept in the hospital nursery. They were fed **on schedule** – given milk at set times and not when they cried. The nursery lights remained on.

After ten days, the Group A babies had begun to be quieter at night. Group B babies remained as active through the night as through the day.

Bedtime routine

By six months, babies can sleep through most of the night. But some take longer to settle into a sleep routine than others. This depends upon many factors including the baby's birthweight, the stress of birth, the diet and the parents' own ability to relax. From a very early age, infants respond to the feelings of their carers. An anxious, tense parent can trigger unsafe feelings in the baby, who then becomes too tense to relax into sleep.

A bedtime routine involves a gradual introduction of a set of patterns. The baby needs plenty of activity during the day. These activities are wound down in the late afternoon. Teatime is pleasant but calm. A relaxing warm bath and then the baby is put into bed. Most infants like soothing lullabies and rocking. Toddlers and older children enjoy bedtime stories and often fall asleep while listening to their favourite tale.

Toddlers can go through phases of wakefulness. This is often related to a new event in their daily routine, such as joining a nursery or playgroup. To relieve the stress, parents can take the toddler

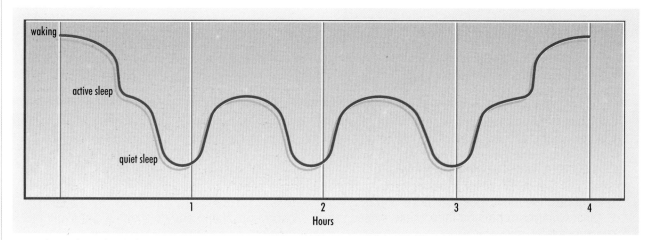

■ Four hours of a newborn's day, averaged over a week

■ An early morning snooze

into their own bed. Or they can sit with the child until it falls asleep. 'Midnight terrors' are very real and painful, and the child needs all the comfort available before it can relax into sleep.

Sleep remains one of the great mysteries in life. It is not known why some people need more sleep than others. More accidents happen when people suffer from lack of sleep. They lose their ability to concentrate and make decisions clearly.

A **time log** is a record of the time required for certain activities. Create a time log of your sleep each night for a week.

— Investigation

Identify the health benefits of sleep.

You will need:

a clock, graph paper, coloured pens or pencils.

a Devise your own sleep log on graph paper using bright colours.

b Record your nightly hours of sleep for one week.

c Estimate what percentage of 24 hours you sleep.

d Describe how you feel when you have not had enough sleep.

e Describe how you feel after a good night's sleep.

f List some disturbances which might wake you from sleep.

g From your findings, do you think sleep is necessary for health? Give reasons for your answer.

— Child observation

If possible, watch a baby during active sleep and describe all the movements you observe. Record the sleep time of your child. Compare this with the findings of other students for children of the same age. Estimate the average sleep time needed. Record any naps taken during the day.

— Questions

1 Explain the differences between feeding on demand and feeding on schedule. From the findings of the sleep study, would you choose to feed a baby on demand or schedule? Give reasons for your answer. Suggest other ways to help a newborn start to develop longer sleep patterns at night.

2 Maxine keeps a time log of her baby's sleep patterns. Her goal is to relieve her baby of having to cry for food. As he emerges from his last phase of active sleep, she is ready to feed him. Explain how the time log helps Maxine achieve her goal. Give your opinion of the value of Maxine's goal.

3 Tracey chooses to do her home-making tasks instead of sleeping when her baby sleeps. Suggest one likely consequence of Tracey's choice on her health. Is an exhausted mother of more value to an infant than a tidy home? Give reasons for your answer.

4 Ravi and Ron enjoy playing with their baby after her late evening feed. They cannot understand why she will not settle when they finally put the lights out. Suggest, with reasons, some arrangements you would make for a calming late evening feed.

5 Investigate night lights to comfort a wakeful toddler.

17 Crying

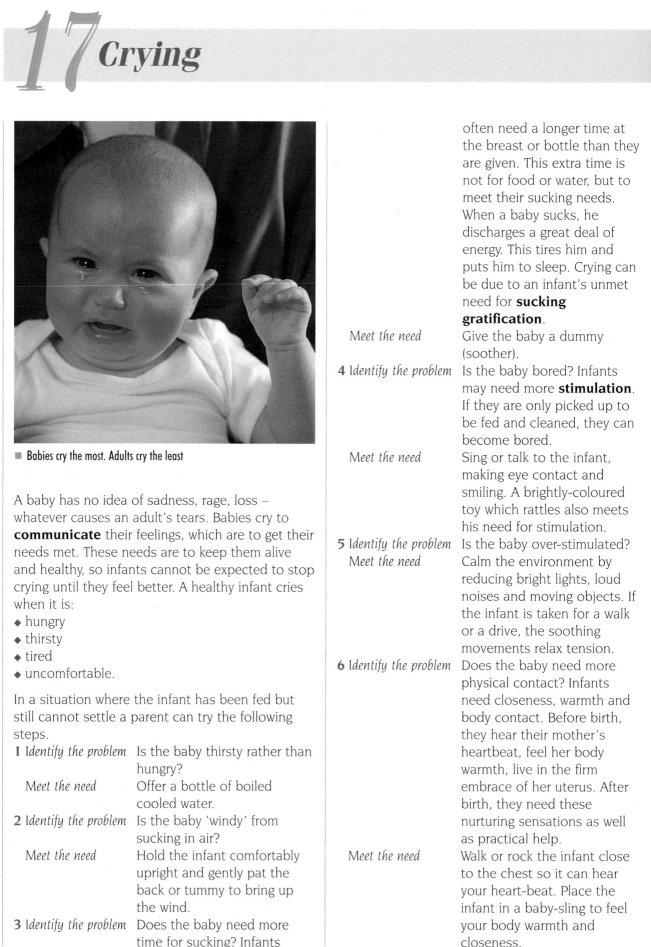

■ Babies cry the most. Adults cry the least

A baby has no idea of sadness, rage, loss – whatever causes an adult's tears. Babies cry to **communicate** their feelings, which are to get their needs met. These needs are to keep them alive and healthy, so infants cannot be expected to stop crying until they feel better. A healthy infant cries when it is:
◆ hungry
◆ thirsty
◆ tired
◆ uncomfortable.

In a situation where the infant has been fed but still cannot settle a parent can try the following steps.

1 *Identify the problem* Is the baby thirsty rather than hungry?
  Meet the need Offer a bottle of boiled cooled water.

2 *Identify the problem* Is the baby 'windy' from sucking in air?
  Meet the need Hold the infant comfortably upright and gently pat the back or tummy to bring up the wind.

3 *Identify the problem* Does the baby need more time for sucking? Infants often need a longer time at the breast or bottle than they are given. This extra time is not for food or water, but to meet their sucking needs. When a baby sucks, he discharges a great deal of energy. This tires him and puts him to sleep. Crying can be due to an infant's unmet need for **sucking gratification**.
  Meet the need Give the baby a dummy (soother).

4 *Identify the problem* Is the baby bored? Infants may need more **stimulation**. If they are only picked up to be fed and cleaned, they can become bored.
  Meet the need Sing or talk to the infant, making eye contact and smiling. A brightly-coloured toy which rattles also meets his need for stimulation.

5 *Identify the problem*
  Meet the need Is the baby over-stimulated? Calm the environment by reducing bright lights, loud noises and moving objects. If the infant is taken for a walk or a drive, the soothing movements relax tension.

6 *Identify the problem* Does the baby need more physical contact? Infants need closeness, warmth and body contact. Before birth, they hear their mother's heartbeat, feel her body warmth, live in the firm embrace of her uterus. After birth, they need these nurturing sensations as well as practical help.
  Meet the need Walk or rock the infant close to the chest so it can hear your heart-beat. Place the infant in a baby-sling to feel your body warmth and closeness.

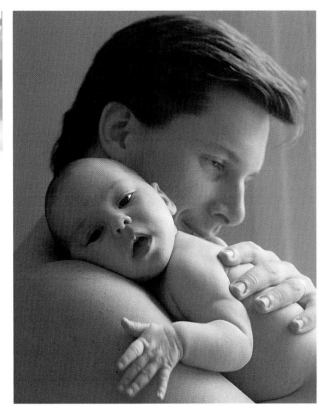

■ Soothing a baby to sleep

The sounds of crying

The cries of an infant are different from the cries of a child. The tone, pitch and frequency keep changing. The sounds are heard as jagged, uneven, intense noise which cuts through to the human brain. In short, an infant's cries cannot be ignored in the way that the more rhythmic cries of an older child can.

When a baby continues to cry after its needs have been met, parents can feel *inadequate* – failing in their parenting skills. They can lose confidence in their ability to help.

New research has found one cause of 'colicky' crying is due to the baby's undeveloped brain and nervous system. The messages the brain sends to the nervous system can get trapped. They travel back and forth along the same nerve pathways without reaching their destination. Crying discharges a great deal of energy and seems to clear the blockage. The baby calms down and settles to sleep when the messages link up again.

Never shake a baby

All babies have at least one time when they cannot stop crying. There is no need for parents to feel inadequate. They can visit the well-baby clinic and ask for advice. A very few parents (and carers) may become so angry that they shake the infant to make it stop. A baby's head is large compared to its body size and must always be firmly supported. When shaken, the head jerks backwards and forwards quite violently. Even swinging a baby without supporting the head or tossing a child suddenly into the air can cause great damage.

◆ The infant brain is quite fragile. When it hits the hard skull, the tiny blood vessels begin to bleed. If the bleeding is severe, pressure builds up and the infant can go into a coma and die.
◆ Shaking can cause a brain injury so severe that it leaves the infant handicapped for life.
◆ Shaking can badly frighten the infant, and make the crying more intense.
◆ Infants under eleven months are most at risk. Older children can be hurt if they are shaken.
◆ Letting the infant 'cry it out' avoids the risk of shaking. The parents should seek help the very next morning. The problem of shaking is linked with problems in the parents' lives. Shaking a baby is child abuse, which is discussed in unit 65.

— *Child observation* —

Ask about any lengthy crying of the child and what the parents' did to solve the problem.

— *Questions* —

1 Give the main reasons for a baby crying. Beside each, write how these needs can be met.
2 Tess felt threatened by her baby's cries. She patted him briefly, then put him to bed and shut the door. Why did Tess feel threatened? State some other options she had.
3 Suggest, with reasons, why parenting is sometimes named 'the greatest detective job on Earth'.

18 Soothing

Empathy is feeling *with* another person; putting yourself in their place, 'walking in their shoes'. **Sympathy** is feeling *for* another person, recognizing their plight, 'feeling sorry for them'. A baby who is held with confidence develops feelings of **security**. Being held gingerly, like a glass that might break, threatens the baby's instinct to survive with terrible fears of extinction (death). Empathic parents replace the firm embrace of the uterus by holding their baby close in a loving embrace.

In fact, babies thrive on cuddles, stroking and other body contacts. Many studies have shown that infants who are not held and touched regularly do not develop at their predicted rate. They are **touch-deprived**. Though they take as much nourishment as babies who are touched, they still fail to thrive. Their physical, intellectual, emotional and social development are seriously delayed.

Low birthweight babies gain weight faster if they are regularly massaged. Human touch appears *critical* for the health and well-being of all infants. It lowers the blood pressure and reduces stress. It may create changes in the brain which help in their **psychological** development (unit 60).

Most babies stop crying if they are massaged with firm yet gentle pressure. This pressure needs to be smooth, rhythmic and persistent. Gentle yet firm pressure releases the tensions which can build up. Soft nervous pats or short anxious strokes can irritate a crying baby more.

Massage

Each step of a massage is completed with the pressure strokes going back towards the heart. This is because blood is pumped out of the heart under high pressure but flows back under much lower pressure. The **veins**, which carry the blood back to the heart, have much thinner muscles which can become sluggish. The person feels not only relaxed but invigorated (stronger, with more energy) from this added help. This same effect occurs after aerobic exercise. Not only the heart rate but the entire blood system is strengthened from a thorough work-out.

Complete the investigation. Describe your sense of well-being before, during and after the massage. From your general feelings of health, explain, with reasons, if you consider a massage is (i) a luxury, (ii) a waste of time, (iii) a soothing comfort and (iv) a benefit to general health. Add any other comments you wish to make. Evaluate your partner's skills.

Many people doze off during a massage. Although infants also feel invigorated after a massage, the pressure of the strokes is much lower and slower. Once the baby's tension is released, the smooth rhythmic movements allow the infant to drift into sleep.

Investigation

Analyse the soothing effects of a massage.
You will need:
a partner, a floor mat.

a Ask the partner to stretch out comfortably on the mat.

b Turn the head to one side.

c Ask for satisfied murmurs when the massage is relaxing.

d Ask for grunts if the pressure is too strong or too weak.

e Before you begin the task, work with your partner to adapt the following baby massage techniques.

Step 1

Using small circular motions with your fingers, massage around the head, then the shoulders and upper chest.

Step 2

Use smoothing strokes along the arm outward from the shoulder, then shake and gently squeeze the hand. Repeat these movements, going back upwards towards the heart.

Step 3

Turn the baby over. Go down the shoulders to the arms, then squeeze the hands gently. Go down the back to the waist. Use smoothing strokes along the legs, starting at the top, then gently squeeze the calves and feet. Repeat these movements, going back upwards towards the heart.

Soothers

Soothers are also named dummies, pacifiers and comforters. Until recently, soothers were not recommended because they were thought to distort the position of the child's front teeth. Many parents ignored this. Others gave their infants a finger or knuckle to suck when the soother was lost or mislaid. Some people still regard soothers as 'common', lacking in aesthetic appeal. In most cases, these people are unaware of the infant's need for sucking gratification.

Infant crying nearly always stops if the following needs are met.

- To be stimulated by being held, carried, touched, talked to and have interesting things to look at and play with.
- To be helped to unwind, relax and fall asleep by gentle, firm, rhythmic and persistent patting, rocking, walking or massage.
- To be helped to bring up any wind by stroking and patting the back or tummy.
- To be held and touched in an environment which feels comfortable and a routine which helps them relax.

─ Child observation ─

If possible, watch a crying baby and describe all the signs of distress. Record the different methods parents use to soothe and relax a baby: holding on shoulder, patting on back, rocking in arms, walking, talking, other.

─ Questions ─

1 Describe one way to soothe a crying baby at night.
2 Name three needs of a baby that a massage meets.
3 Name one need of a baby that a soother meets.
4 'Babies thrive on being held and touched regularly.' Is this statement based on fact or opinion? Give as many reasons as you can for your answer.

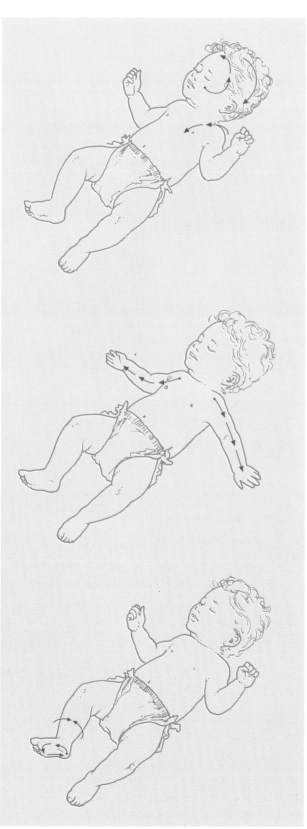

■ Babies find massage soothing

For 23 hours out of 24, newborn babies sleep, lie half-awake, fuss or cry. In the other hour, they lie quietly awake at ten to fifteen minutes intervals, usually around feeding time. They use this quietly awake time to learn about their world.

Newborns cannot use their eyes and bodies at the same time. They either look at their world and study what they see. This is named **paying attention**. Or they make movements and lie quite still. When they pay attention, their eyes shine brightly. When they make movements, their eyes are open but dull, as if staring into space. 'He seems to have fallen into a trance,' parents say.

When newborns are paying attention, their gaze is clear, fearless, direct: 'As if they can see right into your mind!' parents say. It is interesting that, as we observe infants to learn about them, they observe us and our world right back!

Babies have to learn everything, right from the start. They do not know the meaning of 'mother milk food'. They have no idea what is happening to or around them. Any person or object can be a source of fascination. No wonder their eyes shine brightly when they pay attention! But what is happening when they 'fall into a trance'?

Information about the world constantly bombards our senses. Light bathes our eyes, noise our ears, touch our skin, and so on. This information travels along **nerve pathways** from the senses to the brain. Here it is processed, 'translated' as vision, hearing, smell, and so on, and sent back to the senses.

The brains of newborns can **process** only very small amounts of information. When they seem be in a trance, they are taking 'time out' from this constant bombardment. They use this time to learn a little of the new information, to store it in the memory.

Skills for learning

It is not easy to store information in the memory. It requires focus, energy, concentration. **Memory patterns** have to be set down both in the brain and the nerve pathways to and from the senses. This means the information has to be repeated many times before learning begins.

Body and mind learning are interdependent. Each depends upon the working of the other to learn a new skill.

- Information is not easily stored in the memory.
- To learn anything, the human mind must pay attention.
- New information must be studied with full concentration.
- Memory pathways to hold the information must be laid down.
- New stimulations must be repeated until they become familiar.
- New movements must be practised and repeated again and again.

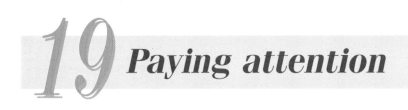

◼ A newborn fitted with headphones linked to a sound machine

A two-day-old girl was fitted with headphones linked up to a sound machine. When she sucked on her soother, the sounds played into the headphones. As she began paying attention, her sucking stopped. This was because she could not pay attention and make movements at the same time. After a while, she began sucking again. The sounds started. Her sucking stopped.

The hearing and vision of newborns are very important sources for early learning. A baby's hearing is the least well-developed of its senses. Hearing becomes fully accurate by age five. The child is then tested to find out if she can distinguish between words such as 'pen' and 'pin'.

Range of vision

A newborn's range of vision is limited. The eyes focus best at 20 to 25 cm. Objects nearer or further away appear shadowy or blurred.

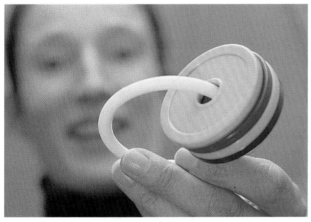

■ A newborn baby cannot focus

▬ *Questions* ▬

1 Give two examples which show that a baby is paying attention.

2 Using unit 5 to help you, answer the following:
  (i) Mandy feels anxious when four-week-old Dan falls into a trance. She brings him out of it by stroking his cheek. Explain why
   a Dan's head turns to the stroking
   b Dan cries though he has just been fed
   c Dan has stopped learning.
  (ii) Mike wants three-week-old Rue to focus on him. She is paying attention to the soft nursery light. In order not to alarm her, Mike waves his hands at arms' length from her face. Explain why Rue fails to pay attention to his waving. Mike then shakes a loud rattle very close to her face. Explain why Rue turns her head away and cries.

3 Devise a simple test to show that a newborn cannot use her eyes and make movements at the same time. If possible, try it out on a baby to see if it works.

20 Stimulation

When any of the five senses is alerted, we say it is **stimulated**. Some stimulations feel 'good': mother, milk, cuddles. Others feel 'bad': mother, undressing, cold. Newborns cannot choose how to respond to either kind of feeling. In child development language, they **orient** to a good stimulation – they turn towards it. They **avoid** a bad stimulation – they turn away from it. These reflex responses are part of the newborn's survival kit.

Newborns respond to stimulation rather than initiate (start) it. They orient to a parent's smile by gazing solemnly back. They avoid a scratchy blanket by frowning or crying. But they do not start new movements. This seeming passivity of newborns has led to the mistaken belief that they do not need stimulation until the special reflexes fade. Yet consider the following:

From the last weeks before birth until age three, the infant brain increases enormously in weight. By age six, a child's brain has grown to 90 per cent of its adult weight.

To learn about their world, newborns do need stimulation. Since they lack control of their body movements, this learning is mainly through sound and sight. They pay attention to voices, music, the tinkling of mobiles and rattle of rattles. They gaze at people and objects as if 'eating them with hungry eyes'.

Eye control

The eyes have fourteen muscles to control each movement. The eyeball is moved in its socket for up and down, and for all-round vision. The lens, which focuses for distance, adjusts for near or far objects. The higher the quality of vision, the better the baby can learn about its world. Most infants (and adults) have slight eye defects. Only one in 30,000 people inherit a flexible, perfect system.

At first, babies cannot control their eye muscles. By three months, they have a wider focusing range and have developed some control over their eye muscles. Squinting can occur, but only for short periods of time. Parents have reason to be concerned only if the squinting always occurs.

As babies grow, their **visual exploration** becomes more selective. They stare longer at faces than at bodies or objects. If the faces are smiling, the baby learns to smile back. If the faces are scowling, the baby learns to scowl back. By six months, both eyes have learned to work together, though brief squinting can still occur. By two years, a toddler has gained the same range of vision as an adult.

From observing newborns, we know that they prefer the small cosy world of the family. They orient to the music of gentle voices, the soft glow of nursery lights, the smooth texture of linen, the familiar smell of mother. They avoid the harsh sounds of arguing voices, the glaring lights of hospital wards, the rough textures of outdoor clothing, the unfamiliar odours of strange places. We know too that newborns can only pay attention for a short while before falling into a trance.

Babies spend their first weeks mainly lying on their backs. Parents hang brightly coloured rings across the pram and gently-tinkling mobiles over the cot to stimulate their interest. Lying on your

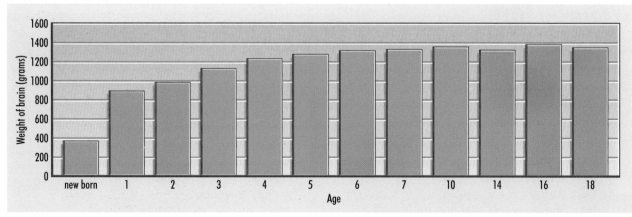

■ The weight of the brain from birth to age 18

■ Which of these diagrams do you find more interesting?

back limits your vision and an older infant needs a wider view of the world. By six to eight weeks, a baby can be propped up with cushions or placed in a bouncing cradle while busy parents get on with other tasks.

— Investigation —

Babies find faces more interesting to look at. Copy the three diagrams onto paper or cardboard. Allow 12 cm between each circle. Watch the movement of the baby's eyes. Record everything you observe. Since not all students will have access to a baby, the findings can be pooled in class.

a At what age do babies start paying attention to the circles?
b Which of the circles do they stare at the most?
c Describe what happens once a baby has oriented to the circles.
d Move the circles. Does this lengthen their attention span?
e From your findings, what conclusions can you draw about the statement that babies find faces more interesting to look at.
f Show the circles to the child you are studying and record its responses in detail.

— Child observation —

Find out if the child 'squinted' in its first year. If there are any sight defects, record them.

— Questions —

1 From the brain weight graph, give the following:
 a the average weight in grams of a newborn's brain
 b the average weight in grams of a eighteen-year-old's brain
 c the weight gain between birth and eighteen years old
 d the weight gain between birth and eighteen months old
 e the weight gain between birth and forty-two months old
 f the greatest period of brain growth in childhood.

2 From the findings of your investigation, comment on the length of a baby's attention span. Did a variety of stimulation (moving the circles) improve this? Comment on the stimulation value of
 a a mobile
 b a rattle
 c a stationary toy.

3 Devise a test to show that infants orient to gentle sounds and avoid harsh ones. If possible, try it out to see if it works.

4 Give your opinion of the theory: 'Early stimulation is essential for learning.'

5 Living things respond to stimulation by **avoidance** or **orientation**. Discuss.

The development of hand skills

Purposeful movement

As the special reflexes fade, the baby's movements show **purpose**. The head is turned purposefully as the eyes follow a moving object. The hands reach for a toy with sturdy purpose. This does not mean the baby is always successful. At nine weeks Kim reaches purposefully for a toy – and misses. She may smack her face or bang her other hand instead! She has not yet developed the ability to move her eyes and arms together. She can manage this at between ten and twelve weeks.

Every child knows the phrase 'Keep your eye on the ball!' When a baby reaches for a toy, the brain sends messages to the eyes to focus on it. This is the **eye-brain** connection. Kim's arm movements must work in co-ordination with her eye muscles before she can actually touch the toy. A baby with poor vision cannot be expected to do this at the same age as a baby with good vision. A child with a brain defect will be slower at learning to write with a pencil.

Hand skills

As Kim gains control of her arm movements, she learns control of her hands. Instead of a little fist automatically closing in the grasp reflex, she learns to hold a toy with purpose. She learns to co-ordinate her hand and eye movements in order to reach for and hold the mobile. This is named **hand-eye co-ordination**.

━ Investigation ━

Analyse some different hand grips.
You will need:
a needle, a can of juice, a cup of water.
a Pick up the needle. Draw the position of your fingers.
b Clasp the can. Draw the position of your hand.
c Raise the cup as if to drink the water. Draw the position of your fingers and hand.
d Now, try to pick up each object using the palmer grip.
e From your findings, explain some drawbacks of the palmer grip.

The palmer grip

The adult grip

■ By six months Kim can hold objects in a palmer grip

Manipulative skills

To manipulate is to handle with skill. Hands become manipulative when they can be used as tools. By seven months, Kim can bang a building block on the table and pass it from hand to hand. By eight months she can hold two blocks at the same time, one in each palm. She may seem a bit puzzled as to what to do next since both her hands are now full.

Kim has a further puzzle to solve since she cannot let go of the blocks. Her **hand release** will not develop until around her first birthday. The only way she can free herself of the blocks is by opening her fists. She loses interest in them as they fall out. She has stopped paying attention to them.

Parents encourage Kim by joining in her game. They cover a toy with a cloth, leaving part of it sticking out. 'Where has it gone?' They stimulate Kim's interest to find the toy. They stop the game when Kim avoids it or falls into a trance. They learn the right amount of stimulation by her responses.

'Out of sight, out of mind!'

Babies between four and eight months lose all interest in a toy when it disappears. They do not make connections between an object being there and not being there. 'Out of sight. Out of mind,' parents say. The reason may be that babies see people and objects as 'extensions' of themselves, rather like an extra arm or leg. Once a baby can make these connections, this stage of development is named **object recognition**.

■ Babies lose all interest in a toy when it disappears

At one year old, Kim shows a huge advance in manipulative skills. She tries to pile one block on top of another. She has developed a **pincer grip** and can pick up small objects. This is still a crude grip and will become refined over the next few years.

Child observation

Draw the grips the child uses when clasping a drinking cup, holding a spoon or crayon, handling a toy.

Investigation

Test the development of object recognition of babies aged four to twelve months.

For a baby between four and eight months make these observations.

a Observe and record what happens when the baby drops a toy.

b While the baby watches you, tuck a toy half in your pocket.

c Drape a cloth completely over a toy the baby is holding.

d Remove the cloth. Record the baby's expression.

e Drape a cloth over a toy which is making a noise and repeat.

The findings can be pooled in class.

For a baby between eight and twelve months make these observations.

a Repeat the above tasks. Comment on the development of object recognition.

b Hide a toy under a cloth while the baby is watching you.

c Hide the toy under a piece of paper.

d Hide the first toy again while the baby watches you.

e Secretly change the hidden toy for a different one.

f Hide the toy in an upturned cup, behind a board, or in a box.

Questions

1 Give the average age at which babies can:
  a reach for a toy in a purposeful way
  b hold it in a crude palmer grip
  c pass it from one hand to the other
  d grasp a toy in each hand
  e develop full hand release (letting go on purpose)
  f pick up a small toy using the pincer grip.

2 Dee's parents want her to be clever. They bombard her with stimulation, even when she falls into a trance. Explain why Dee then gets upset, cries and finally falls asleep.

3 Will's parents leave him strapped in his pram without any toys. Explain why he is late to develop his manipulative skills.

4 'Not too little! Not too much!' Suggest ways in which parents can learn the right amount of stimulation from their baby.

5 'Parenting is a constant learning process in which the baby is often the best teacher!' Discuss.

Motor skills are those which involve large movements of the body. Babies develop control from the top downwards. Their **upper body strength** shows when they can control their neck and shoulder muscles. By six months Dan can use the weight of his head to propel himself over onto his back. As soon as this stage is reached, infants cannot be left unattended on a high surface such as a bed in case they roll themselves onto the floor.

Babies kick strongly long before the special reflexes fade. But their muscles lack the strength to take weight on their legs. **Lower body strength** starts to show at six months when they can sit comfortably if they are propped up. By nine months, they can sit unsupported for ten to fifteen minutes.

Mobility

Between nine months and one year, babies become **mobile**. They crawl, sometimes at great speed. They may prefer to 'bottom shuffle' or 'bear-walk' in order to reach a toy. A few try to pull themselves to a standing position by using the furniture. Parents encourage a baby's motor skills by placing the toy a little further distance each time.

At one year, Dan can lift his body from the lying position to the sitting stance. He sits easily and with confidence. Some toddlers can walk unsupported, without the help of a parent's hands or clutching the furniture. Once Dan can move by himself, he gains a great sense of power. To be able to stand freely is wonderful, a huge progress in gaining body control. He crows with delight at his achievement, before falling flat on his bottom again.

During all this learning, Dan must pay attention to his movements. If his concentration wavers, he promptly falls down. Nor can he progress to further learning, e.g. stepping forward, until he has developed memory patterns for standing.

Helping a child

Early learning can stay in the memory for life. So it is important to learn the correct movements from the start. At three, Dan still gets his feet in a twisted tangle. His parents teach him to pay attention by games of encouragement and praise. 'One step. Two step. Three step. You're good at walking!' Dan continues to be given encouragement and praise until he can walk without having to pay attention to his feet. This is **positive teaching**.

Kay, age four, keeps bumping into objects. Her parents scold, 'Clumsy girl! Why don't you look where you're going?' Kay is not clumsy. She is making mistakes, as all learners do. Because she hates being scolded, she pays attention to her upset feelings and now cannot look where she is going. Kay bumps into more objects until she finally does become clumsy. This is **negative teaching**.

■ This baby prefers to bear-walk

— Investigation —

Identify the value of memory patterns.
a Stand up. Sit down.
b Record which parts of your body moved to stand up.
c Stand again, paying attention to all the moving parts.
d Record all the parts of your body which moved.
e Were you really paying attention the first time?
f List some advantages in not having to pay attention each time you stand up.

■ It takes years before a child can move smoothly and gracefully. Estimate the age of each child

At eighteen months, walks well and can run. Crawls up stairs and comes down backwards. At two years, runs well, stops safely. Walks up stairs one step at a time with one hand on wall, crawls down. At three years, can walk on tiptoe. Climbs on a play frame. Rides pedal cycle and turns wide corners. At four years, walks upstairs with each foot, downstairs with both feet. Can stand briefly on one foot.

At five years, hops and skips on one foot, walks along chalked line, runs up and down stairs, climbs trees.

━ Child observation ━

Record some stages of the child's motor skills. How do these skills match those of the milestones?

━ Questions ━

1 Give the average ages when children can:
   a roll their bodies over
   b sit without support
   c start to crawl
   d stand freely without support
   e begin to walk
   f run well
   g walk along a chalk line.

2 Going forward is easier than going into reverse. Analyse this statement by observing how children manage stairs at different ages.

3 As a class activity, draw up a list of milestones for motor control from observing children playing on the park swings.

4 Why do you think children are so pleased when they become fully mobile?

Play

Exploratory play

Play is not something babies do to fill up their time. It is the way all infants learn. They seek information about their world through their senses of sight, touch, smell, taste and hearing. This sensory exploring is named **exploratory play**.

A baby's first playthings are parts of herself. Rani's fingers are an endless source of fascination. They are stared at, clenched, waved about. Her parents are a very close second. Their faces and clothing are there to be smelled, clutched, rumpled, explored. Rani's mouth is her first source of pleasure. The lips are extremely sensitive, with many more nerve endings than, say, the nose. Because it feels good to suck, any and every object within Rani's reach will be put into her mouth.

'How can she enjoy that?' cries Rani's father when she tries to eat his tie. The most unsuitable objects are **mouthed**: licked, tasted, sucked, chewed, dribbled on. Rani is exploring the tie for information. When she learns that ties are not nice to eat, she still has a **purpose**. She is learning about textures through her sensitive mouth.

Obviously, the first concern when choosing a toy for a baby is safety. The primary rule is 'no toy should be small enough to fit inside a baby's mouth'. The next rule is 'no toy should have small parts which can become detached'.

■ Exploring keys – not the most suitable thing to suck!

Investigation

Analyse early toys for safety factors.
You will need:
a variety of toys.
Visit a toy shop or playgroup, or use the information from a toy catalogue.

a Do the rattles have small moving parts?
b How are the teddy's eyes attached?
c What is the size and strength of the straps, bars or other moving parts?
d Are there any rough edges on the plastic toys?
e Will the toys be easy to clean when they get dirty?
f Comment on their colour, texture, shape, aesthetic appeal.
g Record each hand-eye skill the toy encourages.
h Record its cost and predicted length of use.
i From the evidence of your findings, plus what you have learned so far, choose two toys for (i) a baby of under three months old, and (ii) a baby aged between eight months and one year old. Explain in detail the reasons for each of your choices.

Home toys

Toys do not have to be expensive or even bought. A home is full of them: wooden spoons, plastic cups and plates, saucepans with clangy lids, empty shoe boxes. These are all fine learning toys, especially if one item fits inside another. Older children enjoy dusters and drying-up cloths as 'toys'. Helping with the home-making tasks gives them a sense of value and importance. Old clothes are fun for dressing-up games.

Work or play?

Adults call their play **leisure**. They play when they read, paint, garden, DIY, cook – whatever they enjoy as a hobby and not for payment or duty. For example, people try out new recipes for the fun of cooking. This is very different from working in a canteen or having to cook three meals each day to feed a hungry family.

■ Early toys

A child's play includes these factors:
◆ it is enjoyable and fun
◆ it is chosen by the child
◆ it is exciting and absorbing
◆ it is done for its own sake
◆ it is done because the child wishes to do it and not to please.

Though play needs to include these factors, children are learning at the same time. They have a lively curiosity, a keen desire to uncover the secrets of their world. When an object catches their attention, they mount a full investigation of it. They identify it as a toy, whether it is the gas bill which should not be touched or a real toy. They analyse what they can do with it, whether they push it along the floor or tear it up. They generate new forms of play with it, whether they feed the torn pieces of bill to teddy or collect them up into neat piles. They evaluate it as useful or useless in their play.

Toy play begins in the first year and reaches a peak at six years. After that, children become more interested in activities which involve the company of other children: games, sports and hobbies. At each stage of learning, toys need to meet the progress made in physical, intellectual, emotional and social development. They need to stimulate the interest and then satisfy the curiosity. As children get older, they need toys which push their learning a little further, and which challenge them to try new skills.

Building blocks are favourite learning toys. They encourage:
◆ hand–eye co-ordination to grasp a block firmly
◆ motor skills of crawling to fetch another one
◆ manipulative skills to balance one on top of the other
◆ creative skills to make new shapes and patterns.

— Child observation

Watch the child with a new toy and record:
a the child's first response to the toy
b the time spent on investigating it
c any new games the child generates with it
d the old skills used or new ones learned from it
e any comments the child makes about it
f the child's general evaluation of it.

— Questions

1 What are the main differences between work and play?
2 Name the kinds and size of toys used by the child you are studying, and describe the type of skills they encourage.
3 What is meant by
   a mouthing
   b sensory exploration?

4 Describe three ways in which exploratory play helps a baby learn.
5 Explain the safety rules for early toys. Do you think they should be extended to toys for older children? If so, say why.

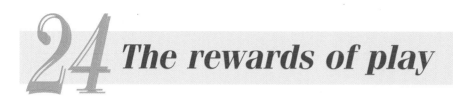

Play is serious work for children. If they are interrupted, they become annoyed or upset. In fact, it would be very difficult to stop infants playing. One classic sign of ill-health in a child is a loss of interest in play.

Play progresses from one stage to the next as the child develops. There is an age sequence for each activity which can be predicted.

Manipulative play is work with the hands: sand and water games; learning the size, shape, colour, texture and weight of things. Sewing cards, threading beads, cutting out, dot-to-dot, tracing, copying shapes and letters; learning hand dexterity and improving hand–eye co-ordination.

Physical play is body work: jumping games, hopping, skipping, climbing stairs, garden frames, trees; learning to develop balancing skills; getting rid of energy.

Social play is people work. Learning to share toys, watching how other children behave, trying to communicate with them, practising behaving in an acceptable way, wanting to belong and fit in.

Creative play is artistic work: making things, drawing pictures, dressing-up, **role-play**.

The joy a child gains in learning a new skill through play is easily observed. Rajan gurgles with delight when he manages to place one block on top of the other. His reward is the pleasure of achievement, nothing else. If the block then topples off, this does not seem to matter. He has achieved what he set out to do, he has reached his goal.

Life is full of challenges: confusions, puzzles and problems waiting to be solved. To meet a challenge and overcome it brings feelings of great confidence. Confidence helps a child to feel more in control of the world. A toy which is too difficult has the opposite effect. Children feel frustrated if they cannot master the new skill or fail to understand what to do with the toy.

Favourite toys are those which are **versatile**, they can be used in many different ways. A plastic duck is fun to sink in the bath and watch it bob up again. But otherwise it is boring. On the other hand, a plastic cup can be used for filling and emptying, for floating and sinking, for pouring and drinking, for banging and knocking. Toys which make noises as well as having many different uses

■ Games of pat-a-cake bring happy feelings

are even more popular and keep a child's attention longer.

Play without toys is popular when it involves people.

'Pat-a-cake, Pat-a-cake, baker's man
Bake me a cake as fast as you can.
Prick it and pat it and mark it with T
And put it in the oven for Tadek and me.'

Games of pat-a-cake involve touching, talking, copying, missing, laughing, trying again. Games of swinging from parents' hands bring warmth, belonging, happy feelings, sharing fun.

Role-play is **imaginative play**, and begins at age two (see unit 40). Children often use role-play as a way to manage their feelings of tension. These feelings come from situations which are stressful. Children try to manage the stress by acting out the situation. For example, Rod is jealous of the new baby. He smiles and pats its head but his inner feelings are in a turmoil. Rod role-plays nursing his teddy as he has observed his mother nursing the new baby. He talks to it and rocks it, sitting cross-legged on the floor. Soon, his whole body is rocking quite strongly as he releases the pain of his tension. After a while, he feels calmer and can pat the baby again.

Play helps a child reduce stress

Clara has returned from her first morning in a playgroup. She enjoyed the fun but she was alarmed by all the noise and constant movement.

■ Role-play helps children deal with difficult situations, such as their first morning at a playgroup

She role-plays the same situation at home, lining up her toys as the noisy children and pretending to be the play leader. Clara is teaching herself to understand what the play leader expects of her. Then she role-plays being one of the noisy children: shouting, running about, bumping into the toys she has lined up and snatching things from them. Clara is teaching herself to become familiar with the way children behave when they are together.

Role-play helps a child become familiar with new situations and so reduces the fear of them.

▬ Child observation ▬

Record a favourite toy of the child and list all the hand and/or motor skills it encourages.

◇

▬ Questions ▬

1 Identify at least three skills a child is learning through the activity of pat-a-cake.

2 Suggest, with reasons, four objects which can be used as toys in many different ways.

3 List the different types of play, with and without toys.

4 Explain the following problems.
a Zac's parents hide his blocks and replace them with a high-tech train-set. Zac refuses to play with it.
b Rani's mother becomes anxious when she sees her daughter rocking in a trance. She picks her up, and Rani bursts into tears.

25 *Pleasure and pain*

A child's first years involve learning body control. But while they are learning, they have many failures. Life can be difficult when your muscles lack strength and your body movements do not obey you. At three months, babies smack their faces when reaching for a toy. At seven months, they topple over when sitting up. At one year, they fall down quite painfully when learning to walk and must get up and start all over again.

Do babies learn more from pleasure than pain? To find the answer, observers studied their brain waves and heart beats. In any stimulation, nerves 'fire' electrical signals which show a *slight* increase in brain and heart rate. These can be measured on electrical machines.

Millions of brain cells 'fire' every second. Each produces a tiny burst of electricity which can be picked up by electrodes (sensors) on the scalp. The signals go to an electromagnet, which drags a pen over moving paper. This is an **electroencephalogram**, EEG. An EEG is a graph of the brain's activity. It records 'brain waves'.

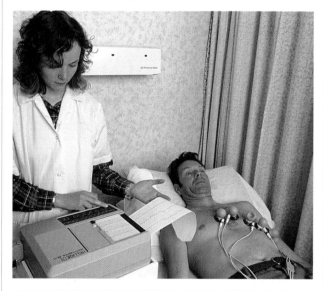

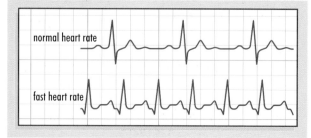

The heart has powerful muscles to pump blood around the body. The same nerve signals can be recorded when the heart muscles contract. A graph of the heart rate is an **electrocardiogram**, ECG.

The observers found that when newborns orient to pleasure, such as 'mother, milk, cuddles', their heart rate and brain waves first speed up. Then they slow to a slightly faster-than-normal rate. This slightly faster-than-normal rate remains steady during the time they feel pleasure. Their energies are directed to learning more about these feelings of pleasure. They are paying attention.

When newborns avoid a painful stimulation, such as being undressed when they are cosy and warm, their heart rate and brain waves speed up and *stay* at the fast rate. They do not slow to the slightly faster-than-normal rate of paying attention. Babies cannot learn till the undressing stops because the energy needed for learning is directed to avoiding the pain.

Paying attention

Paying attention is a natural thing for babies and children to do. They show great pleasure in discovering their world. When they pay attention, their heart rate and brain waves beat at a slightly faster pace than when they are in a trance, dozing or asleep. When they are distressed, hurt or crying, their heart rate and brain waves stay at the fast pace we all experience when we are frightened, hurt or very angry. The slightly faster-than-normal brain and heart rate is **the paying attention rate**.

When the special reflexes fade, babies react to pleasure or pain with **purpose**. They purposefully reach for the things which bring them pleasure. By four months, Glenda crows with delight at being fed, cuddled, soothed and stimulated. She frowns, screams, kicks out, yells when she feels pain.

As Glenda gets older she can choose how to react: 'Do I really hate this feeling of being undressed? Shall I scream anyway to see what happens? Shall I be good and smile because I like my bath? Shall I be more good and help because I love my Mum?'

Being undressed is not painful. Children have the serious task of learning to manage

■ An ECG

■ Learning to manage pain

As children grow, they seek to control more of their world. They wish to be less dependent on the help of parents. 'Me do it!' they say, long before they have the skills to tackle a task safely.

When Glenda gets soap in her eyes while trying to wash her face, her parents reduce the sting with clean water. They reassure her with plenty of comfort and cuddles. This helps Glenda learn that her world is a safe place, even though it gives her plenty of stings and knocks. Her parents then reward her efforts with praise: 'You nearly did that!' They encourage Glenda to try again the next time. 'Now do it this way.' They balance the comfort and cuddles with praise and encouragement. In this way they help Glenda in her natural wish to be more independent.

When small children are stimulated to learn, and when their emotional needs are met, they remain keen to learn.

discomfort. Later, they have the even more serious task of learning to manage pain. (Not all pain is manageable but most adults try to control their responses at the early stages.) With the pain, for example, of having the dirt washed from a cut, children learn that it is worth managing the pain to gain the 'reward' of praise for being brave. How soon a child can control its reactions to pleasure and pain depends upon its early experiences of them.

Interdependence

Newborns cannot choose their responses to pleasure and pain. They feel **devoured** by panic if their needs are not met. Hunger or cold are serious life threats. Even minor discomforts such as being undressed can trigger terrifying fears of danger. Parents learn to speed up any process which causes their baby distress.

Learning and growing are **interdependent**. When the physical needs of babies are met, they remain keen to learn.

— Child observation

Record any painful knock the child experiences and the ways it tries to manage the hurt.

— Questions

1 Copy and complete the following into your folder: The heart rate and —— are powered by electrical impulses. They beat at a slow rate when a baby is sleeping, —— or in a trance. When a baby is learning, this rate speeds up and then —— to the slightly faster paying attention rate. When a baby is upset, this pace —— and does not —— to the paying attention rate.

2 Explain in your own words why babies cannot learn when they are in pain, upset or otherwise distressed.

3 Name three actions of parents which help children remain keen to learn.

Body language

Body language is **non-verbal communication**. It consists of the signals which people use to show their feelings without words. Body language shows in appearance, posture, gesture, expression, distance from another person and state of awareness. A great deal can be learned from observing the body language of infants.

Think of the most disgusting food and show your response. The feeling of disgust causes an unpleasant jolt through the system. If a child believes that the wrinkled skin on warmed milk is nasty, a strong charge of revulsion is felt all over his body.

The lower eyelid is pushed up. The eyebrows lower to shut out the disgusting sight. The mouth pulls down or widens in a grimace of distaste. The nostrils wrinkle though there may not be a bad smell. The child may make a croaking sound as if about to vomit.

If the child is then forced to eat, a further jolt charges through the system. This is anger. The muscles contract in the pullback response. The parent then becomes the 'enemy'. Sensitive parenting includes 'reading' the child's signals correctly and then providing the care which matches the signals.

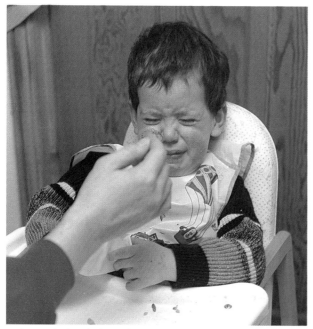

■ A great deal can be learnt from watching children's expressions

The comforter

By four months, 55 per cent of infants suck objects which do not provide food. The comforter is common to children in all cultures. The comforter is any object the child wishes to have near: a blanket, a fluffy toy, a soft rag, a cloth which smells of milk. This object is cuddled, stroked, clutched, clung to and sucked, especially when the child feels strong emotions or wishes to fall asleep.

A **habit** is an activity which has settled in. Adults use comforters too. Pets are ideal for filling this role. They are soft and furry and enjoy being stroked. However, they are not sucked.

― *Investigation* ―

A class survey of sucking habits.
You will need:
volunteers who pen-chew, nail-bite or hair-twist.
a When is the habit most often done?
b How do the students feel at the time?
c Does the habit help with those feelings?
d If so, describe in what ways.

Over 10 per cent of children start sucking habits at eight months. Their comforter may be a thumb, fingers, cloth or soother. They use this comforter to help them manage their feelings. The following shows the frequency of sucking habits in childhood:
47 per cent of two year olds
42 per cent of three year olds
36 per cent of four year olds
30 per cent of five year olds
21 per cent of six year olds
5.9 per cent at eleven years old

As children learn to manage their feelings, they gain a sense of dignity and self-respect. This is closely linked with their progress in body control. Their self-image depends more upon their physical development than their reasoning skills. Parents help children by allowing them personal dignity long before they actually develop it.

Toilet control

Infants have no control over their urine or stools. The feeding reflex relaxes the **sphincters** (rings of muscle) which control these activities. Some infants can be potted successfully after a feed but this does not mean they have developed any control. By eighteen months to two years, toddlers learn to make connections between 'tinkling' in the potty and their inner urges. They may clutch themselves, make signals, or ask for the potty.

Rewards of praise when they are successful speed up learning. Pressure, scoldings or disapproval slow it down. The toddler 'pays attention' to her hurt feelings instead of her inner urges. She can develop **memory patterns** for the toilet as a source of stress.

The child is the only person who can make connections between her inner urges and the potty. Forcing her before her developmental stage of control is both ineffective and an affront to human dignity. By age five, most children are clean and dry.

— *Child observation* —

Watch the child with a comfort object and record the different ways it is used.

Over 10 per cent of children start sucking habits at eight months

— *Questions* —

1 As a class activity, list the various objects children choose as comforters. Identify which common factors they all share. Record
   a the method of use
   b the times of greatest need
   c the response if the comforter is removed or mislaid
   d whether or not this response speeds up its return.

   Suggest ways in which parents can solve the problem of cleaning a grubby comforter without the child suffering loss. Link the need for comfort objects to stages of physical development. From your findings, explain if you would choose to allow a child the use of a comforter.

2 Toilet control cannot be taught, only encouraged. The advice is 'Reward success. Ignore failure'. Comment fully on this advice.

3 Gordon starts bed-wetting at age five. What happens at this age? Suggest, with reasons, ways you would choose to help him.

4 More girls than boys develop sucking habits. Can you think of reasons for this gender difference? If so, what? A study of fifteen-year-old students found two-thirds were (or had been) nail biters. Which group was normal? Complete the following: 'I do/do not think habits in childhood are normal because...'

Saturday morning

'A mother's work is child's play!' scoffs sixteen-year-old Jeff. His mother smiles, 'Then walk in my shoes tomorrow.' Jeff devises the following work plan, with the needs of his sister, Jemma, in mind.

- 20 minutes to prepare and eat breakfast
- 5 minutes to settle Jemma with toys
- 10 minutes to clean kitchen
- 10 minutes to vacuum lounge carpet
- 5 minutes to dust surfaces and tidy
- 10 minutes to tidy bathroom
- 25 minutes for cartoons on television
- 10 minutes to tidy bedrooms
- 10 minutes snack for Jemma and self
- 60 minutes walk in the park, buy groceries for lunch
- 15 minutes to prepare lunch

— Investigation —

Evaluate Jeff's time plan (as listed above).
a Select one task from Jeff's work plan.
b Identify the material resources for the task.
c Plan, time and complete the task.
d Record the time and evaluate your work.
e Is Jeff's time plan realistic?

■ Jeff's plans get off to a bad start when Jemma spills her juice

How Jeff's plan worked out

Jemma spills her breakfast juice, soaking herself and the floor. Jeff takes her to the bathroom, removes her wet clothes and sits her on the potty. While he fetches dry clothing, she 'helps' by tipping the potty contents into the toilet – and misses! Jeff hoses her down in the bath, dries and dresses her.

He tries to settle Jemma to play but she wants to be with him. After ten minutes, he gives up and Jemma helps him fetch the vacuum cleaner. She bangs her thumb and cries for kisses and games of piggy-back. Now it is time for television. The other tasks must wait. Then Jemma wants her mid-morning snack. Jeff fixes it. The milk makes her sleepy. She toddles into the front room and curls up on the carpet. So as not to wake her, Jeff tackles the mess in the bathroom. He has to make two journeys to the kitchen for items of cleaning equipment which he forgot. Each time he walks across the spilled juice, the floor becomes more tacky. As he finishes the bathroom, Jemma wakes. She wants a cuddle, her potty and more games. Jeff is exhausted as the family returns for lunch.

Leisure time

Children are beyond price but the cost of raising them is steep. From birth to age 21, the estimated cost in 1995 was £122,675. Even parents who are reasonably well-off have to make cuts in their lifestyle. Other extremely important costs include the time and energy available to busy parents.

Leisure time is 'the time you have to do whatever you like'. Four-fifths of leisure time is spent in the home. Couples without children have an average 47 hours a week. With children, this is 22 hours a week. Parents say that their time and energy could be saved for much more leisure if older children cleared away their things.

The concept of helping

People need to feel useful and of value. They become depressed if they see their lives as pointless. One long-term goal of parents is to raise an independent and *useful* adult. From a very early age, children feel useful and important if they help around the home. This help can start by learning to put away their things.

When story-time is over, Jill's mother takes her to the book shelf and they replace the book together. They *share* the task of putting things away. Jill, aged nine months, is learning the value of caring for her possessions. By two, she will expect to return things to their proper place.

A three-year-old can clutter the home as messily as a 23-year-old. 'It's quicker to pick up Jack's things than waste time and energy nagging him,' his parents say. This is a short-term goal. Children who learn to be useful around the home also learn to care for the comfort of others. Tasks take much longer while they help and mistakes often happen. But children gain in self-respect when they see themselves as useful. **Infantilism** is the condition in adulthood of thinking and behaving like a child.

■ This child knows he can be helpful by tidying away his toys

— *Child observation* —

Place a box of small items in front of the child. Record the way each object is picked out, handled and examined. As a new game, ask the child to find a special place for each item to go back in the box. Record how the child does this. Pool your findings in class and estimate the average age at which children can methodically return each item separately.

— *Questions* —

1 Name four of Jemma's physical needs during the morning.

2 How did Jeff meet her emotional need for comfort when she banged her thumb?

3 Describe the ways Jemma showed her social need for company.

4 List the tasks not done and the time planned for them.

5 When devising his work plan, what major factor did Jeff forget?

6 Give a rough estimate of Jemma's age from her behaviour.

7 Name one way for parents to save time and energy and the long-term value a to the parents and b to the child.

8 Name another cost to parents of raising a child. 'Possessions which are cared for last longer.' Suggest ways that this statement can be proved or disproved.

28 *Nutrients*

Nutrients are the substances in food needed for health. There are five groups of nutrients: proteins, carbohydrates, fats, vitamins and minerals. Most foods contain more than one kind of nutrient. Human milk contains all the nutrients necessary in the first four to six months of life.

Proteins

Proteins are the growth and body-building nutrients. Babies grow very rapidly. They double their birthweight by four to five months and almost triple it by one year. The word protein is from ancient Greek and means 'I come first'. Every cell in the body is made up of more protein than the other nutrients.

Proteins are built from 22 different **amino acids**. Ten are essential for children and eight for adults. The essential amino acids cannot be made in the body so need to be supplied by food. Foods containing proteins that have all the essential amino acids include milk, eggs, fish, poultry and meat. Proteins which lack some essential amino acids are found in pulses, nuts, seeds and cereal foods such as bread, rice and pasta.

When growth stops in the late teens, protein continues to be needed for cell replacement. Over each seven years, each cell in the body (except the brain and teeth) dies and is replaced by a new cell. The skin sheds dead cells all the time.

Carbohydrates

Carbohydrates are the energy nutrients. Babies are bundles of energy and toddlers are explosions of activity. Carbohydrates provide the fuel the body needs for energy, whether at work, play or sleep. The three types of carbohydrates are:

1 **Starchy carbohydrates** – which are found in cereals and cereal products such as flour, bread, cornflour and pastry; in fruits and vegetables such as yam, potato, plantain, green banana and turnip; in rice and pasta.

2 **Sugary carbohydrates** – which are in cane and beet plants; in fruits and some vegetables such as sweetcorn, carrots, peas and tomatoes; in honey, treacle and golden syrup; in prepared foods such as jams, soft drinks, tomato sauces; in baked products such as biscuits, cakes, sweets and chocolate.

3 **Fibre** – which is the tough part of plants and is not digested. It exercises the muscles of the intestines and helps to prevent constipation. Fibre comes from the cell walls of vegetables and fruit. It is also found in pulses such as peas, beans and lentils; in breakfast cereals such as oats, wheat and bran; in wholemeal bread and pasta, and in brown rice.

During digestion a lot of fluid pours into the intestines. Fibre absorbs this fluid, making the food soft and bulky. This gives a feeling of

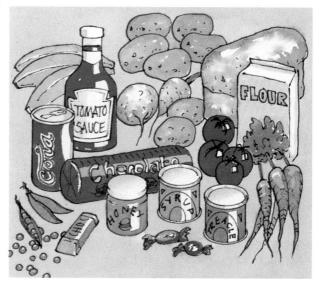

■ Separate these foods into starchy carbohydrates and sugary carbohydrates

■ Which of these protein-rich foods contain essential amino acids?

fullness without adding weight. The softened fibre and waste products of digestion are easily moved along the intestines and there are soft bowel movements without any strain.

Fats

Fats are energy nutrients too. They are essential for the healthy working of body cells. Some fats are visible, like the fat on meat. Others are invisible, like those in eggs, nuts, cheese, mayonnaise and other prepared foods. Fats from plants such as cooking and olive oils are **liquid** at room temperature. Fats from animals such as butter and margarine are **solid** at room temperature.

Fats contain **essential fatty acids**. Breast-fed babies get all the essential fatty acids from human milk. When they start to eat solids, babies under

■ Which foods for toddlers are rich in essential fatty acids?

age two continue to need more fats in their diet than children under age five. Good sources of essential fatty acids come from oily fish and the plant oils in vegetables, fruit and nuts, and cereal products.

During the last few weeks before birth, the unborn baby builds up a store of nutrients, which helps support growth for the first few months of life. Premature babies and those of low birthweight have little time to store enough food. They need food which is **dense** (rich, high) in energy for rapid growth.

- ◆ One gram of protein has an energy value of 4 kilocalories.
- ◆ One gram of carbohydrate has an energy value of 3.75 kcal.
- ◆ One gram of fat has an energy value of 9 kcal.

The milk of the mothers of premature and low-birthweight babies contains more fat, protein and salt but less carbohydrate than the milk of mothers of full-term babies. This enables the babies to obtain the energy they need in a dense form.

─ *Child observation* ─

Record some favourite foods of the child. Ask if they are favourites because of their **taste**, sweet or savoury; **texture**, smooth or crunchy; **smell**, strong or weak; **visual appeal**, colour, shape, size, pattern or other points of interest. Pool your findings in class and list the favourite foods of different-aged children in your area.

─ *Questions* ─

1 What are the functions of proteins in the body? Why are they important for babies and growing children? From what source do newborns get their protein? Name six foods which could be given to ensure there is enough protein in a five-year-old's diet. What are the likely consequences of a lack of protein in the diet?

2 Name three foods which are good sources of
   a starchy carbohydrates
   b sugary carbohydrates.

3 Explain the functions in the diet of
   a fats
   b fibre.

4 Which food group has the highest energy value?

5 Give the average birthweight of a full-term baby. Estimate the predicted weight gain at
   a four to five months
   b one year
   c eighteen months
   d three years
   e five years.

   Refer to units 4 and 7 to help you with this question.

29 *Food requirements*

The word **diet** can mean either what people normally eat or a special eating plan for health reasons. Here, diet refers to the normal intake of food which provides all the nutrients and energy required for health. A **dietitian** is a person who specializes in nutrition and health. **Diet therapy** is the treatment of a disease by changing the pattern of food intake and nutrients and/or energy in the diet.

Energy

All foods provide energy, some more than others. For adults, the energy input from food must equal the energy output by the body. For children, the energy input must be greater than the energy output because they are growing. This also applies to women in the last three months of pregnancy, to provide energy for the developing baby, and to nursing mothers to produce good quality breast milk.

Dietary Reference Values (DRV) are estimates of the nutritional and energy requirements of groups of people with similar characteristics such as age and gender. The energy value of food can be measured in:

◆ **kilojoules** (kJ) – 1 kJ equals 1000 joules
◆ **kilocalories** (kcal) – 1 kcal equals 1000 calories.

DRV charts show the food requirements for groups of people in both ways. When you see kJ/d or kcal/d, this means the amounts required for a group of people each day. (The word kilocalorie is sometimes shortened to calorie in everyday language.)

UK Dietary Reference Values for energy in early childhood				
Estimated Average Requirements (EARs) for dietary energy kJ/d (kcal/d)				
Age	Boys		Girls	
0–3 months	2,280	(545)	2,160	(515)
4–6 months	2,890	(690)	2,690	(645)
7–9 months	3,440	(825)	3,200	(765)
10–12 months	3,850	(920)	3,610	(865)
1–3 years	5,150	(1,230)	4,860	(1,165)
4–6 years	7,160	(1,715)	6,460	(1,545)

Source: Department of Health, 1991

The **Estimated Average Requirement** (EAR) means exactly what it says - the *average* requirement for a group of people. So half the children in one age group will usually need *more* than the EAR, and half will need *less*. This is very important to remember as children have very different energy needs.

The **Basal Metabolic Rate** (BMR) is the rate at which the body uses energy when it is at complete rest. Boys tend to have a higher BMR than girls.

The **activity levels** of children are different too. This will also affect their requirements for energy. A child's natural **appetite** is the best guide for parents. If *the child is thriving, gaining weight and eating well, there is no need for concern over energy intake.* Only if growth slows is there a need for concern.

EARs are usful to work out the food requirements of children in groups, not individual children.

Protein for growth and body-building

A lack of protein in the diet is unusual in the Western world. Children who are eating a wide variety of foods will be getting enough protein.

Reference Nutrient Intakes (RNIs) for protein: children aged 0-6 years	
Age	RNI (g/d)
0–3 months	12.5
4–6 months	12.7
7–9 months	13.7
10–12 months	14.9
1–3 years	14.5
4–6 years	19.7

Source: Department of Health, 1991

Note: RNIs are the amounts which are enough, or more than enough, for 97% of the children in that age group.

— *Child observation* —

Record the food and drink consumed by the child in one day. Estimate the protein content of the diet using food tables or a computer program. Compare your findings with the RNI for groups of children at the same age.

— Investigation

Using food tables or a computer program, estimate the protein content of the following foods for children aged 18 months to $4\frac{1}{2}$ years assuming each portion size to be:

1 slice of wholemeal bread = 35 g
1 bowl of cornflakes = 20 g
1 boiled egg = 50 g
1 carton of yoghurt = 150 g
1 small fillet of cod = 50 g
1 slice of roast chicken = 40 g
1 slice of roast beef = 30 g
1 boiled potato = 60 g
1 tablespoonful of peas = 25 g
Cooked spaghetti = 40 g
1 apple = 100 g
1 banana = 100 g

Which foods contain all the essential amino acids?

Repeat the investigation using household measures to help you gain a better understanding of portion sizes.

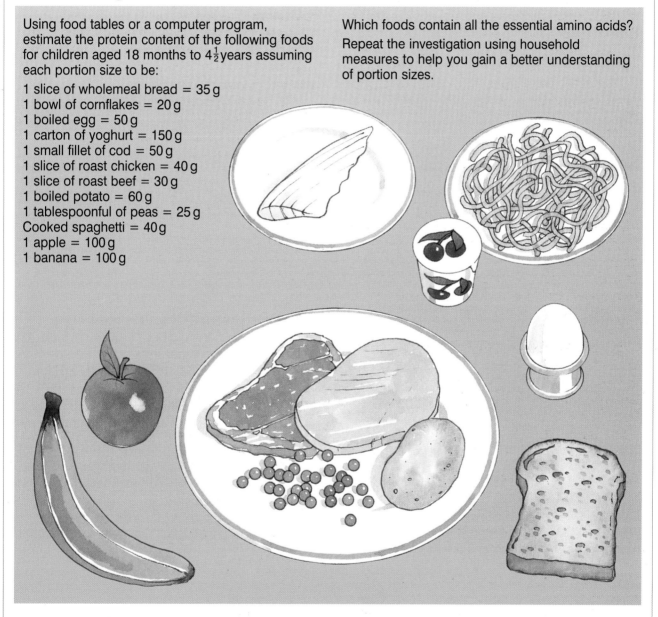

— Questions

1 Give the EAR for energy for
  a a girl aged two
  b a boy aged two.
2 Give the protein RNIs for four-year-olds.
3 Explain the difference between EARs and RNIs.
4 a From which food do babies gain their essential fatty acids?

b What does BMR mean?
c Which gender tends to have a higher BMR?
d What is meant by activity levels?
e Why might a child with a high activity level eat more than a child with a low one?
f Name the signs of health which tell parents that their baby is getting enough of the right foods.

Vitamins and minerals

Vitamins

Vitamins are complex chemicals made by plants and animals (μg is a microgram, one millionth of a gram, or one thousandth of a milligram (mg).

Vitamin A helps the eyes see in dim light. It helps protect the lining of cells over the eyes and the linings over the lungs and upper respiratory tract. The body obtains vitamin A in two forms: **retinol** and **beta-carotene**. The main sources of retinol are whole milk, liver, oily fish, cod and halibut liver oils, eggs, cheese and butter. The main sources of beta-carotene are orange and red fruits, and vegetables such as carrots, tomatoes and peppers. Beta-carotene is converted to vitamin A in the body.

Vitamin A is added by law to margarine. It is also added to some infant foods. It can be stored in the liver and so is not needed at every meal. A great excess of vitamin A can be harmful.

Vitamin B group consists of thiamin (vitamin B1) riboflavin (vitamin B2), niacin, vitamin B6, folic acid (folate) and vitamin B12. In general, they enable the body to obtain energy from food and assist in growth. B vitamins are found in a wide range of foods including meat and meat products; milk, cheese and eggs; cereal and cereal products; potatoes and vegetables. Most diets have an adequate supply. An exception is vitamin B12 (cobalamin), which is essential to make red blood cells and for the nervous system. Vitamin B12 is found only in animal products such as meat, fish, eggs, milk and cheese. Some breakfast cereals have vitamin B12 and other B vitamins added. The B-group vitamins are not stored in the body so a daily supply is required.

Vitamin C (ascorbic acid) is essential to:
- help heal wounds
- help make connective tissue which binds body cells together
- help the body absorb iron from non-meat foods.

Vitamin C may also help to increase the body's resistance to minor infections such as the common cold.

The main sources of vitamin C are citrus fruits and their juices such as orange and blackcurrant. Tomatoes, peppers, green leafy vegetables and potatoes are another source. Fruit drinks are often enriched with vitamin C. Otherwise, it is not widely found in foods. Any extra in the diet is excreted in urine.

Vitamin C is easily lost by long storage and cooking. Quick freezing reduces the loss through long storage. Using a microwave or steaming reduces the loss of vitamin C through cooking.

Vitamin D is essential to:
- develop strong bones and teeth (with calcium and phosphorus)
- promote quicker healing of fractures
- help the absorption of calcium in the intestine.

Few foods contain vitamin D. The main sources of vitamin D are oily fish such as herring, mackerel, egg yolk, liver, margarine, cod and halibut liver oils. Sunlight on skin helps the body make its own vitamin D.

Reference Nutrient Intakes for vitamins: children 0–6

Age	Thiamin (mg/d)	Riboflavin (mg/d)	Niacin (mg/d)	Vitamin B$_6$ (μg/d)	Vitamin B$_{12}$ (μg/d)	Folate (μg/d)	Vitamin C (mg/d)	Vitamin A (μg/d)	Vitamin D (μg/d)
0–3 months	0.2	0.4	3	0.2	0.3	50	25	350	8.5
4–6 months	0.2	0.4	3	0.2	0.3	50	25	350	8.5
7–9 months	0.2	0.4	4	0.3	0.4	50	25	350	7
10–12 months	0.3	0.4	5	0.4	0.4	50	25	350	7
1–3 years	0.5	0.6	8	0.7	0.5	70	30	400	7
4–6 years	0.7	0.8	11	0.9	0.8	100	30	400	–

Source: Department of Health, 1991

Reference Nutrient Intakes for minerals: children 0–6

Age	Calcium (mg/d)	Iron (mg/d)	Sodium (mg/d)	Phosphorus (mg/d)	Magnesium (mg/d)	Potassium (mg/d)	Chloride (mg/d)	Zinc (mg/d)	Copper (mg/d)	Selenium (ug/d)	Iodine (ug/d)
0–3 months	525	1.7	210	400	55	800	320	4.0	0.2	10	50
4–6 months	525	4.3	280	400	60	850	400	4.0	0.3	13	60
7–9 months	525	7.8	320	400	75	700	500	5.0	0.3	10	60
10–12 months	525	7.8	350	400	80	700	500	5.0	0.3	10	60
1–3 years	350	6.9	500	270	85	800	800	5.0	0.4	15	70
4–6 years	450	6.1	700	350	120	1100	1100	6.5	0.6	20	100

Source: Department of Health, 1991

Minerals

People obtain **minerals** from both plant and animal foods.

Calcium is essential for:
- the formation of strong healthy bones and teeth
- normal clotting of blood
- keeping a normal heartbeat
- normal functioning of nerves and muscles.

Foods which are rich sources of calcium include milk, cheese, yoghurt and fish such as pilchards where the bones can be eaten. Other sources of calcium include pulses, dried fruit, green leafy vegetables, oranges, nuts and seeds.

If an adult's diet lacks calcium, it is leeched (taken) from the bones and teeth for other functions. The disease **osteoporosis** (brittle bones) is a loss of bone **density** (thickness, hardness). Osteoporosis can start even in a teenager whose diet lacks enough calcium. If a child's diet lacks calcium and vitamin D, this can lead to the disease of **rickets** (unit 35) which causes deformed legs.

Sodium and chlorine (salt)

Salt is sodium chloride. Salt is essential in tissue fluids and has many other complex functions. It occurs naturally in foods. Too much salt can damage the kidneys. It may cause a rise in blood pressure, which is one of the risk factors for heart disease. Babies should not have salt added to their food because their kidneys cannot cope with excreting large quantities. Nor is it sensible to encourage a taste for salt at the toddler stage.

Other minerals

Iron is essential for making red blood cells. Not enough iron in the diet leads to **anaemia**. An anaemic person feels listless and is easily tired. Women are at greater risk of anaemia than men because of their monthly blood loss during **menstruation**. Iron in liver and red meat is more easily absorbed than iron in eggs and plant foods such as dark green vegetables, cereals and pulses. Vitamin C is needed to help the body absorb iron.

Fluoride helps to protect teeth against decay. It is in the water supply and is added to most toothpastes.

Questions

1 Name two nutrients which work together in the body.
2 Name three foods containing
  a vitamin C
  b vitamin A
  c vitamin D
  d vitamin B12

  e calcium
  f iron
Explain the function of each.
3 Choose three vitamins and three minerals. Give the RNIs for each for the age of the child you are studying.

31 *Milk and weaning*

Weaning is the gradual introduction of solid foods into a baby's diet. The term **mixed feeding** may be used because milk remains a large part of the diet. The Committee on Medical Aspects of Food Policy (COMA) produced the report *Weaning and the Weaning Diet* in 1994. COMA recommends that weaning should begin at between four and six months. Foods given before this age are unlikely to provide all the nutrients which breast or formula milk provides. Other reasons why early weaning is not recommend include:

◆ younger babies have poor muscle control
◆ their kidneys are still immature
◆ their digestive tract is immature.

The composition of human milk

A **deficiency disease** is caused by lack of one or more essential nutrients. Mothers who breast-feed know their babies are getting the right nutrients. They do not need to study the composition of formula milk (unit 11) or worry about which brand will best suit their babies.

Babies need breast or formula milk for the first year during the weaning process.

◆ At 4–6 months they need a minimum of 600 ml daily.

◆ At 6–12 months they need a minimum of 500–600 ml daily.
◆ After one year they need a minimum of 350 ml daily. This must be whole cow's milk. Semi-skimmed milk is not suitable for children under two years because the kilocalories and fat-soluble vitamins A and D are reduced. From two to five years, *providing the diet is varied*, semi-skimmed milk can be given. Skimmed milk can be offered from the age of five.

Weaning happens in three stages. The reasons for weaning include:

◆ to meet the changing nutritional needs of the growing infant
◆ to develop the skills of biting and chewing
◆ to encourage the transition to family foods.

Stage one

Between four and six months the first aim of weaning is to introduce babies to different tastes and textures. The nutritional value of the food is less important because breast or formula milk still provides most of the energy and nutrients needed. Suitable first foods include single-grain baby **cereals** made from rice, cornmeal, sago, millet (e.g. baby rice), and **vegetable or fruit purées**

Composition of human milk (per 100ml)			
Energy (kJ)	293	Lactose (carbohydrate) (g)	7
(kcal)	70		
Protein (g)	1.3	Fat (g)	4.2
Vitamins		*Minerals*	
A (μg)	60	Sodium (mg)	15
D (μg)	0.01	Potassium (mg)	60
E (mg)	0.35	Chloride (mg)	43
K (μg)	0.21	Calcium (mg)	35
Thiamin (μg)	16	Phosphorus (mg)	15
Riboflavin (μg)	30	Magnesium (mg)	2.8
Nicotinic acid (μg)	230	Iron (μg)	76
B6 (μg)	6	Copper (μg)	39
B12 (μg)	0.01	Zinc (μg)	295
Total folate (μg)	5.2	Manganese (μg)	1.2
Pantothenic acid (μg)	260	Chromium (μg)	0.6
Biotin (μg)	0.76	Selenium (μg)	1.4
C (mg)	3.8	Iodine (μg)	7
		Fluorine (μg)	7.7

Source: DHSS, 1988

What a pint of milk (568ml) provides for toddlers aged 1–3 years			
	Proportion of daily needs (% EAR/RNI)		
	Whole milk	*Semi-skimmed milk*	*Skimmed milk**
Energy: Boys	32	22	16
Girls	33	23	17
Protein	129	134	134
Vitamin B2	167	177	177
Vitamin B12	460	460	480
Vitamin A	82	34	2
Vitamin D	2.6	0.9	nil
Vitamin C	20	20	20
Calcium	192	198	202
Zinc	46	46	48
Iodine	126	126	126
Iron	4	4	4

* Skimmed milk is not suitable for children under the age of five because of its low energy content

(e.g. potato, carrot, yam, spinach, banana, apple). Wheat-based cereals contain gluten and must not be given at this stage since they might cause an allergic reaction. Weaning foods must be:

- prepared under hygienic conditions
- smoothed to a purée to avoid the risk of choking
- chosen to avoid the risk of allergies (see unit 33).

Weaning and the emotions

Weaning is a transition stage. It involves change and loss (see unit 64). Food is a source of great happiness for a baby. Being fed from the security of a parent's arms give very deep pleasure. Food on a spoon lacks this loving warmth. Babies have to learn how to take food from a spoon. This is a very different skill from sucking. These are very great changes and babies may cry, refuse the food, or spit it out.

- Cradle the baby in your arms during weaning.
- Give a small feed of the breast or bottle first.
- Use your finger-tip or a plastic spoon not a metal one.
- Put very small amounts of food at the tip of the spoon.
- Talk, smile and encourage the baby gently.
- Remain calm if the baby cries or spits out the food.
- Offer the comfort of the breast or bottle after the solids.
- Wait until the next feed before trying again.

Saving time and energy

The time and energy spent preparing the weaning food for a baby is sometimes wasted. But food should *never* be forced on an infant. It can lead to eating problems later in childhood. However, a little gentle persuasion with huge 'rewards' of smiles and praise can encourage a baby to have another try.

To save time and energy, larger quantities of the food can be prepared and immediately frozen. Small portions can be placed in covered ice-cube trays and stored in labelled bags in the freezer. One or two cubes can then be thawed and reheated at a time. Fresh vegetables or fruit may be added before serving.

— Investigation

Test the following advice:
'Ideal weaning foods are puréed cereals, vegetables or fruit'.

a Prepare a suitable weaning dish for a five-month-old baby.

b Record your results under the headings: taste; smoothness of texture; time, energy and ease of preparation; cost; availability of food; hygiene awareness; other.

c Assuming the baby ate 10 g of the prepared food, estimate the energy (kcal) provided.

d Assuming the baby also had 200 ml of breast milk, estimate the energy (kcal) provided.

e Explain why, during the early stages of weaning, a baby still needs a feed of breast or formula milk.

— Child observation

Ask when the child began taking solids. Pool your findings in class and identify the average age of weaning in your area.

— Questions

1 Explain why the nutritional content of food in the first stage of weaning is not important.

2 Give the amounts of milk needed at each stage of weaning.

3 Name at least two nutrients removed from skimmed milk and why it is not suitable for children under the age of five.

4 Although COMA advises against weaning before four months, the majority of babies are given solids before this time. Refer to units 11 and 12, and suggest some reasons for this.

Stage two

Between six and nine months a wider range of foods with different textures can be introduced. The foods may only need to be mashed or minced rather than puréed. They include fish, poultry, meat, pulses, yoghurt, cottage cheese and a wider range of vegetables and fruit. An egg must be cooked until both the yolk and egg-white are hard to reduce the risk of food-poisoning (see unit 37). Cereals can now be wheat-based, including bread.

Suitable foods from the family meal also save time and energy. But it is important that no sugar or salt is added. **Finger foods** such as pitta bread or chappatti, slices of orange, ripe banana, peeled apple and carrot encourage **self-feeding**. Milk can be given in a feeding-beaker which the baby holds in the palmer grasp.

Choking

Finger foods, lumpy foods and those of an unsuitable consistency can cause choking. To reduce this risk, small foods like peanuts and popcorn should be avoided by children under the age of five. Foods with the highest record of choking among American children under age four are chunks of meat, boiled sweets, popcorn, lumps in peanut butter, raisins and raw carrots.

To reduce the risk of choking requires simple awareness and common-sense. *Never let a child eat unsupervised.*

Stage three

Between nine and twelve months more interesting textures can be given. At this stage, babies can cope with most family foods. However, lumps still need to be chopped or mashed. The aim is to provide three meals each day with snacks or drinks of breast or formula milk between meals. Another aim is to stop the use of bottles by one year to protect against tooth decay (see unit 34). Babies who need more sucking gratification can be given a soother (or dummy).

Family meals

Eating in company teaches babies social skills. They copy the table manners they observe. They learn that mealtimes are for sharing the pleasures of family life as well as for satisfying hunger. A pattern of meals can be set using their appetite as a guide. Enough time must be left between meals so that infants are hungry but not so much time that they become ravenous. A regular eating pattern teaches babies to connect hunger with food, and food with a pleasant feeling of fullness.

Energy needs

Breast or formula milk supplies babies with about 50 per cent of energy as fat. During weaning, the amount of fat intake drops and is replaced by carbohydrate. The aim is to move to a diet which supplies 35 per cent of energy as fat. But adequate energy is essential to sustain growth. Children should *not* skip meals. In particular they need a nourishing breakfast.

After eating, glucose is absorbed into the bloodstream. But the level of glucose in the blood is kept constant since the extra glucose is removed, converted into **glycogen** and stored in the liver. As the glucose level drops, the stored glycogen is converted back to glucose and re-enters the blood.

The time between the evening meal and breakfast can be up to 15 hours. After a night's sleep, the liver's store of glycogen is low. Children who are low on energy feel tired and irritable. They argue, dawdle, fuss; they find it difficult to concentrate. A breakfast of cereals with fruit and milk, an egg and toast will top up these reduced stores and keep children alert, warm, active and keen to learn until lunchtime.

Babies need more fat and less fibre in their diet than adults. Children on a low-fat, high-fibre diet will get full before they have eaten enough to grow.

Malnutrition

'Mal' is French for bad. A child suffering from malnutrition may eat:
◆ too little food – leading to underweight and failure to thrive

Examples of foods containing iron		
Food	*Quantity*	*Iron (mg)*
Family foods		
Well absorbed:		
Minced beef	50 g (3tbsp)	1.6
Liver	50 g (3tbsp)	5.0
Lamb	50 g (3tbsp)	0.9
Pork	50 g (3tbsp)	0.7
Chicken	50 g (3tbsp)	0.4
Sausage	20 g (1 small)	0.3
Meat paste	10 g (thinly spread)	0.2
Corned beef	30 g (1 thin slice)	0.9
Sardines canned in tomato sauce	50 g (2)	2.3
Fish fingers	60 g (2)	0.5
Less well absorbed:		
Lentils (cooked)	40 g (1tbsp)	1.2
Baked beans (or other cooked beans)	40 g (1tbsp)	0.7
Egg	50 g (1)	1.0
Vegetables, e.g. green beans, cabbage, peas, courgette, sweetcorn	60 g (2tbsp)	0.2–1.0
Dried fruit, e.g. apricots, raisins, dates	30 g (1tbsp)	0.4–1.1
Avocado pear	50 g (½small pear)	0.2
Bread	1 slice (35 g)	0.5–0.9
Digestive biscuit	1 large (15 g)	0.5
Fortified foods (typical values)		
Rusk	18 g (1 large)	2.5–3.0
Weetabix	20 g (1)	1.5
Cornflakes	20 g (1 small bowl)	1.3
Rice Krispies	20 g (1 small bowl)	1.3
Iron-fortified jars of baby food	Stage 1: a jar	2.5
	Stage 2: a jar	3.5
Unfortified jars	Stage 1: a jar	1.0
	Stage 2: a jar	1.3
Dried baby foods	10 g (1tbsp)	0.5
Infant formula	150ml	1.0
Follow-on milk	150ml	2.0

- too much food – leading to overweight and **obesity**
- a diet which lacks one or more essential nutrients – leading to deficiency diseases such as anaemia.

Iron

Breast milk is short of iron, but newborns have stores in their body which last for about six months. However, if the mother's diet during pregnancy was low in iron, her baby should be weaned at four months to obtain iron from solid foods. Iron-deficiency anaemia is the commonest nutritional problem in babies and children.

Vegetarians

Vegetarians eat no meat, poultry or fish. Some avoid eggs. **Vegans** eat no animal produce such as milk, eggs and cheese. Both groups must eat a *wide variety* and *enough quantities* of foods to make sure they get all the essential proteins, minerals such as iron and zinc, and vitamins, especially vitamin B12. Soya milk and soya bean products are essential in a vegan's diet.

── *Child observation* ──

Ask about the child's typical breakfast and evaluate it for **a** balance of nutrients and **b** variety of foods.

── *Questions* ──

1 Describe in detail how you would introduce mixed feeding.

2 A two-year-old is given 15 g/d proteins, 5 mg/d iron and 10 mg/d vitamin C. Suggest, with reasons, how to improve this diet.

3 A three-year-old follows a vegetarian diet. Suggest, with reasons, ways to make sure his diet provides enough iron-rich foods.

4 Parents can be too diet conscious. US doctors found babies 'starving on a diet of skimmed milk and raw vegetables instead of the high-energy foods they need'.
   a List the essential nutrients lacking in the above diet.
   b What are the effects of giving a child too much fibre?

5 Survey the breakfast habits of the class and estimate the average energy and nutritional values. Plan, prepare and evaluate a suitable breakfast for a named-aged child.

33 *Some eating problems*

The nutritional needs of pre-school children (age one to five) are slightly lower than in the first year. In general, children in this age group cannot eat large amounts of food at one meal. They need small portions, and suitable snacks between mealtimes. At birth, the nervous system is not well developed. Although the nerves which control the senses are working, the nerves which control body movements are not. Turn back to unit 20 and re-read the growth of brain. **Neuro-development** occurs rapidly during the first two years and a child's diet must be **nutrient dense**.

Food refusal

A recent study found one in twenty babies refusing to eat. At least 180,000 British toddlers were suffering from failure to thrive. Their weight had fallen dangerously below its predicted level. One in three cases went unnoticed by the family doctor. Many of the toddlers had developed other behaviour problems.

Parents become anxious when a child refuses food. When people are anxious, they feel out of control. Parents may try to gain control by imposing stricter rules. Meals are set at rigid times and plates must be scraped clean. If the child is not hungry at the set time, a battle of wills begins. The more the parents pressure the child to eat, the more the child refuses the food.

■ Suggest ways to encourage this child's appetite

Children are people. Their appetites and tastes vary. Some will eat any food at any time. Others have more sensitive tastes and need more freedom of choice over what and when they eat. Hunger is a great motivator to eat. Check that the child is not 'filling up' with snacks or fizzy drinks between meals. The recommended advice is:
- never force a baby or a child to eat
- make mealtimes a pleasant family occasion
- offer a wide variety and choice of finger foods
- make the food look appetizing and fun
- remove textures which can lack appeal, such as the skin on tomatoes or warmed milk
- serve small portions only
- check that the eating utensils are not too big
- remove a meal which is refused, but do not offer snacks between meals
- stay calm, avoid battles starting in the first place.

A child who is seriously underweight fails to thrive. **Casein** can be given as a protein supplement. Casein is the main protein of milk and cheese.

Overweight

Overweight can be damaging to health. The following are some reasons why children become overweight:
- too much food is eaten for the body's energy needs
- too little exercise is taken
- eating becomes a comfort to compensate for a real or imagined loss of love.

Parents need to discuss this problem at the Well-baby clinic or with the family doctor. Overweight children must have a nutrient dense diet for energy and growth. The main aim is to *maintain weight* while the child continues to grow.

Exercise and disability

Some disabled children suffer times of pain or great distress. On a bad day, the pleasure they gain from food may help to provide comfort. If mealtimes are a parent's only chance for closeness and cuddles, the temptation to give extra food can be hard to resist.

With other disabilities, it is difficult for children to take enough exercise. For example, a child with poor muscle control or one in pain may refuse to exercise without supervised help. The less pleasure these children gain from regular exercise, the more likely they are to avoid it, the more overweight they become and the harder it becomes to exercise.

Allergies

The main food allergies are to cow's milk, cheese, eggs, shellfish, wheat and its by-products. About two per cent of the population develop a food allergy. Babies are most vulnerable in the first months of life and allergies are more common in children who were weaned before four months. It takes some while for the body to become **sensitized** to a particular food. Once this happens, each time that food is eaten the allergy becomes worse.

Dietary therapy begins by tracking down the food allergy. This should be supervised by a dietition trained in child health. The offending food is removed from the diet and a substitute for the missing nutrients is added to the diet.

Gluten is a mixture of two proteins found in wheat, oats and rye. It is important in baking because, when mixed with water, it gets sticky and allows air to be trapped. This enables dough to be formed. Gluten intolerance can lead to **coeliac disease** which destroys the villi (absorption cells) in the digestive tract. The baby becomes gravely ill. The symptoms of coeliac disease include vomiting, stunted growth, swollen abdomen, and pale frothy foul-smelling stools. Dietary therapy involves a gluten-free diet.

Because some babies may be intolerant to gluten, avoid giving gluten-containing cereals to all babies before six months. Where there is a family history of allergy, mothers can breast-feed for six months or up until two years. Iron and vitamin D supplements will be advised by the family doctor or clinic nurse.

Child observation

Ask whether the child has a food allergy and find out the therapy to avoid further attacks. Pool your findings in class.

Questions

1 Using the charts in unit 7, which nutrients might you increase in the diet of a boy age four weighing 14.40 kg, and why?

2 Using children's menus from parent magazines, create a day's diet for a four-year-old who suffers from milk allergy. Prepare one dish. Evaluate taste, aroma, visual appeal, cost, time, ease of preparation, and the RNIs.

3 Name the most common food allergies. Role-play how to teach a five-year-old with coeliac disease to refuse all offers to swop his packed lunch.

34 Teeth

Humans have 20 **primary teeth** and 32 **permanent teeth**. All 52 teeth start forming in the unborn baby's jaw. Special tissues in the mouth absorb minerals and begin to harden. At birth, all the primary teeth are in the baby's jawbone, and the permanent teeth have begun to grow.

The crown of the tooth is the part you can see. It is covered with **enamel**, the hardest tissue in the body. Enamel protects the softer **dentine** and **pulp** inside. The **roots** of the tooth grow deep into the jaw. The blood vessels and nerves nourish the tooth and keep it alive.

The roots of the primary (milk or first) teeth start growing at six months and the jawbones get wider. By age three, most toddlers have a full set of primary teeth. These start to fall out at about age six as the permanent teeth begin pressing from behind. This process continues up to about age twelve.

Some babies have no discomfort during teething. Others suffer soreness and pain. Chewy foods such as crusts and carrots can help. If the gums are red and sore, a chilled teething ring cools and soothes. A gentle gum massage with a clean finger is calming. The pharmacist may recommend a sugar-free teething gel to reduce the misery. Sore patches on the cheeks or chin are due to extra dribbling. Extra drinks are essential to replace the lost fluids. Petroleum jelly and other protective skin creams help.

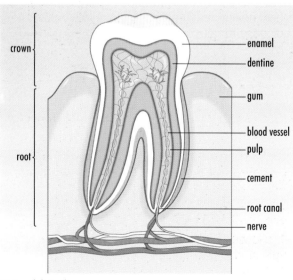

crown
root

enamel
dentine
gum
blood vessel
pulp
cement
root canal
nerve

Sugar

After eating, a sticky film named **plaque** clings to the teeth. If the food or drink contains sugar, the bacteria in plaque use the sugar as fuel and produce acid as a by-product of their metabolism. This acid can dissolve tooth enamel, causing **dental caries** (holes, cavities).

The more often sugary things are eaten or drunk, the greater the chance of tooth decay. If plaque invades the spaces between the teeth and gums, other bacteria can infect the gums. **Gingivitis** is gum disease. As it progresses, pockets of infection cause the gums to shrink and bacteria harm the supporting bones. The teeth become loose and may fall out.

Fluoride

Plaque can appear with a baby's first tooth. The teeth *and* gums should be cleaned with a little fluoride toothpaste on a soft toothbrush. By the age of two, Ami can learn to brush her teeth and gums. This task should be supervised until the age of eight. **Oral hygiene** is more than just cleaning the teeth. It includes the child's diet:

- avoid sugar from the start so that a baby does not develop a taste for very sweet foods or drinks
- never dip a soother (or dummy) into honey or sugar
- never give sweetened drinks in a bottle or feeder
- reduce the *number of times* the family eats sweet things
- clean the teeth immediately after eating sugary foods and drinks
- make sure the diet contains the RNI for bone development.

Dentist

Regular visits to the dentist are very important. Taking Ami before toothache occurs helps to prevent fear building up. She becomes familiar with a routine of regular check-ups and knows what to expect. Watching her parents have minior treatment such as a scraping to remove plaque helps Ami learn that this is a normal part of **oral**

■ An adult tooth

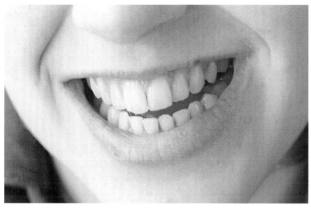
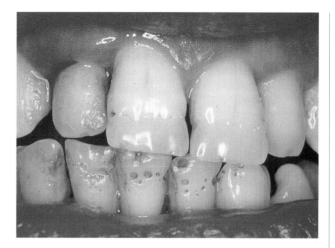

■ A happy healthy smile. The pitted teeth on the right are the result of a rare complication of measles

hygiene. If she does need treatment at some stage, she is more willing and prepared to be patient.

Strong healthy teeth add great appeal to a smile. The short and long-term goals in caring for a baby's milk teeth include:

◆ protection against the pain of toothache and fillings
◆ prevention or early tooth loss through dental extraction
◆ helping the second teeth erupt in the correct position
◆ reducing the loss of second teeth and the need for dentures.

Children with special needs

The consequences of tooth loss are more serious for children with special needs. With a limb deformity, strong teeth are essential to hold drinking straws, reading lights, computer wands and other special aids. Gum disease is a risk for children with conditions which require medicines. Parents can ask for sugar-free drugs and for the names of dentists who specialize in the dental care of children with special needs.

— *Child observation*

Record your child's dental history. Ask which milk teeth appeared first. Which ones gave 'teething problems', and at about what age? What were the symptoms and the effects on the child's behaviour? What did the parents do to relieve the distress? From where did they get the information? Was it perceived to be effective? Does the child clean its own teeth? If so, by what method and when? Has the child been to the dentist? If so, at what age and how often? How does the child respond to any treatment?

Pool your findings in class and draw up an average estimate for each of the observations above.

— *Questions*

1 Explain why primary teeth are often called milk teeth.
2 Name foods which contain nutrients for healthy teeth.
3 Name foods which increase the risk of tooth decay.
4 Suggest, with reasons, three ways for parents to protect a child from the pain of toothache.
5 Pam's parents teach her to brush her teeth but they forget about her gums. Suggest some likely consequences of this.
6 Design a chart to help a two-year-old develop good oral hygiene habits.
7 'Prevention is better than a cure.' Give your opinion of this statement in relation to oral hygiene.

A **balanced diet** contains a wide variety of foods.

Eat more	Eat less
◆ whole natural foods	◆ processed and refined foods
◆ starchy foods for energy	◆ fats – especially saturated fats
◆ fresh fruit and vegetables	◆ stored fruit and vegetables
◆ iron-containing foods	◆ salt, sugar, and sugary foods
Drink more	**Drink less**
◆ plain water	◆ fizzy drinks
◆ fresh fruit juices	◆ squashes

Water

Water is present in all body cells, tissues, and the digestive and blood systems. Oxygen and digested nutrients are transported around the body in the blood. Water is involved in many chemical processes in the body.

Water is found in food as well as drinks, and some is released during the metabolism of foods. Water is not stored in the body. It is lost in urine, stools, breathing out and sweating. The water lost in sweating helps to regulate the body temperature. The daily volume of water intake should equal the volume lost each day.

Babies under six months usually need no fluids other than milk. Natural mineral waters and bottled fizzy waters are not suitable. Still bottled waters can be given to babies over six months. All water given to babies under one year should be boiled. Fruit juices should be unsweetened. Babies taking breast milk as their main drink should be given supplements of vitamins A and D from six months.

Bones

During infancy and early childhood, bones grow very rapidly. Large amounts of calcium are deposited in the bones and so a baby's requirements for calcium are high. Vitamin D is needed to absorb the calcium from the digestive tract. A deficiency of vitamin D in early life leads

■ 'All children have bandy legs at first.'

to soft bones and the development of deformed, bow-shaped legs. This is known as **rickets**.

Vitamin D is present in only a few foods so care must be taken to include these in the weaning diet and throughout childhood. Breast milk is short of vitamin D but the baby has stores for the first months of life. Formula milk has vitamin D added to it. The skin is able to manufacture vitamin D in sunlight.

Children from Asian countries are at more risk of developing **rickets**. Their mothers' diets during pregnancy may have been short of vitamin D. Between the ages of one and five, all children should be given supplements of vitamin A and D unless they have a diet rich in these vitamins and a moderate exposure to sunlight.

Feet

Babies have smooth straight feet with a pad of fat on the instep. Adults have foot problems such as corns, bunions, hammer toes and heel spurs. Soft bones are easily **deformed** (twisted out of shape) by footwear which does not fit.

The following is an estimate by a large footwear store of the minimum pairs of shoes required from

■ A newborn's tiny soft feet

birth to the age of eighteen. (Speciality shoes – smart boots, fashion or ballet footwear – are not included.)

   2 pairs of pram shoes
24 pairs of everyday shoes
14 pairs of sandals
13 pairs of best shoes
22 pairs of trainers
10 pairs of indoor gym shoes
10 pairs of slippers
17 pairs of wellingtons
  9 pairs of tennis, hockey or football boots

— Investigation

Evaluate the following statement:

'Fashion and the cost of replacing outgrown shoes are more responsible for deforming the nation's feet than a vitamin deficiency.'

You will need to research the following by child observation and then pool your findings in class.

a Examine the footwear of children between the ages of one and five. Draw the most popular choices of footwear. Evaluate them in terms of health, safety, aesthetic appeal, costs and care factors.

b If babygros (stretch suits) are still worn, do they allow free range of movement?

c Are outdoor shoes slippery? Estimate the percentage which have no shoe laces.

d Name the material of socks. Do they often slip down?

e Do children try to remove footwear? How often do they go barefoot? Are shoes or socks often mislaid? From these responses, estimate their attitude to footwear.

f List the average heights of children aged one, two, three, four and five. Describe the bow legs of toddlers and the development of an upright posture.

g Use a mail-order catalogue or visit a store to cost the total bill of shodding a child from birth to the age of eighteen.

h Survey the parents' opinions about shoes and socks.

i Name nutrients needed for strong bones and another source of vitamin D. How can this information help a parent's choice of i) winter meals, ii) summer clothing, iii) outdoor play?

j Plan a week's menu for a three-year-old with rickets.

— Questions

1 Give the meanings of:
  a a balanced diet
  b a deficient diet
  c diet therapy
  d a nutrient supplement.

2 Plan, prepare and cost a home-made meal suitable for a four-year-old girl. Evaluate your task at each stage.

36 Prepared foods

Commercially prepared baby foods are popular with busy parents. They save time and energy, and look very attractive on the shop shelves. A great deal of **advertising** thought and **marketing** skill goes into the presentation of prepared foods.

Packaging and labelling

Companies which specialize in **package design** and **labelling copy** (writing labels) use advances in technology to get their message across. First, the pack is designed, passed for approval and a prototype is made. Next, the wording on the pack is designed to have **maximum product** appeal. By law, the labelling copy must include:

◆ the name of the food
◆ the list of ingredients in descending order of weight
◆ the weight of the food
◆ the time it can be kept and methods of storage
◆ the instructions for cooking or other preparation
◆ the name and address of the manufacturer, packer or seller.

Next the **visual design** is created, and the manufacturer's **logo** is added. The different parts are assembled, packed singly or in blocks of 10, 24 or more, and the food is dispatched by road, rail

■ A selection of baby foods

or air to their destination – your local shop. Food packaging adds about 6p to a £1 grocery bill.

Additives

Food technology adds a wide range of synthetic chemicals to prepared foods. Additives include antioxidants, emulsifiers, preservatives, stabilizers, colourings and sweeteners. Additives must be named and the chemical code number given, e.g. flavour enhancer E621. Children are more at risk of developing allergies to additives than adults (see unit 33).

Sugars

Sugars are added to many prepared drinks and foods, even savoury and spicy ones. Babies enjoy what is known and familiar. They recognize the mild sweetness of lactose in milk. Sucrose is the sweetest of all dietary carbohydrates. It should not be added to infant foods and drinks. A taste habit for sucrose can become an addictive craving. The more a child is given, the more it wants, the harder it is to break the habit. Adults can train their taste buds to enjoy seasoned foods: peppers, sour cream, vinegar, hot spices. But if sucrose-rich cakes, jams and sweets are added to a child's diet, one consequence is likely to be a craving **addiction** to sweetened foods.

INGREDIENTS

Water, Skimmed Milk, Apricots, Pineapple Juice, Sugar, Lemon Juice, Modified Cornflour, Eggs, Rice, Tapioca, Vegetable Oil, Vitamin C (minimum 15mg/100g)

Do not use a can opener. If ring-pull fails, return to Happy Meals for a full refund.

Happy Meals desserts are carefully developed by our nutritionists and are the natural complement to any baby's meal. All Happy Meals desserts are suitable for babies aged 3 months and up. Every Happy Meals recipe contains only natural, wholesome ingredients and will help your baby with a varied and nutritionally balanced diet.

PREPARATION: This baby recipe can be served cold or warm. Spoon the required amount into a clean bowl. (Do not add sugar.) To heat, stand the bowl in hot water and allow to warm. Any remaining unwarmed portion can be placed in a suitable container and safely stored in a refrigerator for up to 48 hours. For Happy Meals baby club and safety brochures (UK only), feeding guide or advice, write to our Customer Care Manager at the address opposite. In all correspondence please quote quality code on base.

NUTRITION INFORMATION

TYPICAL VALUES	PER 100g	PER 128g CAN
ENERGY	264 kj 62 kcal	338 kj 80 kcal
PROTEIN	1.3g	1.7g
CARBOHYDRATE	12.2g	15.6g
(of which sugars)	(8.0g)	(10.3g)
FAT	0.9g	1.2g
(of which saturates)	(0.1g)	(0.2g)
FIBRE	0.3g	0.3g
SODIUM	trace	trace

■ A food label from a packet of baby food

Sweeteners

There are two types of sweeteners added to prepared foods. **Bulk** sweeteners are usually less sweet than table sugar (sucrose) and so more is added to the food. **Intense** sweeteners have a sweetness many times that of table sugar and so less is added. Artificial sweeteners and foods containing artificial sweeteners are not suitable for babies and young children. They encourage the development of a taste for very sweet foods.

Sweets

Although the consumption of table sugar has dropped in the past 30 years, sweet-eating remains high. Sweets are prepared foods: chocolates, mints, toffees, pastilles, liquorices, gums and so on.

— Investigation

Identify additives in some prepared foods.

You will need:

labels from a variety of prepared foods and drinks for adults and babies.

a Look for the words syrup, fructose, maltose, sucrose, dextrose, glucose, honey, raw sugar, brown sugar and muscovado on the ingredients list. These are natural sugars.

b Look for the words sorbitol, xylitol, isomalt, mannitol and lactitol. These are bulk sweeteners.

c Look for the words aspartame, saccharin, acesulfame potassium and thaumatin. These are intense sweeteners.

d Identify and name the sweeteners in tomato ketchup, pickles, mayonnaise, baked beans, tomato soup, jam, breakfast cerals, 'diet' yoghurt, 'diet' fizzy drinks, 'sugar-free' squash, and so on.

e Name the types of sugars used in prepared foods for babies. Explain the reasons for this.

f Record any colouring or flavouring additives.

g Record any chemical preservatives.

h Evaluate the labelling copy: is it clear? informative?

i Comment on the visual appeal to entice people to buy.

— Investigation

Research the sweet-eating habits of children. You will need to visit the sweet departments at your local shops.

a Record the name, price and weight of two types of sweets.

b Examine their wrappers for the nutritional value.

c List the sweeters and other additives.

d Comment on the visual appeal of the wrappers.

e If the sweets are advertised on television, make a note of the images, words or musical jingles used to entice children (or parents) to buy.

f Survey parents on the sweet-eating habits of children. When do they eat sweets; how often; what types are most popular; are teeth cleaned afterwards?

g Pool your findings in class. Draw up an information sheet on the sweet-eating habits of children in your area.

— Questions

1 From the food label, name the nutrients for:
   a bone development
   b providing energy
   c healthy vision
   d body-building and cell replacement
   e the formation of red blood cells.

2 Check the labelling copy for the legal requirements.

3 Name likely consequences of adding sucrose to a baby's diet.

4 Cost a prepared baby food. Name three advantages of giving a baby home-made family foods.

37 *Food hygiene*

The name **gastro-enteritis** means food-poisoning. It can be caused by any food or drink which has been **contaminated** with germs. The symptoms of gastro-enteritis are stomach cramps, diarrhoea, vomiting, fever or chills. These can begin soon after eating the contaminated food or some hours later. One serious side effect of gastro-enteritis is dehydration from the loss of fluids as a result of vomiting and diarrhoea. These fluids must be replaced. A special mixture such as 'Dioralyte' replaces the lost salts and sugars, as well as the lost water.

Babies with gastro-enteritis need medical attention. (Toddlers sometimes have bouts of diarrhoea, the reasons for which are not well understood. This type of diarrhoea is not serious *if no symptoms of food-poisoning occur and weight gain is steady.*)

Keep food clean!

Bacteria contaminate food by contact with dirty:
- hands and clothing
- habits: coughs and sneezes, licked fingers and spoons
- work surfaces, sinks and draining boards
- cooking equipment: pots, pans, knives, crockery, cutlery
- cleaning equipment: dish cloths, sponges, tea towels
- flies, rats, mice and their droppings, family pets.

Eggs should be cooked until both the yolk and white are solid. A separate board and knife should be kept for preparing raw meat. Cuts must be covered. Expectant mothers, like babies, are at greater risk from gastro-enteritis. They should avoid patés, cheeses with blue veins and soft ripe cheeses such as brie and camembert.

Gastro-enteritis is more common among bottle-fed than breast-fed babies. The feeding equipment may not be properly sterilized, the hands or work surface may not be really clean, the prepared bottle may not be covered with its protective cap, the milk may be stored too long in the refrigerator, or at a temperature which is not low enough. Unclean soothers (dummies) can cause gastro-enteritis in older babies.

Keep food cold!

Bacteria thrive in warm moist conditions. Food cooked one day is safe to eat the next day if it is cooled rapidly and stored in a refrigerator. The ideal temperature for the coldest part of the fridge is between 0°C and 5°C. Uncooked foods, especially poultry, should be kept away from cooked meats in order not to contaminate them. Foods in a freezer are safe until their expiry date but freezing does not destroy any contamination already there.

■ This fly has found the ideal home!

Keep food fresh!

Foods in a refrigerator will go off if stored long enough.

— Investigation

Analyse the above statement.

You will need:

bread, milk, scraps of different raw and cooked foods

a Wrap each item and store it in an empty refrigerator.

b Record the temperature of the refrigerator.

c Check the foods after two days, one week, two weeks.

d As each food goes off, discard it hygienically.

e Name the foods contaminated with fungus infections.

f State your conclusion about the value of 'use by' dates.

g Clean the fridge carefully.

Keep food covered!

Flies are responsible for a great deal of gastro-enteritis. They breed in open dustbins and manure dumps. They rub their legs and hairy bodies over uncovered food. They spray the food with saliva to soften it before sucking it in through their mouth-parts. They excrete their droppings onto the food after they have eaten. Food should always be kept covered.

— Child observation

Record any attacks of gastro-enteritis the child may have had. Pool your findings to find:
a if one food, or   b one method of storage or
c one method of preparation, is more involved than others.

— Questions

1 Describe all the contamination risks in the pictures and how each can be made safe.

2 The number of accidents in the home has dropped in the last 40 years but the number of food poisoning cases has risen steeply. Suggest ways to reduce this risk when
a buying the food
b storing the food
c cooking or otherwise preparing the food.
d storing any left-over food

3 State, with reasons, two rooms in the home where germs can spread rapidly.

4 A toddler suffers a sudden bout of diarrhoea. Explain
a when a parent need not be concerned
b why extra fluids are needed.

5 Design a chart of hygiene rules to protect the whole family.

Kittens are born blind, though their eyes are perfectly formed. Cats can see. To find out when sight develops, kittens from the same litter were raised in separate rooms. Room A was dark. Room B was light. The kittens in Room A grew up blind. The kittens in Room B developed normal sight. These findings were so surprising that the study was repeated with blindfolds. The results were the same. The study concluded that kittens develop the ability to see only under the *repeated* stimulation of light.

If we analyse this conclusion, we realize that kittens have a *critical* time for learning to see. If their light is cut off, no eye-brain connection is made for sight. Although the kittens' eyes in Room A were normal, their brains could not 'recognize' vision. The ability to see was forever lost.

Do human babies have critical times for learning?

Children alone

Children have been found living in the wild, completely abandoned by their parents. When they were taken into care, they were unable to 'recognize' family values. They behaved like wild animals do in captivity. No matter how much love and attention they were given, they did not become friendly with their carers. A few learned to walk. None learned to talk. They all died before adulthood.

Other children have been found locked in farm outhouses and barns where they were treated like wild animals. They were fed slops, cleaned using hosepipes and treated with much less dignity than the family pet. When these children were taken into care, they *did* recognize family values. They did become fond of their carers. They learned to speak and to read and write. They grew stronger and developed into effective adults.

We do not know why the children in the wild were abandoned. Perhaps they were sickly. Perhaps they were healthy but their parents had too many children, or they hated parenting, or they were terrified because they were unmarried. These are guesses. But we can analyse what we *do* know of the differences between these two groups of children.

The children locked in outhouses were not completely abandoned by humans. They did not struggle alone in the wild, no matter how terrible their 'home' conditions. They were **a** fed and cleaned by humans; **b** clothed in rags and housed by humans; **c** some were locked away at a later stage of development; **d** others were not alone but with a sibling. In short, they all had some **interaction** with humans.

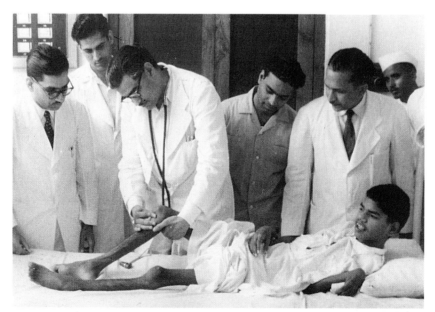

■ 'Wolf boy' Ramu was found living wild in India

■ A father interacting with his baby

Interaction

To interact is to act together with another person. The activity is shared or mutual. Each person 'calls out' behaviours they want from the other person. A handshake is an example of this. Tammy offers a hand in greeting. This is a 'call out' for Paul to take her hand and shake it. The next time they meet, Paul may be the first to 'call out' a handshake from Tammy.

Father smiles. Baby stares solemnly with bright eyes. Father smiles again. Baby tries a smile. Father is 'calling out' a smile from his baby, teaching his child to recognize friendly human interaction. By six weeks, his baby smiles back and may be the first to start a smiling interaction.

Although infants cannot meet their own needs, they can 'call out' love from their parents. They do this by showing their pleasure. **Gazing** and **smiling** are very important bonding behaviours. Some mothers say that when their baby first smiled was the first time they felt the child was really their own.

Blind babies smile at a later date than sighted babies. When a parent comes near, they lie still. Parents of blind babies can mistake their infant's stillness and lack of smiling as a signal that the baby is depressed. But the infant is paying attention by lying still – and 'listening with hungry ears'. For successful interaction, all parents have to learn to read their baby's signals correctly.

Isolation

Children can develop their hand and motor skills with or without people. They can develop certain skills of thinking on their own. But they cannot learn **social behaviours** in **isolation**. Nor can they learn to talk or manage their feelings without people. Children learn these things naturally when they interact with humans.

The studies of children abandoned in the wild suggest that interaction is critical for a baby's development. And it must be *human* interaction, learning *with people*, not from animals. A child can learn from books, television programmes, computer games, friends, walks in the park, and so on. But a baby's brain has not developed enough to process this information. During infanthood, people are the only resource. We can conclude that the level of interaction between parents and babies is of great importance to healthy development.

— *Questions* ——————————

1 Explain what interaction means with an example of your own.
2 Give ways in which an infant interacts with a parent by **pre-verbal** body language.
3 Find the sentence in this unit which shows another reason why parenting is named 'the greatest detective job on Earth'.

4 Find out how Tarzan was raised. Give your opinion of whether these stories are true or the author's imagination.
5 A baby's need for information from humans is critical for its healthy development. Discuss.

Mother says 'Hello, my precious!' Sy gurgles in reply. Mother smiles, 'What a clever noise!' Sy gurgles again and tries to **imitate** her sounds. The result is a cooing noise. Mother talks to Sy directly, making eye contact and smiling her encouragement. She asks, 'Are you hungry? Does the bath water feel good?' long before he is old enough to understand her words, let alone answer. She is teaching Sy one of the ways people **communicate**.

Did you find English (or your native tongue) easy to learn? How do Russian or Greek babies learn their languages? Three year olds do not suddenly know how to speak. They have been hearing and absorbing the sounds of language from pre-birth. Children learn to speak by listening to words, and then practising the sounds they hear. Deaf children also learn to 'speak', but in a different way because they cannot hear words.

Infants communicate their needs by crying. This is not a happy way to ask for help. Crying uses a great deal of energy and makes the baby hot and uncomfortable. Language is more dignified. It makes sense of human behaviour by giving shape and meaning to our vaguest thoughts and feelings. It improves the ability to understand new information and generally enriches the quality of life. Sy's first **vocal** attempts at language are cooing, gurgling and crooning noises. Then he babbles and finally attempts real speech.

Motherese

Adults in all cultures speak to babies in a special singsong way. This is named **motherese**. The words have *pauses* between them. They are *repeated* more often. Each sentence has a *rhythm*: 'Hel-lo ba-by, smile for Dad-dy. Smile, my sweetheart. What a lovely smile!' The *tones* of voice are clearer. The *speed* of language is slower. Motherese is a form of poetry. There is a reason for this.

A newborn's hearing is the least well developed of the senses. Before birth, the fluid that surrounds the baby enters the middle section of the ears. Sy's hearing may be full of echoes or crackly static until the fluid flows away. The poetic pattern of motherese catches his attention. Slower speed and regular pauses separate the sounds from the echoes.

■ There are patterns in sounds

— Investigation —

Is motherese a form of poetry?

a Say: 'I'll huff and I'll puff and I'll blow your house down.'

b Did you stress some words more than others? If so, which ones?

c Say: 'I shall breathe heavily while blowing down your house.'

d Comment on the differences between these two sentences.

e Test your ability to remember each sentence clearly.

f From the findings of this test, suggest ways in which rhythm and repetition might help a baby learn speech.

Motherese is adult speech in simple form. 'Who's my best baby!' It is *not* the nonsense words sometimes spoken to infants: 'Who's my diddums-widdums!' Motherese makes sense. It can be used by adults when they speak to each other: 'See the car, see the cow!' rather than, 'Look brrum-brrum, look moo-moo!'

Talking down to an infant (nonsense words) teaches the child a new and different language. What sense can Sy make of 'Ickle-wickle toesy-woesys?' instead of 'These are your five little toes?' He might become very confused. Later he has to learn the proper words.

Babbling

Infants **babble** long before they know the meaning of the sounds they make. They experiment with a few **key** sounds such as 'dadada' and 'bababa'. Something which is 'key' has a special meaning. But these sounds are meaningless in that Sy will say dadada to greet his Daddy and then point at the cat and say dadada too!

■ Instead of making babbling sounds deaf babies try to imitate sign language

Deaf babies of deaf parents babble at the same age as hearing babies. But instead of making babbling sounds, they make babbling movements with their fingers. They watch their parents using sign language and start their **hand babbles** before they are ten months old. This is the same age as hearing children begin to string key sounds together into wordlike units. This behaviour of deaf babies strongly suggests that the human brain learns language in step-by-step order. Units of sound are first strung together. Later they become meaningful words.

Language acquisition is the development of speech. Children show a great difference in their times of language acquisition. Some jabber strings of words at eighteen months. Others may speak only when they are three years old. Early talkers are not necessarily more intelligent than late talkers. But a child who does not copy the sounds of words by age two may have hearing difficulties. Girls tend to develop language skills earlier than boys. More boys need **speech therapy** when they begin school than girls.

— Investigation

Investigate language acquisition.
Identify the stages of language acquisition either as a class activity or share your individual findings. A tape recorder is useful. Devise ways to find out the following.

a Name some vocalizing sounds of a three-month-old baby.

b State the age a baby orients to the sound of a parent's voice.

c List some babbling sounds used by babies between nine months and a year.

d Name which parts of the face a two year old can point to.

e Name the age when children talk to themselves, or their toys.

f Record some complete sentences of a five year old.

— Child observation

Find out the first words the child spoke. List these as 'key' words for language acquisition.

— Questions

1 List five aspects of motherese. 'A four month old responds more often to motherese than to adult speech.' Devise a way to test this statement. If possible, try it out to see if it works.

2 Describe how poetic forms of speech help in the development of language, giving at least three examples from nursery rhymes.

3 Explain the likely consequences of language development for hearing babies who are not spoken to.

4 Give the gender difference in early talkers. Can you think of any reasons for this? Boys catch up with girls by age three.

5 'Babies need to be bathed in language.' Discuss.

The *best* time for learning the *most* language is long before a child is ready for school. Children who have stories read to them tend to be more successful in learning to read at school. Story time has a special value since parent and child snuggle together for learning. Until children can read, the pictures should enable them to 'read' the plot.

A **homonym** is a word which sounds like another word but has a different meaning: a *herd* of cattle, we *heard* a sound. Homonyms can be confusing and should be avoided. Storybooks contain many pictures to catch a child's attention. The pictures also help to undo these confusions.

At nine months, Shivani sits with her mother and 'reads' a picture book. At eighteen months, she recognizes the pictures and points, saying the words. Her mother praises her, though Shivani mispronounces many words. At two, Shivani is delighted to call out their names.

Symbols are things which represent other things. In public life, symbols are used as shortened 'codes' of communication. The plus and minus signs are a maths code. The letters of the alphabet represent a sound code. When language skills develop at age two, children develop the ability to think in symbols. They enter a wonderful world of **fantasy**: make-believe, creative and imaginary play.

Imagination is the ability of the senses to create what is not really there. Stories are fantasies; symbols of real life. A plate is not a plate but a flying saucer. A child is not a powerless mite but a brave warrior. Or the child is powerless but manages to win by reason and cunning.

Adventure stories are comfort-blankets for Shivani. She feels reassured, develops a stronger

■ Read these symbols for their special meaning

self-image and her anxieties are reduced. However, the level of challenge in an adventure story should not provoke terror.

Problem-solving stories

Stories of mice, rabbits, superwomen, spacemen or robots are really stories of humans in disguise.

'Mary had a little lamb
Its fleece was white as snow
And everywhere that Mary went
The lamb was sure to go.'

Once upon a time, a bat saw a hare at the fork of the road.

Stories are the 'mirrors' of the mind. They reflect an image to the listener of events which cause problems in daily life. They explain the choices which people make to solve these problems. They then describe the consequences of these choices.

'It followed her to school one day,
It was against the rules...'

If Shivani's mother stops, she says, 'What happened next? Did the bad man get caught? Do *go on*!' Mary's lamb is like a younger sibling who always tags along. Children want to know how Mary solves her problem. Sometimes she likes the lamb following her, sometimes she gets cross. She particularly gets cross when the lamb tags along 'against the rules'. These are Mary's 'rules' for when she wants the sibling's company and when she does not.

Listening to stories and talking about their outcome helps a child recognize that:
◆ problems are a normal part of daily life
◆ problems are there to be solved
◆ problems can be more easily solved by talking about them
◆ how to solve problems in their own lives.

Happy-ever-after stories have a **moral**. They help Shivani learn what is acceptable behaviour and what is not. There may be goodies and baddies and a victim. The victim is the powerless child needing to be rescued. Shivani likes to take sides, especially with the goody. She has a strong sense of fair play and identifies with the victim too. 'Stop the Baddy!' she shouts. She wants the Goody to save the victim and the Baddy punished and never be bad again.

Sad stories upset small children, e.g. the little match-girl who starves to death in the snow while watching a Christmas party through a window. But older children can gain some idea of their own good fortune and a wider understanding of life as not fair.

Child observation

Watch a story being read to the child. Record the interaction between the adult and child: points to pictures, turns pages, asks questions, volunteers information, and so on.

Investigation

Analyse a selection of children's books.
You will need:
a variety of both fiction and non-fiction books.
a Record the names of the authors and illustrators.
b Record the books' history from the inside front pages: date of first publication, number of reprints, name of publisher, price.
c Identify tales of (i) everyday experience, (ii) fantasy and (iii) morality. Write a brief summary of the main points of each story and suggest their value to a child.
d Give your opinion of the help provided by the illustrations.
e Identify non-fiction books for learning (i) numbers, (ii) the alphabet and (iii) nursery rhymes. Comment on the illustrations.
f From this task alone, choose, with reasons, a fiction and a non-fiction book for a particular aged child.

Questions

1 Suggest, with reasons, some positive attitudes a child might gain from the following extracts:
  a 'She helped with the shopping, and then went home for tea.'
  b 'Sally went to the dentist. Sally was a brave girl.'
  c 'Joe likes orange carrots. Joe eats red apples.'
  d 'He stopped being cross and played games instead.'

'I keep six honest serving men
(They taught me all I knew)
Their names are What and Why and When
And How and Where and Who.'

Rudyard Kipling

These 'six honest serving men' are **questions** wanting answers. At age three, Mo cannot research in a library for the information she needs. She continues to learn by exploratory play, but now she asks many questions too. This is a more advanced way to collect information than feeling toys with her mouth.

Questions are an important part of problem solving. The more information Mo gathers, the more she can start to make informed choices. 'Why my balloon bursted?' The answer helps her when she wants to play with another balloon but the danger is still there. 'Mo stop play. Make that bad thing all gone.'

Mo's parents are weary of the number of questions she asks, especially when they do not know the answers. 'Where did the flame go when I blewdid the candles?' Children see their parents as all-wise, knowing everything there is to know.

Questions are an important part of learning. Open questions allow Mo a wide range of answers. Closed questions narrow her choice of answers to yes and no. 'Is it late?' Mo has only one choice: to get the answer right – or to fail. The adult knows the answer. Mo senses that this is a test. The conversation stops being fun.

— Investigation

Investigate the difference between open and closed questions.

You will need:

a partner who plays the role of a child.

a Ask: 'Are you happy? busy? good? working hard?'

b Record your partner's answers.

c Ask: 'Why are you happy? busy? good? working hard?'

d Record your partner's answers.

e From your findings, state the type of question which was more effective at allowing your partner a wide choice of answers.

Good conversation is sharing ideas and experiences. It avoids a situation where the adult always asks the questions and the child is expected to answer. Good conversation is equal talk, equal sharing, it is interaction. Children need time to think about the words and adults should avoid jumping in to help: 'Is this what you mean?' or finishing the sentence.

Stammering

Between three and four, words can spill out so quickly that stammering is common. Joshua has exciting events he wants to share. 'Ssssee mmme jjjjjump!' he cries. Joshua's parents watch him jump, then they calm him down. They do not correct his stammer, which will soon pass. Nor do they ask Joshua to pay attention to his words in case he becomes self-conscious and embarrassed. The fun of talking would be lost. He might talk less and the stammering might get worse.

Mixed messages

'Doesn't she look charming with that dirty face!'
   'I'm so proud when my little boy misbehaves in a public place!'

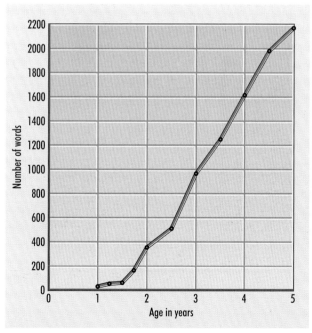

■ The steady increase in a child's vocabulary

■ It helps to crouch at eye level with a child

Exclamation marks tell the reader that the speaker means exactly the opposite. Children are not readers. Mixed messages confuse them. The tone of voice is hostile, yet the words contain praise. Sarcasm confuses a child who is learning speech.

Forms of speech

Adults use idioms, slang, patois and colloquial speech. They use similes, metaphors and personification. They may not even know the meanings of these words, yet they use their forms quite naturally in speech. Children take language literally. Words mean exactly what they have learned they mean.

'Why did that man be a snake?'
'Where do time fly past to go?'
'How do that lady be big for her boots?'

— Investigation

Investigate the difference between talking *to*, *at* or *with* a child.

Working in pairs, take turns at role-playing the small child.

a Say: 'That's interesting. What happened next?'
b Say: 'Sit quietly until it is your turn.'
c Say: 'That is naughty! Now you must clean up the mess!'
d Say: 'Catch! Ho-ho-ho! You have caught me!'
e Describe the likely feelings of the child after each talk.
f Which talk was for
   (i) play and fun?
   (ii) shared conversation?
   (iii) correction?
   (iv) management and organization?
g From your findings, do you think children prefer to be spoken *to*, *at* or *with*?
h Parents speak in all four ways at times. Make up one new example of each.

— Child observation

Speak with the child when you are standing up. Record the child's body language and response. Speak when crouched to the child's height. Record the child's body language and response. From the difference in your findings, if any, give reasons why parents spend a great deal of time in the crouch position. From the graph, estimate the number of words the child is likely to know.

— Questions

1 Design a 'do's and don'ts' chart for talking with a child.

2 When Mo's parents do not know an answer, should they
  a make up one
  b say she is too young to ask
  c say they will find the answer in a big dictionary book
  d give another answer?
Give reasons for your decision.

3 Explain the difference between open and closed questions.

4 Practise tones of voice for putting exclamation marks into speech. Explain why sarcasm and irony are difficult for a child. Suggest reasons why exclamation marks are used both
  a for play
  b for correction speech.

Listening

Listening to children is different from listening to adults. Adults nod to signal when they have understood a point. They may interrupt to ask for more details or add their own point. But when listening to children, the adult pays attention to what the words really mean, does not interrupt, allows plenty of time before responding sensitively. One of the best ways to observe this is by watching the way adults interact with a child who has a **hearing impairment**.

A child with a hearing impairment may be profoundly deaf or only slightly deaf. When the telephone rings, the profoundly deaf child has no idea why the adult suddenly jumps up and speaks into the receiver. The child with a mild hearing impairment can make sense of this. Telephones can be fitted with a light switch when the bell rings so an older child can answer the phone.

A hearing impaired child can learn to lip read too. The adult and child must face each other. Eye contact is essential so that the adult can see from the child's responses that the words have been understood. Sound travels by vibrations in the air. There must be no background noise since it adds to speech vibrations.

Persistent loud noise is a pollutant and a health hazard. Noise intensity is measured in **decibels** and the maximum safety level is 87 decibels. Music played at teen concerts is much louder than this. Some people have very acute hearing and suffer real pain, becoming anxious, tense and stressed as they try to avoid the sounds. Noise which is relentless or sudden does the most damage. Some young people already suffer upper-range hearing loss.

— Investigation —

Analyse the problems of background noise
You will need:
a vacuum cleaner, a blender, a radio, ear plugs
a In turn, switch the machines on. Speak above the noise.
b Record what happens to the level of your voice.
c List the machines which produce noise pollution in the home.
d Now plug your ears and repeat a and b.
e From your findings, does background noise create more noise?
f Suggest ways to reduce noise from technology in the home.

Seeing

A child with **visual impairment** may be blind or have a slight vision problem. When a blind child hears a dog barking, he cannot learn more about the dog. He cannot tell if it is large or small, friendly or fierce, held safely on a leash or about to jump. A child with a slight visual impairment can see the dog but may not be able to tell if it is friendly or fierce.

Children with good vision can be frightened of dogs. A blind child can be terrified. Fear of animals other than family pets is very strong in children between the ages of eight months to three years. Parents find it is more helpful to explain events before they happen. 'Fear can be reduced by information.'

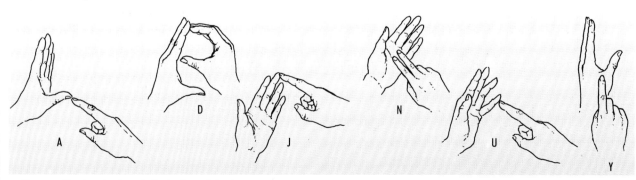

■ Finger spelling is a simple and effective form of sign language

■ Teaching disks are a new resource to help slow learners read

All learning is **interdependent**. The body, the mind, the feelings and the social situation are involved. A frightened child pays attention to his fear. A child in a noisy home cannot hear words clearly. A sight impaired child may speak fluently but is slower to learn reading and writing. A hearing impaired child is slower to speak. These are **secondary** problems. The **primary** difficulty is solved by special help.

— Investigation

Can fear be reduced by information?

In turn with a partner, role-play the frightened child. After each sentence, record the feelings it produces.

a Say: 'It's only a dog. Most people like dogs.'

b Say: 'It looks very friendly. Like your toy dog but bigger.'

c Say: 'Dogs are forbidden in this park. I'll report its owner.'

d Say: 'If you want to pat it, you can. I'm here. You choose.'

e From your records, choose the information you think most helpful to a frightened child.

f List the other three sentences in order of priority for you.

g Make up two further pieces of information which might help a child. Give reasons for your choices.

— Child observation

Ask about any fears the child has and the ways the parents help solve the problem.

— Questions

1 You are planning to give a child a donkey ride. List, with reasons, some of the things she needs to know first.

2 Working in pairs, communicate by lip reading. Convert a simple word into sign language. Evaluate your successes.

3 Explain how pictures and definitions on the TV monitor help a hearing impaired child with reading and comprehension. Compare this with a hearing child's story book.

4 Beth aged five cannot see the blackboard. She is too shy to tell her teacher. Name a secondary problem Beth might develop if her primary problem is not solved. Create and role-play a sensitive scene to help Beth overcome her shyness.

5 Sam stops wearing his spectacles when his friends call him 'four eyes'. Suggest ways his parents might solve this problem. Sam's parents are cross when he loses his new expensive frames. Suggest ways to help Sam remember to look after his spectacles.

6 'Most fear comes from the unknown.' Discuss.

7 Write an essay on the *interdependence* of developmental skills.

8 'Nobody reads anymore. Children live in a world of television and computer games. Who needs old-fashioned books!' Discuss.

A **concept** is an idea, a general notion. In this unit, a concept is an idea of things belonging in groups. Objects can be compared and **classified** into different **categories.** For example, Wendy's pet is a dog. At age two, when she sees a cat she thinks it is another kind of dog. Gradually, she develops the concept of cats and dogs belonging in different groups. Then she recognizes that some animals are bigger than family pets, and they roar and live in jungles and are named 'liars-san-tigers'. Wendy cannot explain the difference between a cat and a dog until age six or seven, but she understands the concept of classifying things at a much younger age.

Concepts are difficult; they require **cognitive** (thinking) skills. They include numbers, colours, shapes, sizes, weights, measures, space and time.

The concept of time

Wendy shows her first concept of time when she can place one event before another. Breakfast comes before lunch. For toddlers, things happen now, in the immediate moment, or not at all. By age three, this has changed. Wendy asks her parents:

'When are we going out?'
'Later.'
'When is later?'
'This afternoon.'
'When is this art ... arter ...siz arternoon?'

Wendy has learned that she must wait, but she has no concept of how long she must wait between her question and this afternoon. Past and future events get confused in her mind. 'I seed the Zoo tomorrow,' she may say of an outing which happened last week. Some five year olds still have difficulty with concepts of tomorrow, yesterday, next week. When told that a new baby is coming, they ask Mummy to hurry it up and then lose interest long before the event. By seven, children are learning to tell the time on a clock.

The concept of space

This is even more difficult. Wendy 'sees' objects which are close to her as larger than they really are. Close objects take up more of her immediate attention. Distant objects seem much smaller. The ability to judge long distances accurately may not be fully developed until age eleven to thirteen.

Space, size and shape are closely linked. At six months, some children can see the difference between circles, triangles and squares. By two years, they often put shapes into the correct hole. By three, they may be able to match objects by shape. 'This star and this star is the same.'

The concept of right and left is very difficult for some children. They may not grasp the idea before the age of ten. 'It's by your right side,' says the adult. The child wonders what is its wrong side, its guilty side. Children with a left-hand preference can find this concept even more confusing since many objects are made only for right-handers.

Weight can be judged by the size of the object. Children expect a small box to weigh less than a large one. When they can pay attention to materials as well as size, they learn that, say, a large packet of cornflakes weighs much less than a small tin of peas.

Beaker A contains water. Beaker B contains milk. The volume of liquid and shape of beakers are exactly the same. When children between ages five and seven were asked 'is milk bigger than water?' they replied:

Yes, because the milk tastes more.
Yes, because there is white in it.
Yes, because it makes teeth grow.
Yes, because you buy it with money.
Yes, because you don't have your bath in it.

Logic is reasoning which makes sense. Children have a special logic for viewing their world which makes sense to them. It makes sense to reason

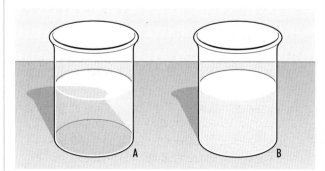

■ Children learn difficult concepts quite naturally during play

■ Explain how these toys help children learn to classify objects

that milk is bigger because it has more taste, more colour, and so on. At another level of thinking, children know that their parents put more value on milk than water.

The home background of a child cannot be separated from its intellectual development. They interact. Children often answer questions in the way they think will please the questioner.

— *Child observation* —

If possible, repeat the milk test with orange juice instead. Record the child's responses and pool the choice of words in class.

— *Questions* —

1 Devise a way to test the following:
   a by three, children may know their age
   b by five, they know their bedtime and have some idea of the days of the week
   c by six, they know the time they get up.

2 Using different shaped toys, find out at what age a child can categorize objects by
   a their shape
   b their colour.

3 Suggest, with reasons, one way to help a five year old identify which is her left and right shoe.

4 Find and quote from songs, games and nursery rhymes which help a child to learn numbers. For example,

'One potato, two potatoes, three potatoes, four. Five potatoes, six potatoes, seven potatoes, more'.

5 Suggest, with reasons, why it is unhelpful to tell a young child that his reasoning is wrong.

6 'Children have a particular logic for their world which makes sense to them.' Discuss.

Art and writing skills

Art represents real or imagined life. It uses symbols which can be difficult to understand. The letters of the alphabet are symbols which look like a set of squiggles. It takes a long time to 'crack the code' of each letter, to match each different shape with a different sound, to learn that – if they are placed in a different order – they form different words: cat can be shaped into act.

Greek		Russian		Chinese	
α	= a	a	= a	⼀	= ee
β	= b	б	= b	⼆	= er
γ	= g	г	= g	三	= san
δ	= d	Д	= d	四	= szu
ζ	= z	3	= z	五	= wu
λ	= l	Л	= l		

■ The letters of the alphabet are codes to be cracked

Pencil control

Learning to draw helps learning to read and write. The skills of **pencil control** have to be mastered first. Scribbling starts at one year. Progress is made when the child can lift the pencil from the paper to draw lines in different directions. Because all learning is interdependent, drawing skills develop in much the same stages as the hand manipulation skills. As the table below shows, each stage follows a set sequence.

The tadpole person

A child's first attempts at art usually represent a human figure. The **tadpole** person is the key drawing for children everywhere. They draw what is most familiar and most important to them. The tadpole person has a head, arms and legs, but no body. The arms and legs sprout from the 'face'. 'Mummy!' Sharon says, patting her mother's body to gain her attention, 'Look!' Adults may wonder why there is no trunk. To the child, the 'face' also represents the body mass and makes sense in non-adult logic.

Stages in the development of writing skills

Age	Crayon control	Records on paper
15 months	The crayon is grasped half way up, and held in the palm with the fingers wrapped around it	Imitates a scribble if shown
18 months	The thumb and first two fingers may be used in a primitive tripod grasp. May show preference for one hand. May draw with both	Scribbles to and fro. Makes dots
2 years	May hold the pencil close to the point in the tripod grasp	Makes circular squiggles plus to and fro. Copies a vertical line, perhaps makes a V
2½ years	Has an improved tripod grasp, pencil in preferred hand	Scribbles and starts to name the scribble as things. Copies a horizontal line and circle, can sometimes make letters T and V
3 years	Holds pencil well with good control	Copies a circle and the letters V, H, T
4 years	Holds pencil like an adult. Maintains good control	Copies V, H T, O and a cross. Starts to trace over words and may copy some simple words
5 years	Good control	Copies squares, triangles, V, T H O X L A C U Y. May write own name and copy some words

■ A tadpole person

■ Zoe can write her name. Estimate her age

Once the tadpole stage is familiar, other objects are added to the picture. The sun is a favourite, smiling happily down, often with radiating lines of sunshine. Dogs and cats look rather like a person lying on one side, only with four legs.

Houses may look more like the pictures in storybooks than the child's actual home. Trees all look the same. These drawings are representations of images in the child's mind rather than the reality. It is much the same as classifying all men as Daddies.

By age five, the child draws a recognizable person with a body, fingers and toes. The house has a door and windows. Cats and dogs begin to look less like people.

By age six, more detail is added. The person is given clothes, a car may be in front of the house. Children draw what they expect or know will be there rather than what they actually see. The car is given four wheels though only two can be seen.

Investigation

Find the key features in children's art.
You will need:
the circles used in unit 20.
Continue to share your findings in class.

a At about what age can children begin to draw the circles?

b Which of the three do they draw (or paint) most often?

c Which of the facial features does a child draw first?

d Which parts of the person are drawn last?

e From your findings, name the key features in children's art and suggest reasons why they have special meaning for a child.

Child observation

Ask the child to draw an object suitable for its age and stage of development. Interact with the child to gain information about the picture. Record the child's level of satisfaction with the finished artwork.

Questions

1 What skills and pleasures might a child gain from drawing?

2 Children may not show a left or right handed preference until two or two and a half. Explain how you could you check this statement.

3 Why do you think children first try to write their name? You can turn back to unit 1 to help you.

4 Write holding a pencil too near the point and explain the disadvantages. Investigate good lighting and where it should fall.

Child interaction

Peer friendships

By eight months, babies smile at other babies they are familiar with. They may vocalize to call the other's attention. Once crawling starts, they follow each other around the floor: touching, poking, trying to learn more. This early interaction is very limited. Touching can be pulling the hair. Poking can be directed at the eyes.

Between eighteen months and two years, children may hug and pat each other. On a good day, they will share their toys. They show sympathy for tears and may try to comfort their weeping friend or otherwise help. If they fail, they themselves become distressed and seek the help of an adult. From age two, familiar children may interact more with each other than with adults.

Adult friendships are based on liking the other person. The friendships of children are based on knowing the other child, recognizing them as familiar though the other child has not met their needs. 'I likes Zoe because she's there,' Zac proclaims. Having access to a child of the same age seems more important than liking. 'Me and Zac fight. He's my friend,' Zoe stoutly insists.

Parents can be baffled by these **peer friendships**. 'But Zoe, you don't even like him,' they say. Zoe does not understand this. Zac meets her need for same-age company. The fighting is all part of learning, and of not being alone.

Twins seem like mirror-images of each other. This can make it difficult for each child to develop

■ Twins are good company for each other

a clear self-image and sense of identity. Because they are good company, they may get less attention from their parents. Their progress may be slower than other children, especially in language skills, because their close interaction reduces their need to struggle for words.

Like all children, twins cannot move forward without adult help. Each baby needs a whole relationship with his parents. Even identical twins are *not* the same. Studies show that the work of raising twins does not double – it multiplies! Parents may have less time and energy to respond sensitively to each child.

Birth order

The order in which children are born plays a large role in their development. Research shows that **siblings** often learn as much from one another as they do from their parents. In some cases, they learn more. Sibling play covers a wide variety of roles. An older sibling can switch from being a wise teacher to a fun playmate, from being a kind comforter to a cruel tormentor. Cruel behaviour is usually kept for the home. The older sibling takes the role of protector when the younger sibling is teased outside the home.

Siblings tend to have strong feelings about each other. They squabble and fight for their parents' attention. This is named **sibling rivalry**. They battle fiercely for the possession of toys. Yet several studies show that siblings share more

■ Babies having fun together

friendly and loving interactions than unfriendly and hostile ones. Adults tend to remember past hurts more clearly than they remember past pleasures.

Siblings can show as strong an attachment to each other as to their parents. The increase in step-families can mean that a sibling is the main source of security – the only person who is always there. By eight months, a baby may cry if an older sibling leaves the room and smile on the sibling's return. By fourteen months, they go to an older sibling for comfort. By two and a half, an older sibling can comfort a toddler effectively and becomes another secure base.

Some parents say they were more tense and 'pushy' with a first child. With a second child, they were more relaxed. They tended to over-indulge a last child. Studies show that a first child is more likely to be anxious and an over-achiever. A second child is more likely to suffer from low self-esteem. A last child is more likely to under-achieve but knows how to get her own way. But children and parents have different temperaments. It can be very dangerous to forget this – see unit 60.

The single child

'Only' children may have advantages that children from large families lack. They may have all their parents' love, time, energy and attention. They may have more conversations, more toys and a more expensive upbringing. They may become so used to adult company that they find it difficult to make friends with children of their own age.

Only children can be lonely children. They benefit from the company of **same-age** friends.

They can practise their social skills, learn more about acceptable behaviour and sharing, and they suffer less boredom.

Jealousy

To be jealous is to be anxious of losing your rights. When you suffer jealousy, you feel resentful of other people who seem to be taking attention away from you. An older sibling is jealous of the new baby who seems to be taking all the parents' attention. A younger sibling can be jealous because her older sibling can do everything better. Since she was not the first-born, she feels she must work harder for her parents' attention. Even a single child can suffer jealousy when a friend comes to play and gets more attention.

Since jealousy comes from the need for attention, it can be reduced be respecting this need. An older sibling is encouraged to help with the baby. A younger sibling is reassured that being second does not mean 'second-best'. Children have to learn they are *not* the centre of the universe. Child experts believe it is better to learn this painful lesson in the home than at school.

— Child observation

It used to be thought that children under age three were not able to interact. Devise a task to prove or disprove this theory by child observation. Evaluate your task by testing it out.

— Questions

1 'Only child, lonely child.' Students who are only children can share their experiences in class. What kind of pleasures did they feel they were missing? What advantages might they have gained from being a single child.

2 Twins are such good company they are often left on their own. From the text, suggest a more practical reason for this, and ways to test it.

3 'There will always be sibling rivalry.' Explain the meaning of this term and whether or not you agree with the statement.

4 What does birth order mean? Describe how you might feel as a parent if your child blames you for her birth order. Can parents ever get family life totally right? Suggest, with reasons, two other criticisms of parents which may not be fair.

Over 98 per cent of households have a television set, and 43 per cent have more than one set. Over 63 per cent of homes have video recorders. Television, home movies, rented videos and pre-recorded programmes are part of family life. Radio programmes lack visual appeal for children, but they are part of family life too. Radios may be switched on at breakfast for the morning news, and housework may be done while listening to music or a favourite talk show.

The revolution in entertainment technology has changed the structure of many children's lives. Instead of learning to amuse themselves, they can sit back and be entertained. Their fun is **passive** rather than **active**: cruising the TV channels, playing computer games, changing the VCR, relaying continuous music. Some of this passive entertainment helps with learning. Children gain a wider knowledge of their world and computer games, for example, improve their hand–eye skills. But, if for example they watch the daytime or early evening 'soaps', they learn in a highly dramatic way that not all parents are wise and benign. Some are foolish and many more are 'bad'. The long-term effects of this on the basic trust of children in the wisdom of their parents are not well understood.

Music

Music enriches the quality of life. But if it is relayed non-stop into the home, this background noise can reduce the amount of conversation. Children have different levels of sensitivity, and some can be over-stimulated by constant exposure to noise.

Making music is active learning. Sing-alongs are fun before a child becomes self-conscious and realizes that she may be out of tune. Percussion instruments such as tambourines, xylophones and drums are fun for making rattling and banging sounds. Wind instruments include tin flutes, whistles, combs with tissue paper stretched across their teeth. A few two year olds learn to play string instruments such as the violin. Electronic toys with programmed keyboards can switch on a child's interest in making music.

■ Percussion instruments are great fun for children with partial hearing

Television

Television is a visual medium and its messages are powerful to a child. A 1994 report from the Broadcasting Standards Council (BSC) found that, in a typical week on British television, there were 246 killings and a further 549 people were injured. Apart from the killings, the most frequent violences were:

    pushing and throwing people 15 per cent
    shooting them 13 per cent
    threatening them 10 per cent
    hitting people with objects 7 per cent
    punching them 7 per cent.

Rape was a common theme of drama programmes.

Bad language is broadcast every nine minutes. In one survey week, there were 1154 words of abuse against religion, women, minority groups and the disabled. Most of the murder, rape, violence and bad language is kept for peak viewing hours. But in some homes, the television set is used as a 'babysitter' and children spend more time viewing than they do with their parents.

A 1990 survey for *Options* magazine found that 52 per cent of under-fives could record and watch their favourite programmes without help from their parents. One-fifth of children younger than two could operate a VCR and 72 per cent of four year olds could manage fast-forward, rewind and pause. Other trends observed included an increase in swearing; 44 per cent of the mothers reported that their two to four year olds used bad language. They were concerned about the effects of television on their children.

Investigation

Analyse television programmes for the under-fives.

Plan this task along the same lines as your research into their storybooks.

a Record the names of the programmes, the times they are broadcast, how long they last, whether or not they are repeats.

b List tales of fantasy, everyday experience, happy ever after and problem-solving.

c Analyse the programmes for their types of speech content: motherese, open and closed questions; mixed messages; talking to, at or with a child; help with different ethnic groups; arousing fear then calming it; reducing fear by information, and so on.

d Identify the introduction of difficult concepts: maths skills for numbers, sorting into categories of weight, colour, shape and size; writing skills for letters of the alphabet; hand skills for water, sand, drawing and creative play.

e Record any encouragement for children to follow through after the programmes by active play.

f Comment on the design and visual appeal of the clothing, sets and general appearance of the actors or puppets.

g Analyse scenes for sheer fun and enjoyment, nothing else.

h Identify and describe any factors which you think unsuitable for under-fives, giving reasons why.

i From your findings, select two programmes which you think help children learn, giving reasons for each choice.

Investigation

Conduct a survey to find

a the most popular television programmes for the under fives

b parents' opinions of these programmes.

Analyse your survey findings in the light of your own findings. Discuss any differences and suggest some reasons for them.

Child observation

Record the average time spent by the child viewing television a on weekdays and b at the weekends. Pool your findings and estimate the average viewing time of children in your area. Find out how many children have access to computer games and which games are most popular. If possible, analyse their contents. Record any musical instrument the child plays.

Questions

1 Describe some differences between active and passive learning as it applies to music in the home.

2 Was any bad language used on children's television? Suggest, with reasons, two other places where a three year old might hear bad language.

3 'Parents have to be "watch-dogs" over a the quality, b the amount and c the suitability of entertainments coming into their homes.' Write a short essay, discussing each point.

Primary education covers three age ranges: **nursery** for the under fives, **infant** for the five to seven or eight year olds and **junior** for the seven or eight to eleven or twelve year olds. Most primary schools take both girls and boys in mixed classes.

Special schools meet the needs of children who are seriously disabled and cannot manage learning in an ordinary school. Special schools may be day or boarding. The number of children in these schools is about 86,900. Each child receives an **assessment** and **statement** of its special needs. The statement helps parents choose the right sort of educational care for their child.

Nursery schools and nursery classes

These are run by the Local Education Authority. They take children between ages three and five. Their services are free, though a charge is made for lunch. Nursery schools may be purpose-built. Nursery classes may be part of an infant school. Both types are staffed by trained nursery teachers and nursery helpers. They are usually well equipped with learning materials and play space, including an outdoor play area. They are open during normal school hours and close in the holidays. They may have places for disabled children. State-run nursery schools and classes usually have a long waiting list.

Private nursery schools provide similar services but have to charge fees. They may be run by voluntary or religious organizations and should be registered with the local authority. They may have less equipment and some lack an outdoor play area. They may take disabled children, depending upon the type of disability and the facilities available. Some children attend for the whole of an adult's working day. Others attend part-time, depending upon their parents' needs.

The Pre-school Playgroup Association (PPA)

The PPA was set up to meet the needs of pre-school children and their parents. It is funded by a government grant and local groups get a small grant from their local authority. The playgroup

■ Structured play is based on learning

must be registered with the local authority and the playgroup leader trained by them. Parents whose children are the **consumers** also help run the group. They are **active citizens** participating in community self-help.

The PPA takes children age three to five but they may take younger siblings. A small fee is charged for each session the child attends. The sessions last a morning or afternoon, not the whole day. The PPA aims to provide learning experiences through structured play. Parents are involved in all aspects of running the playgroup. Funds are short, so money for toys and equipment is raised from local businesses, car boot sales and other events. This creates a network of parents with strong community ties. Parents gain skills to manage committees, read balance sheets and organize publicity. Some choose to train as playgroup leaders themselves.

Rising fives

The term 'rising fives' is used for children who are nearly, or recently, five. The following are some skills gained by the rising fives.
◆ To feed themselves easily and without too much mess.
◆ To drink from a cup using one hand only, sometimes two hands.

- To co-operate by passing food, plates or other utensils at table.
- To interact with their home life and help with domestic tasks.
- To dress and undress, but they may need help with buttons or zips.
- To change their shoes but are unlikely to manage shoe laces.
- To go to the toilet alone, wash and dry their hands afterwards.
- To know simple arithmetic such as sorting, grouping, counting.
- To name four colours, and match others they cannot name.
- To recognize their name and write some letters of the alphabet.
- To create simple pictures using pencils, crayons and paintbrush.
- To listen to simple instructions and carry them out.
- To take part in adult conversations they find interesting.
- To sing along with music and chant their favourite nursery rhymes.
- To have some idea of time, and the days of the week.
- To give their full name, age and home address.
- To have their own friends and invent games with them.
- To protect and (sometimes) look after younger children and pets.
- To comfort their friends when it was not they who upset them.
- To understand the reasons for rules and fair play (see unit 61).

Lonely children

Research carried out recently found that children are lonelier than in the past. They are less likely to have siblings and to play freely outside. This last is due partly to the increase in traffic and partly to the increased fear of **child molestation** – see unit 65. If both parents work, the children may not get much attention at home either.

— Child observation =

a Record the type of pre-school education attended by the child (if any). Survey one type and make notes on the following:
  - **ratio** of children to adults
  - activities in groups or with a single child
  - indoor and outdoor play space
  - hours of opening
  - fees
  - distance from home, and so on.

b Photograph or draw sketches of the general layout, cloakrooms, washrooms, eating and rest areas. Mark and label the safety features of each.

c Comment on the aesthetic appeal of the layout. Is it cosy? fun? bleak?

d Is there easy access for children with disabilities?

e Who cleans and maintains the building?

f Do the children seem happy and relaxed? Are their needs being met?

g Suggest, with reasons, how parents might use your information.

h Design a play area on chart paper.

— Questions

1 Place each skill of the rising fives under headings: physical, intellectual, emotional and social development. Some skills will fit into more than one group. Try to explain why.

2 Give two reasons why children are more likely to be lonely than in the past. Suggest ways in which pre-school education might help solve this problem.

3 Suki's parents both work office hours. Suggest, with reasons, a choice of pre-school education for Suki.

4 Didi longs for friends but cannot manage being separated from her mother. Suggest, with reasons, suitable pre-school education for Didi.

Infant health

A baby girl born 50 years ago could expect to live to age 67. Today she can expect to live to age 79. This huge increase in **life expectancy** is due to improvements in:

- the care of newborns which has reduced **infant mortality**
- the care of women during pregnancy and birth
- choices of diet with more information on nutrition
- safety and protection factors in the home and workplace
- hygiene, sanitation and more knowledge of disease
- more **immunization** programmes in the first years of life.

The National Health Service (NHS) began in 1948. It provided free medical and dental care for everyone. **Maternity and child welfare clinics** were set up, sometimes named **mother and baby** or **well-baby** clinics. **Health visitors** are nurses with special training in family welfare. They give advice on pregnancy and child care. Immunization programmes protect children from diseases such as polio, tetanus, whooping cough and diphtheria.

Sadly, not all infant deaths can be avoided. For every 1000 babies born alive in the UK in 1992, 5.7 girls and 7.4 boys under age one died. These figures, though tragic, are a great improvement on 30 years ago when 18.2 girls and 26.3 boys per thousand live births died under age one.

A baby boy born 50 years ago could expect to live to age 62. Today this has risen to age 74. About 120 boys are conceived for every 100 girls. This drops to 110 boys for every 100 girls during the nine months of pregnancy. Live births are 103 boys to 100 girls, but more boys die in the first year of life. Twice as many males than females ages 15 to 39 die from injury or poisoning. From the cradle to the grave, men suffer more ill-health and serious accidents than women.

Cot death

A few babies who seem perfectly healthy die suddenly and without warning. This is **Sudden Infant Death Syndrome** (SIDS). Many theories have been suggested for the causes of SIDS but none have been proved. Newborns have simple **haemoglobin** – the chemical that absorbs oxygen in red blood cells – which only matures after birth. One study found that immature haemoglobin seems to linger in SIDS babies.

Cot deaths are rare, but the risk is seven times greater in the first six months of life. This risk is one of the most harrowing fears of parents. In 1992, the number of SIDS cases dropped to 0.7 per thousand live births when babies were placed to sleep on their backs. Other advice is not to smother the baby in blankets but to keep the room warm. Dummy sucking might help to keep the airways open. Avoid exposing infants to cigarette smoke during pregnancy and after the birth.

Post-natal care

At birth, each baby is examined to make sure all is well. Its reflexes are tested to check that the sensory system is working (see units 5 and 7). Its measurements are recorded on a chart (see units 4 and 6). A hip examination checks that the thigh

Causes of death by age and gender, 1992				
Cause of death	Percentages			
	Under 1		1–14	
	Girls	Boys	Girls	Boys
Infectious diseases	4.3	4.8	4.8	5.1
Cancers	1.5	1.0	18.0	17.3
Heart diseases	5.6	4.0	4.0	4.0
Breathing diseases	10.6	11.9	5.6	5.1
Injury and poisoning	16.8	17.6	25.8	34.2
All other causes	61.3	60.8	41.4	34.2

■ This baby is placed safely in the cot

bones are set in the hip sockets and not dislocated or unfirmly fixed. A blood sample is taken and screened for certain disorders.

Hypothyroidism is a hormone disorder of the thyroid gland. The baby does not produce enough thyroxine, which is essential for growth. Thyroxine is given daily to replace the missing hormone.

Beta thalassaemia is a blood disorder in some Mediterranean families. Not enough red blood cells are made for the baby to thrive. Screening at birth helps the doctors plan long-term care for the child. Beta thalassaemia is rather similar to **sickle cell anaemia** (see unit 56), which is also screened for at birth.

Phenylketonuria (PKU) is a disorder of protein metabolism. The amino acid phenylalanine is not broken down and stays in the blood. PKU damages the developing brain, causing metal handicap. Babies are screened for PKU at about one week old. Dietary therapy begins at once. Their food has proteins from which phenylalanine is removed.

Birth defects

One in every 1000 full-term infants is born with a birth defect. Many of these defects are minor **impairments**. The major birth defects are listed with the most common first.

Heart	Heart or blood vessel defects can be treated by surgery. A few babies have been operated on while in the uterus.
Clubfoot	A foot in the wrong position is corrected by surgery or a cast. Physiotherapy speeds up the process.
Cleft lip/palate	An opening in the upper sides of the mouth is corrected by surgery and speech therapy.
Limbs	Shortened or missing limbs, fingers or toes are helped by physiotherapy and technological replacements.

A **disability** can be mild or severe. The table below shows the average numbers of children in England and Wales with certain disabilities. Over 2 per cent of pre-school children have some physical or **mental disability** so severe that their development is delayed. A few have multiple handicap. A child with severe Down's syndrome falls into this group (see unit 84).

Average number of children with disabilities (England and Wales)	
Disability	**Number of children**
Blind	1,200
Sight impaired	2,500
Deaf	3,800
Hearing impaired	5,000
Physical disability	14,000
Mental handicap	28,000

— Child observation —

Record any impairment the child may have, any problems this causes, and ways the child manages them.

— Questions —

1 Explain what SIDS means. Name the highest period of risk and three methods to protect against it.

2 Disabilities can be placed in three categories: physical (the body), sensory (the senses) and psychiatric (the mind). From the table above name
   a the largest
   b the smallest
   group of children with disabilities and the category of impairment.

3 A severe disability, e.g. loss of limb movement, keeps a child in a wheelchair. Using role-play, identify and describe ways in which this can affect the quality of a child's life.

Infections

We share our bodies with millions of living things so tiny that they can only be seen under a microscope. Hence their name, micro-organisms. They live on our skin, hair and eyelashes. They inhabit the mouth, nose and throat. Colonies breed in the large bowel. In general, they do us no harm. Some do good. The microbes in the large bowel are a source of vitamin K.

Germs

The micro-organisms which cause disease include **bacteria** and **viruses**. Bacteria multiply at a very fast rate if the conditions are right. Each one becomes two every 20 minutes in warm, moist, unventilated places. They produce **toxins** (poisons) which damage the infected area and which may travel in the bloodstream to other parts of the body.

Viruses are even smaller than bacteria. They breed only in living cells. They multiply inside the cell, which bursts, releasing the viruses to attack neighbouring cells.

The first drug (medicine) to cure a bacterial infection was made from fungus in the 1940s. These drugs are **antibiotics**. They are powerless to destroy viruses. Medical research for new drugs continues non-stop because bacteria have ways to defeat the latest cures. For example, the sexual diseases caused by bacteria can be cured by antibiotics. But the bacteria can develop **resistance** to antibiotics. Or they **mutate** (change their structure) and attack in different forms.

Thrush is a yeast infection which can grow in any of the body openings.

The common cold is a frequent illness in childhood. It is caused by viruses which mutate, sometimes from year to year. An **epidemic** is an outbreak of disease in a community. **Epidemiology** is the study of the over-all patterns of disease.

Diseases are **transmitted** (passed on) in the following ways.

Droplet infection The cold virus can be sprayed from the mouth and nose by coughing, sneezing, laughing, even talking. Illnesses spread by droplet infection mainly cause **respiratory disease**.

Contact A disease can spread by direct contact: kissing, shaking hands, close contact on a crowded bus. It can spread by indirect contact: sharing drinking cups, spoons or towels which are contaminated. An illness transmitted by contact is named a **contagious disease**.

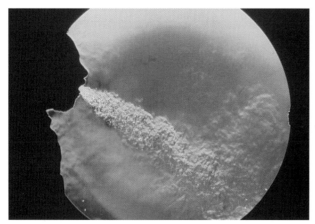

■ The distance travelled by spray from a cough

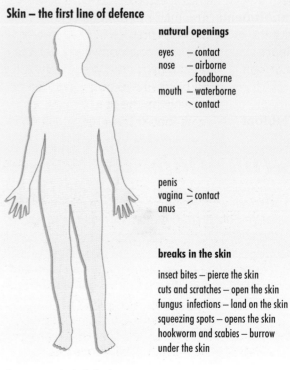

Skin – the first line of defence

natural openings

eyes — contact
nose — airborne
— foodborne
mouth — waterborne
— contact

penis
vagina — contact
anus

breaks in the skin

insect bites – pierce the skin
cuts and scratches – open the skin
fungus infections – land on the skin
squeezing spots – opens the skin
hookworm and scabies – burrow under the skin

■ Germs enter the body by these routes

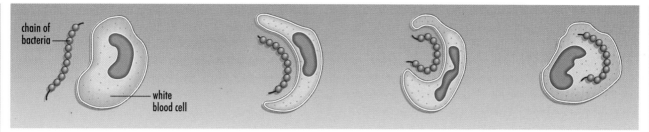

■ White blood cells are part of the immune system. They 'gobble up' germs

The immune system

People do not always catch a cold when they are exposed to the virus. This is because the body has its own system of defence. When germs invade, the immune system produces antibodies which attack and destroy them. Different antibodies have to be made for different germs. Once a disease is defeated, the antibodies remain and provide **immunity** if those germs attack again.

Some people catch colds more often than others. These are some of the factors which increase the chance of infection.

Age The young and old have weaker immune systems, and are more vulnerable to infections.

Diet Poor nutrition lowers the body's resistance to disease. A malnourished child is at greater risk of infections.

Emotions Stress upsets the body systems and lowers resistance. Studies show happy people have fewer infections than unhappy ones.

Wounds Germs enter cuts, spots and scratches. Once the skin is broken open, there is a chance of **secondary infection**.

Illness Conditions such as diabetes, blood disorders and AIDS carry a high risk of secondary infection.

Addiction Substance abuse weakens the immune system. Shared needles pass HIV and other infections.

Environment Unventilated or overcrowded homes, unclean food preparation and storage, poor personal hygiene.

The unborn baby lives in a protected environment. At birth, the environment is no longer **sterile**. Though newborns have little resistance to disease, they are protected by the antibodies in their mother's milk.

— Child observation

Ask about the first illness of the child.

Questions

1 Copy and complete the following sentences:
   a Humans are **hosts** to harmless ....
   b The main harmful micro-organisms are ...
   c An outbreak of disease in a community is an ....
   d The search for new cures is non-stop because...
   e Respiratory diseases are spread by ...
   f Contagious diseases are transmitted by ...
   g Newborns are protected against disease by ...
   h Happy people catch ... infections than ... people.

2 'A few germs won't hurt!' says Jo, coughing as she picks up the baby. Role-play how to protect the baby without hurting Jo's feelings. Discuss two ways to reduce the spread of infection.

3 Thrush in the mouth is more common in bottle-fed than breast-fed babies. Suggest
   a where the infection may come from
   b what parents can do to avoid thrush.

4 Explain clearly what is meant by secondary infection.

Immunization

As babies grow, they become more exposed to germs and build up their own resistance to disease. But some germs are powerful and can defeat the immune system. Babies are helped to build up their resistance by **immunization**. They are given **vaccines** which contain either weakened parts of the viruses or bacteria which cause the disease, or very small amounts of the toxins they produce. The vaccine triggers the immune system to produce antibodies and this gives the infant immunity from a real attack.

Some antibodies remain active for life, others wear out. **Booster shots** make sure the growing child stays immune.

Hib is an influenza virus which causes a range of illnesses:
- a type of meningitis (infection of the brain linings)
- a severe swelling in the throat and difficulty in breathing
- blood poisoning (septicaemia)
- infections of the bones and joints
- pneumonia.

Before the Hib vaccine was available, one in 600 children caught the virus before the age of five. Hib was responsible for about 65 deaths and 150 cases of brain-damaged children each year.

Polio is a serious disease of the spinal-cord which can paralyze the muscles.

Measles, mumps and rubella (MMR) may seem like mild diseases. But they can cause serious **complications**. Measles can lead to convulsions (fits), brain inflammation (swelling) and deafness. Mumps can lead to deafness and meningitis (infection of the brain linings). If a pregnant woman is exposed to rubella, the germs can cause her baby to be born deaf, blind or brain damaged.

After immunization, some children feel unwell for a while. They are irritable and develop a mild fever. The medical staff advise parents on these reactions and how soon they will pass.

Contra-indications are conditions that suggest there might be a bad reaction to a vaccine (or other medical treatment, especially drugs). Whooping cough is a serious disease for babies. It causes breathing difficulties, with long painful coughing fits, up to 50 times each day. The coughing often ends in vomiting, the baby loses weight and becomes exhausted. The complications include ear infections, pneumonia, convulsions and brain damage.

Whooping cough spreads rapidly by droplet infection. Before the vaccine was discovered, epidemics were common. By 1976, these epidemics were rare. Yet between 1977 and 1983, some infants died and many more suffered long-term complications from whooping cough.

What led to such a terrible epidemic? Study the table below showing the drop and rise in immunization over 20 years.

Name the years when parents stopped having their babies immunized against whooping cough. In 1976, a national study found that the vaccine itself caused brain damage once in 100,000 babies. This was higher with a family history of epilepsy.

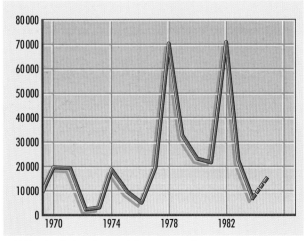

■ Epidemics of whopping cough happen every four years

Immunization	Percentages				
	1971	1976	1981	1986	1991–2
Diphtheria	80	73	82	85	96
Whooping cough	78	39	46	66	88
Poliomyelitis	80	73	82	85	94
Tetanus	80	73	82	85	94
Measles* (mumps and rubella)	46	45	54	71	91

* measles only vaccine. The combined shot for measles, mumps and rubella only became available in 1988.

Immunization only works if most children are vaccinated. If too many parents decide against one vaccine, the disease spreads rapidly through the baby community. Parents face the difficult task of making an **informed choice**. Some choose not to risk their baby being harmed by the vaccine – although the baby is then at risk of catching the disease itself. Some choices are always a risk and painful to make, even with all the health information.

The recommended schedule for immunization issued by the Health Education Authority and the Department of Health is shown in the table on this page.

Date	Immunization	Type
2 months	Hib	one injection
	diphtheria whooping cough tetanus	DTP one injection
	polio	by mouth
3 months	Hib	one injection
	diphtheria whooping cough tetanus	DTP one injection
	polio	by mouth
4 months	Hib	one injection
	diphtheria whooping cough tetanus	DTP one injection
	polio	by mouth
12–15 months	measles mumps rubella	MMR one injection
3–5 years	diphtheria tetanus	booster injection
	polio	booster by mouth
girls 10–14 years	rubella	one injection
girls/boys	tuberculosis	one injection (BCG)
school leavers	tetanus diphtheria	one injection
15–19 years	polio	booster by mouth

◇

Child observation

Make an immunization history of the child, giving its age now. (The dates are not necessary.)

Questions

1 At what age is the first polio vaccine given? Explain the reason why booster doses are needed, and give the ages. Suggest a reason why some school leavers are more keen to have the polio booster than the booster injection of tetanus and diphtheria.

2 Grace missed her MMR immunization because she was abroad. Now age fourteen, she chooses not to have the MMR vaccine. List the risks she is taking and the consequences of her choice.

3 Between 1978 and 1992, the cases of measles dropped from 200,000 to 17,000. State, with reasons, if you think a national programme of immunization works.

4 'Good hygiene and immunization are effective against diseases transmitted by personal contact and respiratory route.' List some hygiene rules to protect a child from diseases passed by droplet infection.

5 Investigate, in detail, one of the above diseases mentioned in the text. Identify how it is transmitted, the incubation period, the symptoms of disease, the methods of home nursing and any complications which can arise.

An infectious illness

Symptoms

The symptoms of an illness are the signs which can be observed: the rash of measles, a wheezy cough, a rise in temperature. The stages of an infectious illness are **incubation**, **fever and recovery**. During the first stage, the germs breed rapidly. The immune system begins producing antibodies to fight them. The child may seem healthy at this time.

Fever is the high point of battle between the germs and antibodies. The immune system is working flat out. Not only must all the viruses be destroyed, the damaged tissue and toxic waste must be removed. This battle produces extra heat, which shows in a child's flushed face and burning skin. The body temperature rises and causes sweating. The doctor must be called if there are aching limbs, headache and feelings of dizziness or confusion.

Taking the temperature

Modern technology has led to improved methods of taking the temperature. A feverscan is made of a series of heat-sensitive strips which change colour to show the level of body heat. The scan is held across the baby's forehead and this avoids putting a glass thermometer containing mercury in the infant's mouth. A more expensive method

■ The feverscan thermometer

records the level of body heat by using a mouth thermometer.

A child's temperature is not taken under the tongue. The armpit is the usual place while the child is held on the lap. A lullaby or soothing story helps pass the time. Avoid taking the temperature after a hot drink or bath since the reading will be falsely high.

Not all rises in temperature are symptoms of disease. Upset feelings can cause over-heating too. Children need the skills of nurturing rather than nursing to calm them down. The advice is to take the temperature only when there are symptoms of ill-health. In very young babies, the doctor must be called if the temperature is high.

Over-heating

Fever is 'good' in that the infection has reached its peak. But even a small increase in the temperature can bring on a fever-related **seizure** (fit, convulsion). The first goal is to *bring down the temperature*. The child is undressed and tepid water is sponged over the flushed face and burning skin. As the water evaporates, it removes heat. This not only cools the body, but soothes the mind. Cold water must *never* be used since it can cause shock. The child should then be dressed in a lightweight absorbent garment.

The second goal with fever is to *avoid dehydration*. Plenty of fluids must be given to replace those lost

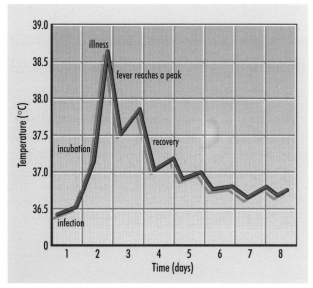

■ Temperature changes during an infectious disease

in sweating. Influenza (flu) is a common childhood illness. The early symptoms include ear, nose and throat (ENT) infections. A child whose throat hurts may refuse drinks because swallowing is painful. Sugary juices and fizzy colas, even bribes help. The consequences of these have less priority than getting fluid into the child.

Aspirin is an anti-inflammatory drug, which means it reduces swelling. Aspirin must *never* be given to reduce fever in a child. The drug is linked with a rare but fatal childhood disease, named Reye's syndrome. The general advice is to not give drugs because they all have side effects and can

■ One litre of fluid needs to be taken over each three hour period

damage the liver. However, a dose of paracetamol syrup may be advised for babies who run a fever after immunization.

Diet has an important role in recovery. Colds and fevers burn up the body's resources of nutrients. A child in recovery has a very poor appetite. Solids lack appeal since they require effort to chew. Homemade soup is a favourite and some parents keep a ready supply in the freezer. Ice-cream is cooling and nutritious too.

Vomiting

Infants bring up a little milk after most feeds. This is named **posseting**. They tend to suck in air with milk and feel more comfortable after a burp. Toddlers and older children go through phases of having a 'delicate' stomach. They retch or actually vomit if they become over-excited. They need to be calmed down. Talking about their feelings and being reassured can help.

Vomiting is a symptom of illness when the child is repeatedly and properly sick. With diarrhoea, this indicates food poisoning. Take a child who vomits repeatedly to the doctor's surgery.

— *Child observation* —

Ask if the child has had an infectious disease and the first symptoms which the parents noticed.

— *Questions* —

1 Give reasons why you would:
   a nurse a feverish child by giving a tepid sponge bath
   b avoid dressing the child in wool-mix clothes afterwards
   c encourage the child to drink more fluids
   d always hold a child while taking the temperature
   e avoid taking the temperature at the first sneeze or cough
   f avoid giving a child any drugs
   g always call the doctor for a baby who seems unwell.

2 List some nutrients in chicken soup. Identify the food values in a scoop of ice cream. State, with reasons, why you might offer these foods to a child at the recovery stage. Plan a day's menu, or prepare a dish, giving reasons for your choice.

3 Investigate fever-related seizures (convulsions, fits).

Sick children need the comfort of bed. A quiet, darkened room helps them fall asleep. They need familiar people when they wake to find their illness still hurts. They need reassurance which is both calm and encouraging: 'Let's make you feel better' is more positive than 'Let's see if a sponge bath works.'

Babies cannot pay attention while they are in pain, but most children can. This depends upon their temperament, the type of illness, and how long it lasts. Instead of progressing in their learning, sick children can **regress** – their behaviours return to a younger age. Some children regress by as much as two years. The concept of illness and getting well again is difficult to grasp. Children live in the present, and the present hurts.

As children recover, they need both company and quiet times. This can be solved by nursing them on the sofa where they can play games or drift into sleep. Suitable television or video programmes will distract their minds from the pain and keep them contented. They need lots of tender loving care and 'babying' if they fuss and fret.

First Aid

When children say 'hurt', identify the problem first. The 'hurt' may be emotional. Their feelings may have been wounded and need to be soothed. When the 'hurt' is a tiny scratch, their feelings may also need soothing. Some children believe they only get better if the scratch is taken seriously and covered with a plaster.

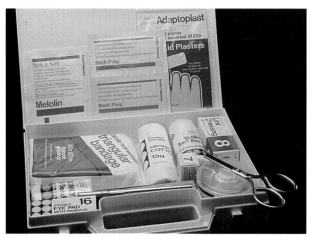

■ The contents of a First Aid box

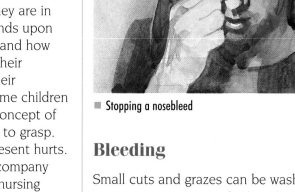

■ Stopping a nosebleed

Bleeding

Small cuts and grazes can be washed in cold water to remove any germs. Antiseptic creams and sticking plaster can keep a wound moist and delay healing. If a dressing is required, it must allow the area to 'breathe'. A nose bleed is stopped by pinching firmly just under the bridge. Keep the pressure steady for ten minutes.

Severe bleeding can be stopped by pressing firmly down on the wound. You need a course in First Aid to learn this. The other priority with severe bleeding is to get medical help urgently.

Stings

Soothing ointments help the child feel better. Calamine lotion is comforting for nettle-stings. For bee or wasp stings, only use creams which are recommended for infants. The anti-histamines in other creams may not be suitable. A few children get a severe allergic reaction to a bee sting. Watch a stung child's progress over the next few hours.

Burns and scalds

Burns are caused by dry heat from a fire or touching hot objects. Scalds are caused by wet heat from liquids. For small burns and scalds, the priority is to reduce the heat by plunging the area in cold water for fifteen minutes. Avoid ointments; they delay healing. The blister which may form over a burn must not be pricked since it keeps out germs.

■ It's very dangerous to have hot drinks near small children

Over 75 per cent of serious scalds to one to four year olds are spills from cups, teapots, kettles and saucepans. *No hot drinks should be taken with a child sitting on the adult's lap.*

Choking

The priority with choking is to remove the object stuck in the airway. Hold a baby *firmly* upside down by the legs and pat his back. Bend an older child over and slap between the shoulder blades. If this fails, a short sharp squeeze to the stomach will push the object out. Like mouth-to-mouth resuscitation, these skills can be learned at a First Aid course.

Emergencies

Rush the child to hospital immediately without waiting to call a doctor for: severe bleeding, severe burns and scalds, difficulty in breathing, swallowing poison or a dangerous object like a pin, a fit or convulsion, a severe fall or a blow on the head.

■ Choking requires immediate action

— Investigation

Practise a simple First Aid skill.
You will need:
a partner, a First Aid box, freshly-washed hands.
a Choose, with reasons, a dressing for a grazed elbow.
b Choose, with reasons, a cream for embedded dirt.
c In turn, clean each 'wound' and apply the dressing or cream to a partner.
d Become familiar with the contents of the First Aid box.
e Develop a sensitive and calm approach.
f Demonstrate how to treat a minor scald.
g Name, with reasons, one hygiene rule to observe.
h Evaluate each other's nursing skills.

— Child observation

Ask the child to tell you about any small cut or hurt it has experienced.

— Questions

1 List six items you would expect to find in a First Aid box. Give a use for each.
2 Name the first task if a child complains of pain. Describe how to treat
   a a cut
   b a minor burn
   c a sting.
3 Describe one likely consequence of drinking a cup of tea with a child sitting on your lap.
4 Explain the reasons why children need more comfort, love and attention when they are ill. List the symptoms which you would regard as an emergency and describe what you would do.

53 Protection at home

The word **accident** means chance, fate or luck. It suggests that safety in the home is random and that parents cannot protect their child from danger. But many accidents can be prevented. Every year, some 600,000 children aged from a few months to four years are hurt badly at home and have to go to hospital.

— Investigation

Analyse the term 'accidents waiting to happen!'

a Study the pictures below for their dangers.

b Identify each hazard to a child's airway.

c Suggest ways in which each hazard can be avoided.

d Create a powerful warning title for each of the pictures.

e Explain the term 'accidents waiting to happen!'

Once children can walk, they become human dynamoes. Toddlers show the thrill of freedom by charging madly around. They dash from one place to the next with no thought for their safety. They get stuck on the climbing frame, but refuse help. 'Me do it!' They push away their parent's restraining arms.

By eighteen months, toddlers have had enough knocks and bumps to develop **expectations** of things as threatening. But they cannot make the right **connections** between past warnings and now. When the hot plate on the cooker glows invitingly, they climb on a chair to touch this exciting thing. If they say 'hot, hurt' after a nasty burn, it does not mean they have made the connections for the future. Memory is still developing. *Toddlers do not 'learn a lesson' by pain.*

A lovely snuggly pillow!

Prop feeding saves time!

Learning by sucking!

Hunks of food for a hunky toddler!

This dummy is safe from getting lost!

Open-weave nylon and ribbons look pretty!

Plastic bags are fun for play!

■ Young children need to be protected from these dangers in the home

Fire!

The controlled use of fire is valuable in human life. It only becomes dangerous when people take risks. The **point of ignition** (where the fire starts) is the point where *human behaviour* and the *risk of fire* meet.

The table shows the main causes of ignition. In the fires recorded in the table, 262 people burned to death, 533 died from breathing fumes and 6947 were rushed to hospital with severe burns.

Fires produce **choking smoke** and **deadly gases**, mainly carbon monoxide. The smoke and gas cause 60 to 90 per cent of fire deaths. The person is overcome by the fumes and cannot escape the flames.

Flame-resistant clothing gives only slight protection from heat and flames. Fibres in home furnishings can be highly **flammable**. They burn fiercely, giving off a mixture of deadly fumes. It is thought these fibres add to the problems of most home fires.

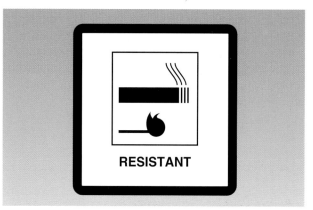

■ This is the fire safety symbol used by the furnishing industry

Main points of ignition for household fires		
Cause of fire	*Number of fires*	*Percentage*
Cooking appliances	20,800	45.8
Cigarettes	6,200	13.7
Electrical appliances	5,900	13.0
Matches	4,600	10.1
Space heating	4,500	9.9
Electrical wiring	3,400	7.5

Investigation

Test the burning properties of various fabrics.

This investigation must only be carried out in the presence of a teacher and with a fire extinguisher to hand.

You will need:

a suitable *safe place* for this task, small fabric squares, a retort stand, a stopwatch, a taper.

a Hang a square by one corner from the retort stand.

b Light the taper. Apply to the lowest corner of the fabric. *Stand well back!*

c Record your findings under: fabric name, time to ignite, time to complete combustion, amount of smoke, smell, drip.

d List the fabrics in order of their **flammability**.

e List them in order of their dangerous products of combustion.

Questions

1 Peanuts have become a popular food for children. Suggest one reason why death by choking is on the increase.

2 Create a list of rules to protect a child from burns.

3 Draw and name the safety labels to watch out for when buying products for children.

4 Using resources, describe the emergency procedures for
a house fires
b small fires
c chip pan fires
d clothing.

5 'Fire is a good servant and a poor master.' Discuss.

6 Investigate overhead sprinklers.

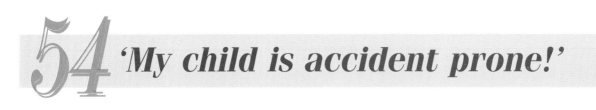

People who have many accidents often suffer stress. They cannot 'pay attention' to their own safety because they (unconsciously) pay attention to the stress. Give an example when you mislaid or forgot something important because your mind was on other things.

Some children seem **accident prone**. They walk into walls, fall off stools, catch their fingers in doors, long after they have learned to avoid these things. These children may not be suffering from stress. They may be more active so they take more risks. Parents can seek advice from the health visitor about a child who seems accident prone.

For every death, 500 people are injured. People *interact* with their environment. An unprotected home can be full of 'enemies'.

The table below shows the main kinds of accident in the home in one year.

Category	Number	Percentage
Falls	24,124	44.8
Cuts	10,018	18.6
Struck by object	6,699	12.4
Burns/scalds	3,202	5.9
Poisoning	1,385	2.6
Choking/suffocation	705	1.3
Electric current	64	0.1
Others unknown	7,698	14.3

Poison, beware!

'I keep telling Yasmin not to touch the medicine cabinet.' Objects which are forbidden become even more exciting. Toddlers feel left out when they observe a parent swallowing coloured 'sweets' (pills) and not sharing them. They know where the secret hoard is kept. The parent believes the medicine is safe in the locked cabinet. Keys are fascinating. *Toddlers do not learn the rules of home safety by warnings.*

Each year, 10,000 children are treated in hospital for suspected poisoning. The main **poisons** are **common household chemicals**. Some children suffer only minor effects but use hospital resources urgently needed for others. Packaging and labelling Acts were passed to make sure that the warnings on toxic products are clearly marked. Medicine containers are designed

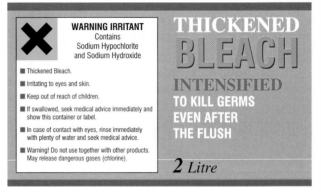

WARNING IRRITANT
Contains
Sodium Hypochlorite
and Sodium Hydroxide

■ Thickened Bleach.

■ Irritating to eyes and skin.

■ Keep out of reach of children.

■ If swallowed, seek medical advice immediately and show this container or label.

■ In case of contact with eyes, rinse immediately with plenty of water and seek medical advice.

■ Warning! Do not use together with other products. May release dangerous gases (chlorine).

THICKENED BLEACH INTENSIFIED
TO KILL GERMS EVEN AFTER THE FLUSH

2 Litre

■ The label on a bleach bottle indicates that the contents are toxic

to be childproof, though some youngsters can open them. But the casualty rate stays high.

Supervision around water

Children can drown in just three centimetres of water. Two recent deaths occurred from nappy buckets left without the lid on. A girl of 22 months fell into a fish-tank and drowned. Her parents had placed it in her bedroom so that the bubbling noises would soothe her to sleep. The Royal Society for the Prevention of Accidents (RoSPA) warned: 'This accident is a reminder to all parents that children are very ingenious when it comes to exploring and need constant supervision around water.'

■ Watch out for hazards!

■ Hazel has managed to push the stool over to the sink to explore the medicine cabinet!

— Investigation

Analyse the labels on some common household chemicals.

You will need:

hair dyes, glues, insecticides, cleaning agents.

a Compare packaging, directions for use, warnings on labelling.

b List the substances in order of clear warnings, ease of storage and use.

c Select one you think could be improved. Design your own label.

d Evaluate your results in class.

— Child observation

Record any accidents the child may have had, and whether or not a hospital visit was involved.

— Questions

1 Name the main type of accident in the home and two groups of people who might be unsteady on their feet. List ten objects in the home which can cause falls and suggest ways to avoid them.

2 What makes the kitchen the most hazardous room in the home? What factor in the kitchen makes the use of electrical appliances particularly dangerous?

3 Draw the kitchen in the illustration opposite with the hazards removed, or corrected.

4 List the hazards in the bathroom above. Draw the same room with the hazards removed, or corrected. Suggest three other places to keep the key to the medicine cabinet. Name one other type of accident this child is risking.

5 Mel and Meg are very aware of accidents. They tie their toddler's legs to his chair to keep him safe. Name some likely consequences of this restraint. Suggest more suitable ways in which Mel and Meg can solve their problem.

6 Some teenagers seem accident prone. Suggest, with reasons, at least three skills they can develop to reduce accidents. In what ways might these skills be applied to small children?

7 Death by poisoning reaches its peak in the late teens and twenties. Suggest some substances which lead to these deaths.

8 *If only...!* Helen put a corrosive chemical in an empty juice bottle. She warned her husband. He forgot to tell his mother who was baby-sitting. 'Give the baby juice if she's thirsty,' he said, and ran to catch the bus...

Complete this tale of the terrible burns their baby suffered to her mouth and airway. Describe how each adult probably felt. A neighbour, filled with pity for the little girl, wanted to tell somebody off. She asked which family member was to blame. All three said they were. Discuss this, and whether or not family members really benefit from a telling off after such a terrible accident.

9 Investigate
   a safety gates
   b playpens
   c safety film for glass.

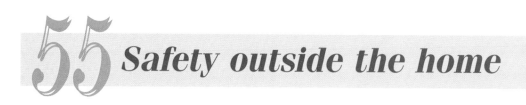

Street wise? A study by the World Health Organization found that 30–50 per cent of accidental deaths in the one to fourteen age group occur on the roads. The peak times for child road deaths are between 8 a.m. and 9 a.m., and later between 3 p.m. and 4.30 p.m.

A Scottish study into road safety attitudes found that children age five to seven 'decide if a place is safe purely on whether they can see cars from where they cross. They choose the shortest, most direct, route. They reason the less time on the road, the safer they will be.' The study concluded, 'Children under age nine show remarkably little awareness of dangerous factors. Our results suggest they cannot make such judgements for themselves.'

Buckle up!

Each year, hundreds of children are injured or killed in car accidents. **Restraints** can reduce the risk of injury by about two-thirds. From birth to six to eight months depending on size, the choice is between the rear-facing baby carrier and carrycot restraints.

■ And baby travels safely too!

Reins

'My child is a person, not a horse! I cannot put him in reins!' Hundreds of children are injured or killed each year when walking or playing in the street. The parent above believes reins are not dignified and holding hands is safe. She crosses a busy street with heavy shopping in one hand and her child suddenly pulls away from her other hand.

— Investigation —

Has the parent quoted above, who dislikes putting her child in reins, got her values confused?

a Role-play this scenario with your school bag in one hand and a partner in the other.

b Can hands get slippery and easily pull apart?

c Where else can a parent also secure the reins?

d Why might a parent with heavy shopping lose concentration?

e Decide, with reasons, if reins are more effective than holding hands.

f Where should this parent have crossed the road anyway?

g Why would you not place a child's dignity above its safety?

h Name one likely consequence of the value this parent places on her child's sense of dignity.

■ Reflective strips, bands and belts can be seen for 300 metres. What else should he be wearing to protect him?

■ This toddler is safer being held by reins

At the doctor

Studies show that pre-warning a child before therapy helps. The more Stevie **participates** in her treatment, the less anxious she becomes. Warning that an injection may sting may not reduce the hurt, but it allows Stevie to keep her dignity if she loses her courage and screams. One **paediatrician** (a doctor who specializes in child health) says: 'This will sting a bit. Would you like to sit on your hands? Just in case they fly up in surprise?'

In hospital

Research has found that a single hospital admission of more than one week, or repeated short admissions before age five, are related to a rise in behaviour disorders from age ten onwards. This damage can be reduced when parents stay with their child.

Hospital staff work under pressure. Some still believe in the attitude of 'get it over quick'. To the child, this is brutal and bewildering. She lives in terror of when the next attack will come. Her **basic trust** in her parents can be seriously weakened. Why have they left her here, alone, in this terrifying place?

In some cases, surgery can be performed on an 'out patient' basis. Parents can investigate this. In other cases where the hospital staff seem unfriendly, the child's treatment may be an emergency and their priorities are to meet this need.

— Child observation

Visit a children's ward and describe the toys and decorations to interest a bored, sick child. Note the comfort objects the medical staff seem friendly? Are day-long family visits allowed? Does the company of other children seem to increase or reduce stress? Is there pre-warning of painful therapy?

— Questions

1 State why a child must be restrained in a car. Suggest reasons for using reins in a supermarket trolley. Name two other seats from which an unreined child can fall.

2 Identify and draw road safety clothing for children in the winter months. Contacts: RoSPA, Child Accident Prevention.

3 Clare is rushed to hospital after a fall. Her mother can only stay a short while because her father wants his dinner cooked. State the priorities of her parents and one likely consequence.

4 Using books and other resources, copy and draw the First Aid procedures for
   a poisoning
   b shock
   c the recovery position.

5 'If an infectious disease were killing our children in the numbers that accidents do, people would demand a vaccine be found at once and this killer be stopped.' Discuss.

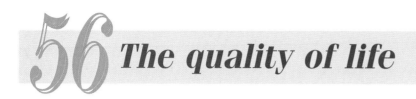

Attitudes

Case Study 1 Anna has cerebral palsy. She cannot control the movements of her limbs. Her parents are very upset. The doctor, midwife and health visitor explain the disease in great detail. Anna's parents listen and get over their shock. At home, they have a dreadful time with their neighbours, but gain support from the family. Anna develops an active mind and a loving nature, though her physical development is slow. Her family love Anna dearly and take great delight in each step of her progress.

Case Study 2 Peter also has mild cerebral palsy. His parents react in the same way as Anna's. The hospital staff are less effective at helping upset parents. They explain Peter's illness, but his parents cannot accept it. At home, Peter is hidden from view. His physical needs are met, but he is not loved or played with. Peter develops **secondary** disabilities. He becomes slow to learn and emotionally disturbed.

Studies show that parents of a disabled baby need time to mourn their 'loss'. They need to let go of their dreams of a perfect infant and accept the real one. With severe handicap, there is so much to learn about therapy and management that the baby's emotional needs can be forgotten. Some infants spend their first weeks in hospital, or return at regular intervals for more tests or surgery. Parents miss the fun of handling and cuddling the baby.

Disabled children used to be cared for in institutions. Today, all but the most severely handicapped live in the community. The 1981 Education Act brought children with physical disability back into mainstream schools. They can be with their friends and receive extra teaching support. Slow learners and children with certain disabilities have **Special Educational Needs** (SEN).

In most families, it is the woman who faces the hard work of caring for a disabled child. Suggest some reasons for this. Often one or both parents feel guilty about the disability. There is no need for guilt. Most disorders just happen; and nobody knows why.

Sickle-cell anaemia

This is an inherited condition which affects the Afro-Caribbean community and, in a different form, families from some Mediterranean countries. It is now classified as a British disease because the people with the anaemia are born in the UK.

The red blood cells change from their normal round shape to a 'sickle' curve. The immune system tries to remove them, and the child becomes anaemic. Some cells get stuck in the small blood vessels. The blockages cause pain in the arms, legs, back and stomach. The hands and feet swell, and the joints hurt. A bad attack of anaemia is a dangerous 'sickle crisis'. In babies, it can be fatal.

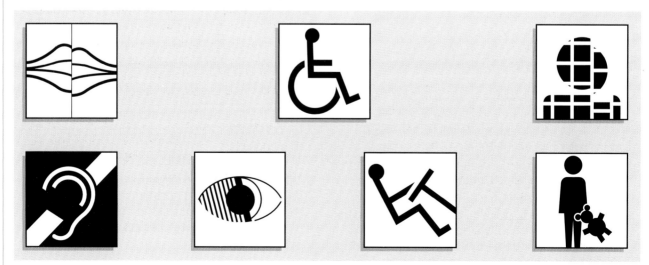

If a baby inherits the condition from one parent, she is a carrier but has no symptoms of the disease. If both parents are carriers, there is a one in four chance each baby will have it. Not all children suffer to the same extent. Some are very ill. Others lead a nearly normal life.

Because of the anaemia, the child has a higher risk of infections. She quickly chills when swimming or at other sports, and on cold wet days. She risks getting dehydrated, and must drink more liquids and more often than other children. This can cause constant visits to the toilet and bed-wetting until the teens.

The child's intelligence is not affected (except in rare cases). She can participate in normal school activities. But is it easy to concentrate with pain? Is there much energy with anaemia? For some children, regular hospital visits are essential. Is it easy for the child to keep up with school work?

'The same number of people suffer from haemophilia [see page 173], but more is known about it, and there are better support groups. Black people should organize things for themselves,' said

footballer Garth Crooks and pop singer David Grant. 'This is one more area where the community can stand up and say we have a voice, we have a power and we are going to do something.'

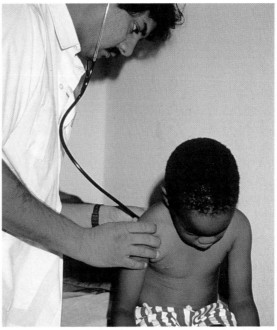

■ A child with sickle-cell anaemia

— Questions

1 Is sickle-cell anaemia caught like flu? Explain your answer.

2 Why should a child with sickle-cell anaemia be fully immunized?

3 For a child with sickle-cell anaemia suggest some drawbacks to
   a drinking lots of plain water
   b buying flavoured drinks.
   Create a tasty and cost-effective drink.

4 Choose, with reasons
   a a winter coat
   b a heating appliance
   c a 'learning' game for a sickle-cell child.

5 All children need love, encouragement and stimulation. List some consequences to a disabled child deprived of these needs.

6 Are the symbols opposite easily recognizable? What does each mean? If one is not clear, design a more effective symbol.

7 State, with reasons, why some disabled children need regular visits from a **physiotherapist** (see unit 66).

8 Community help in the form of home adaptations, mobility allowance and so on can be confusing. Using the list of resources, state where parents can obtain this information.

9 Extra stimulation of mentally handicapped children can produce great advances in their learning, though it is always slow. Name some rewards you think parents hope to gain.

10 Each year, 10,000 children in the UK are disabled in accidents. Suggest two types of accidents in the home which can result in disability and explain how each can be avoided.

11 'The true nature of a society shows in the care available to its weakest members.' Give your opinion of this statement in essay form.

12 Investigate: eczema, asthma or cystic fibrosis in children.

57 *Infant bonding*

Human emotions are extremely complex. Love feels different from one person to the next. It feels different from one life stage to the next. Grandparents love the baby in a different way than parents do. Parents love each other in a different way than they love their baby. By studying the emotions of infants, the following theories have been formed. But they remain **theories**, since infants cannot tell adults how they feel.

At first, a baby has no concept of love. The people who nurture six-week-old Chloe seem to be **extensions** of herself, rather like an extra arm or leg. Sometimes these extensions bring her pain such as the 'bad' feeling of being undressed when she is cosy and warm. Sometimes they bring her pleasure and she may smile when they do.

Baby humour?

Although infants smile at human faces by six weeks, they smile just as sweetly at faces on paper. At four months, they laugh when their parents laugh. But they laugh just as cheerfully at odd noises. An odd noise may be funny when silence is expected. But an odd noise on its own is strange rather than funny. Paper faces cannot interact. Before eight months, infants have no real sense of what is amusing and what is not.

Before something can be funny it must be familiar. There must be **expectations** of how it *should* be rather than the strange way it turns out to be. Babies cannot recognize humour because they do not know what to expect. Everything is strange so everything is accepted as 'normal'.

Baby fear

The brain waves and heart rate of the baby in the photo increased, then dropped to the slower 'paying attention' rate. Her face showed no fear, only a lively curiosity. But if she is startled at eight months, her brain waves and heart rate increase and continue to race. Her face shows real fear. She has developed expectations that strange things might harm her. She looks around for parents to protect her.

If the parent is near, her brain waves and heart rate slow to the 'paying attention' level. The fear leaves her face. She feels safe enough to begin playing with the jack-in-the-box. She has developed expectations of her parents as protectors. They are the people who keep her safe from harm.

Isn't she adorable?

She's much more adorable in her photograph

■ Do you find the cartoon amusing? If so, why?

■ A four-month-old baby is startled by a jack-in-the-box

The most common fears of children before age two are loud noises, sudden movements, the dark, animals, high places, pain and strange people, places and objects.

The huge world outside the child is exciting, delightful and *scary*. He recognizes that his parents are the one **stable** and **secure** base in his life. He also recognizes that, if his parents are not part of him, they might easily disappear. Though he cannot reason any of this on a conscious level, he fears that he could be **abandoned**.

The theory of infant bonding is based on these two feelings: the *pleasures* a child gets from his parents and the *pains* from his fears of losing them. These two opposite and intense emotions drive the baby towards the feeling we call love. This is a simple way to describe the **attachment theory**, and how it develops into love.

Attachment

In Child Development, infant bonding is named attachment. Infants show their attachment to their parents (or familiar carers) by eight months. Before then, Chloe can be picked up and nurtured by anyone. However, the more she is nurtured by the same carers, the more she pays attention to them and the pleasures they bring. She orients in special glee to her father's voice. She shows extra delight at her mother's approach.

'Of course Chloe knows us!' her parents say. And perhaps she does. But it takes a long time for children to gain a sense of their own identity. First Chloe has to become familiar with these caring extensions of herself. Then she has to separate from them and gain a sense of 'self'. Both recognition and separation happen more quickly if a child receives **continuity of care** (unit 9).

■ *Questions*

1 Why are new jokes funny, but not so amusing the second time? Write or draw an old favourite which still makes you smile.

2 Explain why a four month old does not show fear. At about what age does a child show fear? Why?

3 Give the age at which infants show attachment to their carers.

4 Name the two feelings which produce the emotion, love.

5 Name the pain which stops if parents are near at eight months.

6 'Out of sight. Out of mind!' Link the stage of development in unit 21 to an infant's emotions at eight months.

7 From what you learned in unit 18, explain why a baby needs not only loving cuddles, but the same loving cuddles from the same carers, and the same teddy in the same bed.

8 Explain the role of **familiarity** in attachment. What conclusions can be drawn about a baby's need for continuity of care and a stable home in the first year of life?

9 'Humour occurs when the familiar and strange come together in unexpected (odd, unsuitable, nonsense) ways.' Analyse this statement by working through some jokes you enjoy.

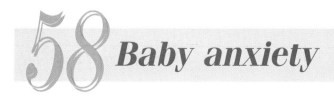
Flight or fight?

Imagine you are alone on a dark night. You are alert to trouble but not afraid. Your heart rate and brain waves increased then dropped to the paying attention rate. Now you hear footsteps behind you. They come closer. You feel seriously afraid, very *threatened*. Your heart and brain waves speed up again. Other changes happen so strongly that you feel them. Your mouth dries. Your stomach clenches. Sweating breaks out. The pupils of your eyes dilate (widen).

This is the 'flight or fight' response to help you survive. It is an automatic reflex to a *serious* threat. The bloodstream is flooded with the hormones **adrenaline** and **noradrenaline**. They speed up the breathing rate so that extra oxygen is rushed to the muscles which then produce extra energy for flight or fight. All the body systems not needed for survival close down. This is why the mouth dries and the stomach clenches shut. The sweating is to prevent over-heating and the pupils dilate for a clearer, wider range of vision. The feelings are like a mild **panic attack**.

At the same time, the mind is making frantic choices: should you take flight as speedily as you can? Should you turn and fight the threat as strongly as you can? The extra energy is to empower whichever choice you make. The flight or fight system puts your body on Red Alert. You have no control over this.

Once the threat is over, your body must return to its normal steady state. The systems which were shut down are triggered by opposite hormones to start working again. This is why, once the threat is over, your mouth floods with saliva and your stomach feels as if it has been dropped from a great height. There can be a small loss of urine as the muscles of the bladder relax.

Stranger anxiety

A baby's fear of abandonment shows at eight months. This is the age when the fear of strangers develops. The fear produces the reflex 'flight or fight' response with its extra surge of energy. For example, Lauren recognizes her parents as her protectors, but she cannot recognize strangers in that role. She makes a terrible fuss if she is left with a person she does not know. The fuss is so terrible because it is fuelled with the extra surge of energy. It brings Lauren's parents speedily back to her side.

Lauren does not choose this behaviour. It is an automatic response to her fears of abandonment. A few strangers may not have Lauren's best interests at heart. Stranger anxiety is 'good' in that it helps a child survive.

Separation anxiety

This fear is slightly different from stranger anxiety, though it begins at the same age. With separation anxiety, the child cannot bear to be separated

■ The flight or fight response is automatic

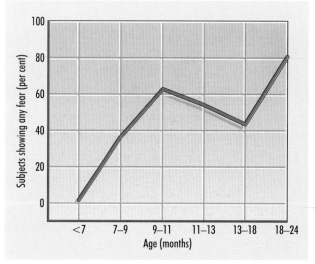
■ This graph shows the development of fear of strangers

from his parent or carer during his waking hours. For example, when John's mother leaves the room, he tries to crawl after her in a panic of anxiety. If the door is closed against him, he screams with all the extra energy to get near her again.

'He's driving me crazy!' John's mother tells the clinic nurse. 'I can't even use the toilet without him following!'

'He'll grow out of it when he's three,' the nurse soothes. 'In the meantime, let him be with you until he feels more secure.'

'**Separation anxiety**? Never heard of it!' says Lauren's mother. 'Not with all my family wanting to play with her!'

Separation anxiety is rare if parents are not **isolated**. If they have an extended family or friends, the toddler has more than one person to depend upon. But for nuclear or lone families, the problem of separation anxiety can be acute. All the toddler's emotions are focused on his mother. He *cannot* let her go. If he is shut out, his anxiety becomes intense. He may try to reduce the pain of this by the 'fight' response; he struggles and fights to hold onto her. Or he may try the 'flight' response; he struggles to avoid being held by her in case she leaves him again.

Parent and Toddler groups

To reduce isolation, Parent and Toddler groups are run by social workers, health visitors or the Pre-school Playgroup Association. Lonely parents can make friends, while their toddlers learn to play together. Company can reduce the worries of child care and can increase its delights.

■ This child is suffering feelings of abandonment

— *Child observation*

Watch a toddler being examined by a clinic nurse, or a child moving from the parent's side. Record any signs of anxious behaviour you observe.

— *Questions*

1 Sam's mother works at night and leaves Sam with a babysitter. She makes a soothing tape of her voice and leaves it by Sam's bed. When Sam falls asleep, the babysitter switches it off. Explain the ways in which Sam is helped by the tape of his mother's voice.

2 When Sam's grandfather babysits, he thinks, 'Mustn't mollycoddle the boy.' He switches off the tape, closes the sitting room door and switches on the television to full volume. Give your opinion of the fear of 'mollycoddling'. Role-play sensitive ways for Sam's mother to change his grandfather's attitude.

3 At what age does **a** object recognition and **b** separation anxiety develop? Explain why stranger anxiety also begins at this age.

4 In what ways might Parent and Toddler groups help an isolated parent through this stage?

5 'Separation anxiety is an issue of nuclear and lone families.' Discuss.

59 Baby anger

The unconscious mind

At the turn of this century, the psychiatrist, Sigmund Freud, showed how the **unconscious mind** controls much of human behaviour. The unconscious deals with our basic instincts and emotions. If these feel 'good' in early life, Chloe will be 'gooder because I love my Mum' at her predicted stage of development. If these feel 'bad', Chloe's behaviour remains controlled by her basic instincts and emotions even though she may want to be good.

Our basic instincts are to get what we want, when we want it and how we want it. Older children have to learn that this is not possible. Their needs must fit in with the needs of other people. While they are learning to fit in, they suffer **frustration**. When people are frustrated, they feel angry.

Anger

From eight months, Lauren knows when a toy is taken from her. She knows who did this frustrating thing and she knows it was done deliberately. The reason why it was taken does not interest her. She may scream at her parents, trying to bite and kick them with all her fury and might.

If parents do not know how the emotions develop, they can become angry in return. They too get an extra surge of energy for 'fight or flight'. Some parents respond by 'fight', they shout at the child or hit back. Others respond by 'flight', they keep their distance, or they distance the child by dumping him in his room to scream it out.

Being anxious or angry is part of the human condition. They are normal emotions and only cause stress if they are *mismanaged over a long period of time*. If Lauren can never **express** (show) her anxiety or anger without being punished, she may get the idea that these feelings are 'bad'. She may then try to **repress** them. Instead of learning how to manage them, they become buried in her unconscious mind. The extra energy for 'flight or fight' is needed to keep them buried because these emotions are very powerful and long to be expressed.

Reduce stress – increase security

Lauren develops a sense of security from understanding that her parents are *on her side*. They are there to help her, not hinder her. Their task is to protect Lauren from unnecessary frustration and pain. No parent can protect a child from bad feelings all the time. But they can:
- reduce the times they have to frustrate a child
- remove the objects she is not allowed to play with
- plan ahead to avoid most problems before they arise
- let the child express her feelings so they can be got rid of
- control their own bad feelings.

When Sam cries, his mother goes quickly to meet his needs. 'Mummy is here to take away your pain.' When he screams because he is hungry, she **empathizes**. 'Does your tummy hurt? Mummy is late with lunch. Chew this juicy carrot until it is ready.'

She finds him playing with a fragile vase. 'Oh-oh, that is a grown-up toy.' She looks for something to replace it, an object which is equally interesting, yet safe. The next time she swaps the vase for a safe toy, Sam is not fooled and screams with rage. She lets him express the hurt of his anger and then plays jumping games to release his extra energy. She admits her mistake. 'Mummy should have learned not to leave the vase within your reach.'

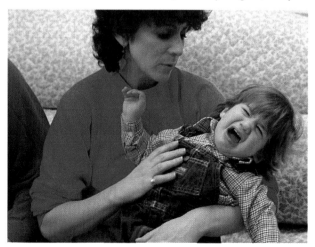

■ 'I get quite frightened by her anger at times'

■ Who is really responsible for that broken vase?

Reduce security – increase stress

When John cries, his mother does not understand the value of going to him quickly. She is afraid of spoiling him. She thinks he will become *too needy, too greedy*. 'I'm not your slave,' she tells John. 'Yes, lunch is late. I'm hungry too.' John feels insecure. His mother does not seem to be on his side.

When she finds him playing with the fragile vase a second time, she smacks his hand. 'I told you not to play with grown-up things.' John screams with rage and smacks her back. She weeps, 'This child is out of control,' and dumps him, still screaming, into his cot. 'Your Daddy can deal with you when he comes home. Bad boy!'

Basic trust

Children need to develop basic trust in their parents. They need to recognize that Mummy and Daddy are on their side. This helps them learn that when Mummy and Daddy do get cross something very important has happened. They try to pay attention to what that thing is, and not to do it again.

Children are very frightened of losing their parents' love. Frightened people become anxious people. *Anxiety is the fear of loss*. Underneath the anxiety there is anger. Children are no different from adults; they want to be happy and have fun. They feel angry if they are always being told off. Anxiety and anger bring feelings of tension and stress.

In *The Future of Illusion*, Freud made a direct link between mismanaged feelings in childhood and emotional problems in adulthood. He wrote that a child cannot successfully complete its development without times of great upset. 'So many instinctual demands which will later be unserviceable cannot be suppressed by the rational operation of the child's intellect but have to be tamed by acts of repression.' Put simply, this means someone has to help a child manage its upset feelings. Parents and carers benefit from knowing that children who develop basic trust can (slowly) learn to manage their upset feelings.

▬ *Questions* ▬

1 Examine the power of your anger and the longing to express it by describing a time when you were frustrated and how you felt before you got your anger under control.

2 What does empathy mean? How might it help Sam develop basic trust? Why did his mother blame herself for the vase? Does she seem in control when Sam is angry? Give reasons for your answers.

3 When John's mother says, 'I'm hungry too' try to analyse what she is really feeling. Is John 'bad' for playing with the vase, and why? Which parent would you choose to be, and why?

4 Sam is pulling the cat's tail. His mother stops him when the cat begins to growl. Give **a** one safety and **b** one moral reason for stopping Sam.

5 'Minimize stress, maximize security.' Give your opinion of this advice to parents.

6 If parents bring more pain than pleasure, the child is more likely to avoid them than orient to them. Name two emotions this arouses and why they prevent children learning how to behave well.

Parent–child interaction

Balance

Happy feelings are the opposite of anxious or angry feelings. The eyes widen to see 'good' things better, or they crinkle to show a lovely smile. The voice may be higher than usual, the laugh can sound ready to tip over into tears. Toddlers rush to share their happy feelings by snuggling in close, squeezing and hugging. An older child bounces up and down excitedly.

Children feel their emotions very strongly in their bodies. Too much happiness (like too much sadness) cannot be contained. It builds into stress. 'Don't over-excite Sam,' his parents warn. They help Sam move from his state of high tension to a calmer state of pleasure and contentment. The emotions are so powerful that children need help to *balance* them. Parents can help their child back to calm and content feelings if they feel calm and content themselves.

Parent–child interaction

'She's as different from her brother as chalk from cheese!' Babies are born with different temperaments. Some psychiatrists label these 'easy', 'difficult' and 'slow to warm up'. Parents can have the same or different temperaments as their children. If they are very different, the child's signals can be 'misread'. Without meaning to, the parents provide unsuitable care.

When people interact, they **influence**, **alter** and **change** each other's behaviour. By one year, the interaction between Sam and his parents cannot be separated. It is no longer possible to tell if Sam 'calls out' behaviours from his parents, or the other way around. However, parent–child interaction is based on many other factors, any of which can change with changes in family life.

Factors that influence interaction

1 Culture

The values of a culture play an important role in parent–child interaction. For example, American culture encourages children to be assertive and outgoing. 'Be your own person! Just do it!' Oriental culture encourages children to be more restrained.

■ Happiness!

'Family first! Never lose face!' So an 'easy' American child may seem 'difficult' to Japanese parents. And a 'difficult' Japanese child may seem 'easy' to American parents.

2 Environment

The home conditions also play an important role in interaction. An unsupported parent who is made homeless has little time or energy to respond sensitively to her baby's signals. She has more immediate priorities. If her housing needs are not quickly met, a stressful interaction can start between mother and child.

3 Family history

Patterns of child-rearing are passed on in families. Parent–child interaction is strongly based on what

■ Cultural factors play an important role in parent–child interaction

happened in the parents' own childhood. Even parents who intend to raise their children very differently can find they repeat the same patterns. What is learned at an unconscious level in infancy is not easy to change.

4 Gender

A *role* is a part you play, depending on who you are with. You stand, speak and behave differently with a stranger than with a friend. Parents are **role models** for their children who 'model' their behaviour on the behaviour they observe at home.

To **stereotype** someone is to put a label on them. For example, all adults can be stereotyped as bossy and all children can be stereotyped as noisy. People can also be stereotyped by their gender. All teenage girls can be gender stereotyped as 'fashion crazy' and all teenage boys as 'football crazy'. Yet many teenagers find fashion and football boring.

Gender-role stereotyping begins early in life. Parents can treat girls and boys differently. Fathers play tougher games with their sons than daughters. Mothers calm girls if their behaviour seems 'tomboyish' and excite boys if their behaviour seems 'cissyish'. In subtle ways, both parents encourage independence in boys and discourage it in girls.

By eighteen months, children know their gender identity. By age three, they become anxious if they are mistaken for the other gender. They have learned rules about how girls and boys should behave from their gender role models. These rules are reinforced by the gender-role stereotyping they see in the media and wider social groups. Gender-role stereotyping is harmful when it limits the choices available to children.

■ The 'football crazy' teenage boy is an example of a gender-role stereotype

The psyche

The word psyche (pronounced sigh-key) means both the mind and the emotions. **Psychology** is the study of how the mind and emotions interact. A mental illness occurs when this interaction breaks down and the person loses touch with reality. **Psychiatry** is the study and treatment of mental illness by doctors with specialist training in psychic disorders.

Stress

Stress is pressure on the psyche. Life is full of pressures, many of which are good. Stress is **positive** when it challenges a child to enjoy learning more difficult ideas and feelings. Stress is **negative** when the challenge is too great, or otherwise unsuitable for that particular child. Effective parenting is detective work. It involves 'reading' the child's signals and providing suitable and balanced care.

Questions

1 You are tickling a child who starts sobbing with laughter. Describe, with reasons, what you would do next.

2 Do you think British parents prefer babies with 'easy', 'difficult' or 'slow to warm up' temperaments? Think carefully before you answer.

3 'Putting labels on people is both dangerous and wrong.' Give your opinion of this statement.

4 Parents with dependent children are given priority on local authority housing lists. Suggest some reasons for this.

Autonomy

Autonomy means self-government. Adults have the right to govern (rule) themselves. Children are dependent people. Until they reach eighteen, their parents are responsible for their behaviour and choices.

The drive for autonomy begins early in life. Megan wants to make choices, be in control, govern herself. This gives her a sense of dignity and self-respect. But because she does not have enough information, she cannot always make *informed* choices. An *informed* choice is one which helps Megan behave in an effective way. An *effective* behaviour is one which keeps Megan happy and healthy.

Children depend upon adults to:
- provide them with the information they need
- guide them towards effective choices and behaviour
- help them develop a moral sense by setting out clear rules
- make rules which teach the difference between right and wrong.

A moral sense

A survey by Trinity College, Carmarthen, found that many school children are confused between right and wrong. One in seven (16 per cent of the study group) thought that there was nothing wrong with travelling on public transport without a ticket, 6 per cent felt the same about shoplifting and

■ This toddler insists on feeding himself

fewer than three in ten (28.9 per cent) said they had never stolen anything.

The government issued guidelines to schools on moral teaching in 1993. Children as young as five must know:
- that it is wrong to lie, cheat, bully, deceive, be cruel and be irresponsible
- that it is right to tell the truth, keep promises, respect other people's rights and property, act considerately, help the less fortunate and be responsible for their own behaviour.

Positive teaching

From eighteen months, Megan tests the limits of what she is allowed to do. She whines, sulks and throws **temper tantrums** to get her own way. A temper tantrum is a child's way of defending her new self-image. As Megan learns that she is separate from her parents, she learns that she is an independent person with choices of her own. She becomes self-conscious. By turn, she is defiant and obedient; aggressive and shy. If she is handled with **guidance** and **discipline**, Megan slowly learns that the rules are there to help her, not hinder her. If she is handled with **punishment** alone, she may continue to test people and rules, perhaps for the rest of her life.
- Firmness: 'You know that is not allowed.'
- Consistency: 'If it was wrong yesterday, it is wrong today.'
- Calmness: 'I am not cross with you, just a bit surprised.'
- Empathy: 'Perhaps you forgot that is not allowed?'
- Fairness: 'If you choose to scream, do it in your room.'
- Reward: 'Because you chose to stop, come and have a hug.'

Choice

The concept of choice helps a child learn self-control. Once Megan knows she can choose her behaviour, she knows she can choose to change it. She also knows that if she chooses not to change it, she has opted for the consequences, e.g. being sent to her room.

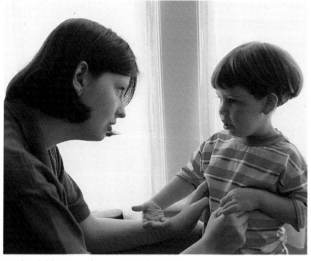

■ This child is given firm yet loving discipline

Children need to be **socialized**, to learn what is acceptable behaviour and what is not. This helps them fit in comfortably with other people, and gain a feeling of belonging. Some parents teach by **punishment**, such as slaps or scoldings. They say that punishment works more quickly than guidance and discipline. Punishment is a short-term goal to stop the behaviour. The long-term goal is to raise a child with a strong moral sense.

The table below shows the main differences between people who can govern themselves (autonomous) and people who cannot (dependent).

Dependent person	Autonomous person
Has short-term goals	Has long-term goals
Wants pleasure now	Delays pleasure now for future goals
Finds choice difficult	Enjoys choice and responsibility
Has brief attention span	Sticks to task until complete
Avoids boring tasks	Works hard at unpleasant tasks
Uses conflict to win	Uses conflict for personal growth

Parents are advised to *reward acceptable behaviour*. When Megan chooses the long-term goal of brushing her teeth rather than the short-term goal of avoiding a boring task, she is rewarded with praise. Because this makes her feel 'good', she feels encouraged to be 'gooder' the next time she wants to test the rules out.

Parents are advised to *ignore unacceptable behaviour*. This advice is based on the theory that paying attention to bad behaviour usually makes it worse.

— *Investigation* —

Test the 'ignore unacceptable behaviour' theory.

a Role-play a scene in which a teenager shows-off.

b Everyone else completely ignores the behaviour.

c Role-play the same scene when the behaviour is greeted with tellings off, jeers and other fuss.

d Describe the feelings produced by each kind of response.

e How long was the person able to keep up the behaviour?

f From your findings, give your opinion of the above theory.

g Think carefully, then try to work out why some people need to show-off more than others.

— *Questions* —

1 Describe your feelings when you are rewarded with praise. Give your opinion of this method of socializing a child.

2 Give the values, if any, of hitting a weaker person.

3 List the goals for teaching children a strong moral sense. Do you agree with the guidelines on teaching morals in schools? Give reasons for each guideline in as much detail as you can.

Lying

Children have a logic of their own and use it to make sense of a world that often makes no sense. Why did that balloon bang and turn into a nasty bit of rubber? 'I didn't do it!' Emily cries. 'Mrs Nobody did! I seed her.' This is not lying. It is Emily's way of protecting herself against anxious feelings from an event she cannot understand. It is also part of her fantasy life. 'Me and Mrs Nobody play spacemen on the moon.' Small children cannot separate their fantasy world from the real one.

If Emily says, 'Yes, I brushed my teeth,' when she forgot, she is protecting herself against anxious feelings that she might lose her parents' approval. Her 'fib' is also a way to keep them feeling happy about their little girl. A small frown from the parents is usually enough to bring on tears as Emily scrambles to the bathroom to clean her teeth. Although children are not really capable of lying before age seven, they must learn that it is wrong.

Obsessions

Some children have stages of wanting every person and thing to be just so. Any break in the normal routine brings on feelings of stress. If Mummy changes her hairstyle, Daddy shaves his beard, Emily's fork and spoon are not in their exact place, she feels anxious and insecure. 'Put it back!' she cries. 'Now! Do it now!' Hair will not grow 'now', but Emily's parents help her by making sure that her possessions remain in their exact place.

During an obsessional phase, children who are not helped to feel secure can develop phobias about the dark, animals, noise, outdoors, heights and so on. A **phobia** is normal anxiety which has developed into extreme fear. It is a mental illness.

Stealing

Stealing can give a child pleasure for a while. Taking coins from Mummy's purse or sneaking biscuits behind Daddy's back gives Jack a sense of power. But his pleasure is short-lived because he has painful feelings of guilt too. When the painful feelings become greater than the pleasures of stealing, the behaviour stops.

Persistent stealing is serious, a sign that the child is in some way stressed. Parents become detectives to identify what is causing the stress. Perhaps the new baby? Perhaps the new playgroup? Perhaps the move to a new home? They know Jack is stealing from them to replace something he feels he has lost.

Persistent stealing should be disciplined, but not punished. 'Put the money back, Jack, because I want a cuddle from my good boy.' This helps Jack manage his guilt by replacing the object. The reward of a cuddle reinforces his desire to be a 'good boy'. During the cuddle, Jack's parent has a chance to find out what is wrong. Now his 'badness' is known and his parent still wants a cuddle, Jack feels more confident about saying what is wrong.

Restlessness

Can you remember being fidgety as a child? Did you squirm in your seat? talk too much? start one activity before you finished the last? Were you impulsive? easily distracted? How do you rate now?

These behaviours are some of the criteria for **Attention Deficit Disorder Syndrome** (ADDS). Children with ADDS cannot pay attention long

■ Breaks in the normal routine can cause feelings of stress

■ Persistent stealing should be disciplined, not punished. It is a sign that the child is stressed

enough to learn. It is thought they have a brain chemical which is over-active. Their restlessness is sometimes called **hyperactivity**.

— Investigation

Test the attention span of television viewers.
You will need:
a watch that shows seconds.
a Time the length of a single scene in a named programme.
b Time the length of six single scenes in that programme.
c Work out the average time of a single scene.
d From your findings, give the average attention span of television viewers.

Television is largely based on entertainment. Single scene shots which last more than three minutes bore or irritate the average viewer, and cause channels to be switched. Restlessness is not an unusual behaviour in adults.

Attention-seeking

Children cannot stand, sit or stay in one place for long. Their nervous system has not developed enough for the more sedate life of a student. If they are happy and well, they discharge energy in constant movement which may seem strange and purposeless. Their attention span is brief.

When is a child being hyperactive or just a child? A wrong diagnosis can do real harm. The drugs used to treat ADDS have serious side effects. They slow down growth and intellectual development.

Doctors have to consider that some **attention-seeking** children get too little attention and this is so painful that they seek it by bad behaviour. They choose scoldings or slaps to being ignored because their need is so great. Parents can solve this problem by giving **unconditional** love. Children need warmth and praise not for anything they do, but just for existing – for being themselves.

Some attention-seeking children get too much attention. This leads them to believe that they are the centre of the universe. 'I want! So I must have!' the child thinks. Parents can solve this problem by teaching their children the rights of others.

— Investigation

Watch children at play.
Record the numbers of times they say 'mine'. Then observe the ages when they can say
a 'yours'
b 'theirs'.
Pool your findings and try to work out the average age when children learn about possessions and respect for the rights of others.
Observe their role-play. Is there a gender difference – do girls role-play more home skills than boys? Record how often the words 'good' and 'bad' are used. Do children praise and encourage each other more or less often than they criticize? Write in detail about the functions of role-play in emotional development.

— Questions

1 Unhappy (anxious, angry) children tend to discharge energy in stranger ways than happy ones. Try to think of reasons why.

Parents in full-time work cannot give their babies full-time care. To solve this problem, they choose a carer whom the baby knows. Family members are the first choice. Extended families share the care between aunts, grandparents, brothers, and so on. Nuclear families and lone parents have a more difficult choice.

Child minders are used when no kin or friends are available (unit 67). Parents can take the comfort object, the special baby rug, favourite toys, familiar feeding equipment and changes of clothing to the childminder to help the infant feel secure.

Sharing the care

Young children suffer distress when their mothers first go out to work. But this distress is less if the child has been raised with familiar carers. If a full-time mother goes into hospital, the father and close relatives are the first choice of carers. Neighbours and close friends are also asked to help. For everyday activities such as keeping a dental appointment, sharing the care among a social network of friends is not unusual.

The numbers of carers used by a family ranges from one to about six. As the child gets older, this number increases. One study found that grandparents were the parents' first choice of

■ Feeling happy and safe with grandparents

carers for one-third of the children and the second choice for a further third. Just under half the children had stayed with their grandparents overnight without their parents.

The reasons why grandparents were the first choice include:
◆ they loved the child and the child felt secure
◆ they wanted to spend more time with their grandchild
◆ they expected to be used as babysitters
◆ they refused payment in cash or other favours
◆ they were trustworthy and competent.

Problems with grandparent care include rivalry for affection and arguments over handling the child. The most common problem is related to spoiling. Grandparents may give sweets, let the child watch too much television, or otherwise upset the family routine.

Friends with children of the same age provide **play-based care**. The children are company for one another. The friend may be more aware of today's attitudes to diet, sleep, safety and stimulation needs. Play-based care helps prepare children of the same age for pre-school education.

Nannies are trained and qualified people in child care. They live in the home or visit it each day. They are expensive for a single child but, where there are siblings, the cost to the parents can be about the same as other child care. Some families share nannies during the week and the parents return to work part-time.

Au pairs have no training in child care. They are usually young people coming to Britain to improve their language skills. They live in the home, are less expensive than nannies and may do a small amount of housework. They must be allowed free time for their studies, and a few may have no interest in the children they care for.

Choosing a babysitter

Babysitters can be male or female. The child has a secure base since it remains in its own home. A sitter for a young baby must be old enough to understand the importance of meeting a baby's needs quickly. A sitter for an older child must be known, liked and trusted by the child.

■ At home with the new babysitter

The babysitter should meet the child at home. She can share the tea-time routine and help prepare the child for bed. The parents, babysitter and child get to know, like and trust one another. Queries which arise can be sorted out there and then.

Debate the following generally accepted advice.

◆ During the first year of life, the most effective approach is to respond quickly to a baby's needs.

◆ Ignoring babies' cries for fear of 'spoiling' them is likely to cause feelings of anxiety and anger.

◆ Keeping older children to their usual routine is likely to calm and soothe them.

Investigation

Test your skills as a babysitter

a List, in order of priority, the things you would check if the baby starts crying.

b Describe all the actions you would take if the baby is wet.

c The baby is dry and well-fed, but cannot seem to settle. Give, with reasons, two sources of comforts you could provide.

d Choose a suitable game or activity for an older child to calm and relax her before bedtime.

e After two hours' sleep, the child wakes complaining of thirst. What types of drink would you offer, and why?

f The child then refuses to go back to bed. Suggest, with reasons, one way to manage this situation.

g You smell burning from an another room. List, in order of priority, the things you would immediately do.

Child observation

Talk with the child about a favourite babysitter. What is liked best about the sitter? What is liked least? What games are played? Are the parents' rules obeyed? What happens if the child breaks the rules?

Questions

1 Describe how you would prepare a child between ages two and five to meet a babysitter.

2 Draw up a list of instructions for the babysitter to follow about the child's bedtime routine.

3 Explain the value of keeping to this routine
   a for the child
   b for the babysitter.

4 Name three emergency services you would list before leaving home.

5 Arrange the following in the order of priority which you think most suitable for a babysitter: kinship, friendship, familiarity with the child, being trustworthy and competent, having children of the same age, being available and willing, not requiring payment.

6 In sleep, the conscious mind is no longer in control. Stress is released and unexpressed feelings can break out as nightmares. Suggest, with reasons, how you might help a three year old who regularly wakes up screaming at night.

Attachment

Secure attachment

By eighteen months, Pam is **securely attached** to her parents and familiar carers. A child who is securely attached has developed basic trust. This comes from the way her parents responded to her needs *before* she was eighteen months. Because they went to her quickly and brought her pleasure, Pam has developed **memory patterns** for basic trust. Now she has **expectations** of the world as a 'good' place.

A securely attached toddler seems happy, is rarely cross, loves to touch and snuggle into her parent. During exploratory play, her heart rate slows while she is learning. She checks to see if her father is there, and follows him instead of screaming when he leaves. She makes her needs known by vocalizing and pointing rather than crying. When asked to do something, she usually obeys!

By five, the securely attached child seems confident. She enjoys learning. Her self-image is developing and her self-esteem is high. At times she behaves as if she is 'king of the castle'! But she is aware of the value of others, and she is learning to respect their needs. As an adult, Pam is open to love and can help her own children develop basic trust.

Transitions

A transition is a change from one role to the next. Children have many transitions. They change roles from the baby in arms, to the toddler who explores, to the child starting playgroup, to the older sibling when a baby is born. Transitions are exciting, but they also involve loss. Children lose the comfort of the known role for the challenge of the unknown role.

Pam's first transition was learning to separate from her parents. To manage this loss, she attached to her comforter. It became the **transitional object** of security. It helps Pam face the challenge of the new roles she must play. Other transitions include being left with unknown carers, a hospital stay, a family break up, a parent's remarriage or when a child is placed in care (see unit 68). All children need to be prepared

for a transition. The Children Act (1989) suggested the following guidelines.

- Read story books or watch videos about the transitional role.
- Role play the doctor, the nurse and the sick child in hospital.
- Take the child for an early school visit so that she knows what to expect. Listen to any new queries she may have.
- Invite the unknown carer into the child's home and encourage the two to become friends.
- Talk to the child, explaining honestly what is going to happen.
- Listen to her queries and help her express her anxieties.
- Comfort her fears and reduce her anxieties by reassurance.

Expectations

Some parents feel out of control with a baby. The newborn's helplessness and demands take them by surprise. Other parents can manage a baby but feel out of control with a toddler. Family size is now smaller and many parents have no experience of children. Their expectations of what parenting actually involves are based largely on what they learned in their own childhood.

Continuity of care means getting the same type of nurture from the same type of people in the same type of environment. A baby who plays on a different surface each day pays attention to the new surface, not to the play. A baby who is nurtured by many different people finds it difficult to attach securely to them. Infants need familiar carers, known places and favourite things.

Attachment disorder

Attachment happens whether or not children develop basic trust. But if they suffer repeated let-downs *before* eighteen months, they are at risk of developing serious behaviour problems. The main causes of repeated let-downs are the death of parents, frequent changes of carers, emotional neglect and child abuse.

There are two kinds of attachment disorder. Both kinds are seen more often in children who

■ *Where are the sweet smiling babies in the advertisements?*

have been fostered or adopted. The **anxiously attached** toddler often seems worried. When Nigel is picked up, he 'fights' by clinging. Or he takes 'flight' by stiffening, pushing away, hitting. During exploratory play, his brain waves and heart rate slow for brief moments only. If his mother leaves, he screams but rarely follows her. When she picks him up, he continues to scream and may squirm to be put down.

The **unsocially attached** toddler often seems angry. Mary throws toys or hits her parents for no obvious reason. When her mother leaves the room, Mary appears calm. Yet her heart races. When her mother returns Mary ignores her, or moves towards her then stops. Her heart continues to race for a very long time.

Love

Love is full of hidden dangers for these children. Relationships are a constant struggle to get their needs met without too much pain. The attachment disorder can range from mild to severe. It takes different forms in different children. Girls tend to be less violently disruptive than boys. Boys tend to be less emotionally frozen than girls. When asked to do something, there is only a 50 per cent chance that these two groups of children obey.

As adults, these children can be anxious or mistrustful of warmth and closeness. They find it difficult to be open to love. They tend to choose partners with similar problems. If they choose secure happy partners, they may make the relationship impossible by behaving in unacceptable ways.

Patterns of love pass down from generation to generation. Parents with memory patterns of basic trust accept that their role is to help their children pay attention to the happy sides of life while protecting them from needless pain. Other parents see their role as controlling their children from the start so that they do not become difficult later on.

Attachment disorder is now recognized by the World Health Organization. The problems it causes can be so serious that it is on the International Classification of Childhood Diseases. In Britain, a **self-help group**, mainly of adoptive parents, was set up in 1994. The numbers are increasing rapidly as more distressed parents hear of the network.

Mental illness

The 1995 figures from the Department of Health showed a 50 per cent increase over three years in the numbers of children below age ten admitted to hospital for mental illness. There are now more than 1000 children being treated for psychoses, severe depression and eating disorders.

The Child and Adolescent Psychiatry Department at Cambridge University estimates that as many as 20,000 children of school age are suffering from serious depression. Family breakdown, a sense of isolation, poor parenting and increased pressure at a much younger age to perform at school were involved. Schools report rising numbers of children with behaviour problems and seek the help of **therapists** and even the Samaritans for pupils as young as four.

▬ *Questions* ▬

1 What does secure attachment mean? How is it achieved?
2 Name some advantages
   a for a toddler who is securely attached
   b for the parents of the child.
3 When asked to do something, there is only a 50 per cent chance that an attachment-disordered child obeys. Suggest some reasons why.
4 Explain the meaning of a transition.
5 Give reasons why learning about emotional development can help
   a parents   b schools   c society?

Child abuse

Child abuse includes death, serious or moderate harm, and failure to thrive due to **neglect**. Neglect is not only lack of physical care. It can be lack of love, company and happy feelings, too much criticism, coldness and emotional starvation.

Rejecting parents are cold and unloving. Their children may be well fed and clothed, but they are emotionally starved. As they grow, they may try to please others too much in order to win love or approval. They may see the world as a cold, heartless place.

Inconsistent parents punish or praise according to their mood. Their children are treated as objects, and this robs them of human dignity. They become anxious and insecure, not knowing when their actions deserve praise or punishment. They may have difficulty in learning right from wrong.

Over-strict parents are afraid of their own emotions. Their children are punished when they struggle for autonomy. Their will is 'broken' by beatings or being terrified in other ways. They may grow timid or full of hate, and long to revenge themselves on the cruel world.

Neglecting parents may be one or more of the above.

Defence mechanisms

'Who needs friends?' thinks the lonely person. 'They're all against me,' thinks the rule breaker. 'My baby is naughty on purpose,' thinks the child abuser.

These are **defence mechanisms**, comfort excuses people make up to avoid their own pain. Everyone uses defence mechanisms from time to time. They are harmless if the person accepts that they are excuses. But they can do untold damage if the person **projects** them onto other people as reasons to fear and hate them.

Theories about child abuse

There are five theories relating to child abuse.

1 Projection Abusive parents see the baby as part of themselves. When they feel the pains of terrors, guilts or rages, they project these feelings onto the baby. 'The bad things in me are in my child. I will be harsh, strict, controlling to stop them coming out.'

2 Lack of empathy Abusive parents misread their baby's signs of pain, hunger or distress. They try to force a child who is crying from pain to eat. This unsuitable response makes the situation worse. The parent feels frustrated because the child will not feed. As frustration builds, so does the risk of child abuse.

3 Feminist Women who are dependent on men feel powerless. So they seek power over their children. Boys grow up terrified of women. Girls grow up afraid of their mothers yet **repress** their own daughters.

4 Infant mortality For our ancestors, life was savage, and full of terrible fears and insecurities. The high death rate of babies made it too painful to love a child. Without love, the difficult task of child-rearing is open to abuse.

5 Sadist Sadists are people who get pleasure from giving pain. They delight in torturing their victims and listening to their screams of agony. Some sadists delight in humiliating their victims by cruel jeers and verbal insults. But the majority of child abusers are not sadists. Of all the criminals in prison only 8 per cent have been found guilty of crimes of sadism.

Theories as excuses?

Society is based on the belief that citizens are responsible for their actions. No theory of child abuse excuses it. No adult who inflicts cruelty on a child is free of blame. When they damage children, they are accountable for the abuse both morally and in law. Studies by the National Society for the Prevention of Cruelty to Children (NSPCC) have found that 'marital conflict is the biggest single factor in child abuse'. They also found that 'abusers often had abused childhoods themselves'.

Sexual abuse

It is unlawful to have sex with a child. **Incest** is the crime of sexual abuse by a member of the child's close family. Parents, older siblings and grandparents can force a child into sexual activity. **Sexual abuse** can be by a person not related to but known to the child: a step-parent, family friend or neighbour. Parents may fear that their child will be snatched from parks or playgrounds by child molesters. But *the most common place for the sexual abuse of children is within the home*. Babysitters and child minders can also commit this crime.

Sexually abused children may show no signs of violence. They find it difficult to report what is going on. The abuser forces them into silence with bribes or threats: 'This is our secret. I'll be angry if you tell.' Or the child is made to feel too dirty, damaged and ashamed to speak out: 'You filthy little slut. It would break your mother's heart if she knew.'

Children can be taught that they have a right to personal privacy. They have a right to say, 'Stop that! It's not allowed. I'm going to tell.'

Baby-battering

The physical abuse of children is also known as baby-battering and '**non-accidental injury**'. These terms are used when children have been injured on purpose. Because many parents hide their misdeeds, many cases of physical abuse go unnoticed.

Children on child protection registers in England, Wales and Northern Ireland, 1993: by category and gender		
Category	Boys (%)	Girls (%)
Physical injury only	34	27
Neglect only	23	20
Sexual abuse only	15	27
Emotional abuse	11	10
Grave concern	10	9
Multiple categories	6	7
Number of children (=100%)(thousands)	17.6	17.9

◆ The Royal College of Psychiatrists estimates that 3000 serious injuries and 40,000 minor injuries occur each year in the UK as a result of child abuse.
◆ The British Paedriatric (child) Association estimates that child abuse is the fourth most common cause of death in children under five. In the first year of life, 400 cases of babies with brain damage are caused by violent shaking, kicking or beating.
◆ The NSPCC estimate that, on average, 'one to two children under five die every week following abuse or neglect'. The estimates from Europe and the USA are equally high.

Questions

1 Discuss the following quotes from adults who were abused:
   a 'Adults who "possess" children *use and abuse* them.'
   b 'In all cases of sexual abuse, the child is *never* to blame.'
   c 'Lack of respect and verbal humiliation are forms of abuse.'
2 A strong urge to control others comes from an unconscious fear within the people that they are out of control. Discuss.
3 Child abuse is a complex issue. Invite a social worker who specializes in child welfare to give a talk to your class.
4 'Due to changing pressures, parenting is no longer simple. Yet we still pretend this difficult job comes naturally.' Discuss.

The needs of a local community are met by the **National Health Service** (NHS) and the **local authority** or **council**. Local services include:

- **Personal:** health, housing, schools and personal social services
- **Protection:** police, fire, ambulance, consumer affairs
- **Environment:** street cleaning, refuse collection, public toilets
- **Amenities:** leisure parks, playgrounds, sports centres, libraries.

Child-care services

The following services to children are personal.

The **nursery nurse** provides care for babies and small children in full-time or day-care nurseries.

The **well-baby clinics** and **child health offices** provide screening, advice and information on developmental needs.

The **education welfare officer** checks school attendance. Frequent absences of children can suggest problems at home.

The **educational psychologist** assesses the mental and emotional development of children with behaviour problems or special needs.

The **school nurse**, **dentist** and **doctor** check children in the first year of school, and at regular intervals after.

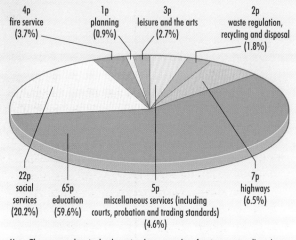

4p fire service (3.7%)
1p planning (0.9%)
3p leisure and the arts (2.7%)
2p waste regulation, recycling and disposal (1.8%)
22p social services (20.2%)
65p education (59.6%)
5p miscellaneous services (including courts, probation and trading standards) (4.6%)
7p highways (6.5%)

Note: The money values in the chart give the cost per day of various services (based on a band C charge for county council services of £397.85, or £1.09 per day).

Source: Oxfordshire County Council, 1995

The **physiotherapist** helps children with disabilities to improve and strengthen their mobility skills.

Participation

Extra money for a community's needs comes from the **council tax**. The decisions made by a local authority when spending council tax directly affect people's health and happiness. Active citizens are those who **participate** in how these funds are shared out. For example, when a **detoxification unit** was closed for lack of funds, the parents of young drug addicts formed a **pressure group**, collecting information on local drug abuse. They then met with representatives from the local authority.

The pressure group questioned the reasons for closing the unit. They explained the need for a local unit because drug abusers have lost control of their lives, and will not travel to a distant unit for the therapy they so urgently need. They argued that funds should be taken from other services to keep the local detoxification unit open. After many meetings and discussions, the pressure group won.

▬ *Investigation* ▬

What are the services in your neighbourhood?
You will need:
a map of your local area and information sheets on the different NHS and local authority departments.

- **a** Trace or copy a simple outline of the map.
- **b** Find and mark one local authority service you already know.
- **c** Using the scale, measure its distance from your home.
- **d** Measure and mark the distances from your home to the nearest baby clinic, hospital, junior school, library, playground.
- **e** Explain why these distances may be very important to a parent with young children.
- **f** Mark in the Town Hall/Council Office and Register Office. Fact-find two things which happen at a register office.
- **g** Write briefly on the work of each local authority service.

A birth certificate

Voluntary services

This is unpaid work done through a group or for an organization: raising money, running events, helping less fortunate people. Anyone can participate.

Numbers of clients using counselling and advisory services		
Services	1981	1993
Al-Anon Family Groups	7,300	12,000
Alcoholics Anonymous	30,000	47,000
Citizens Advice Bureaux	4,514,600	8,253,000
Disablement Information and Advice Lines	40,000	184,000
Law Centres Federation	155,000	525,000
Samaritans		2,400,000
Youth Access	30,000	250,000
Relate	38,000	76,000

— Child observation

Find out when and where the child's birth was registered.

— Investigation

How is the council tax shared out?

Study the chart on the opposite page.

a How much does it cost to run the fire service?

b Which is the most expensive service to run?

c How many teachers and other staff are employed at your school? Do they pay council tax?

d Discuss the interdependence of citizens in a community.

e Suggest ways for people at home to reduce the cost of recyling.

f If you had to reduce one service, which would you choose? Why?

— Questions

1 Do you think citizens should participate in local issues? Why?

2 James dislikes making a fuss yet wants to participate in his local community. Suggest, with reasons, suitable voluntary work for him.

3 'People are more prepared to seek help with their problems.' Name two agencies which offer support and counselling.

4 Suggest a safe place to keep birth and marriage records in the home. Study the 'Births, Deaths and Marriages' columns in your local press. Design a birth or wedding announcement, and cost it.

The personal social services

These services help individuals, not groups. Education, a service for all children, involves the personal social services when a disabled child needs special transport to attend school.

Housing

The Children Act (1989) gave the social services department (SSD) a duty to provide for children in need. Housing can be a major problem for parents on low incomes. Overcrowding in damp and dangerous buildings can lead to accidents, poor health, the spread of infection and reduced hygiene. The parents may feel depressed. These factors, and lack of play space, create an unsuitable environment for children.

The home help

' "They don't want to know about **home helps**," I said. But the man from the council persuaded me. I do ordinary housework, nothing fancy. I clean and shop, the usual things you do in a home. Mostly it's for old or disabled folk. They tell me their troubles and we have a gossip. It cheers them up.

'Mrs Davies comes out of hospital with her second baby today. She had an operation and needs her rest. Washing nappies isn't my favourite thing but I get to cuddle the baby. I cleaned her place when she had her first. A really happier home you can't imagine.

'I meet all sorts – health visitors, community nurses, chiropodists, doctors, physiotherapists – when they visit my clients. The council pays my wages, only average, but I wouldn't be a daily again for twice the money. Job satisfaction is what they call it, getting pleasure from your work.'

The child minder

'I started childminding with Sally's boy. I enjoy kids and, with two of my own, it wasn't much extra work. Then the clinic said I had to be **registered** with the social services department. I don't like people nosing in my business, so I told Sally it was no go.

'Then this social worker came round. Cheeky, I thought. But *she* wanted *my* help! She said how

■ Structured play with the childminder

they needed good **child minders**; how they **trained** and helped you – even sending you clients. I went to the training meetings and really enjoyed them. There are skills in helping your children I hadn't even thought of.

'She checked my home for **safety and hygiene**. I nearly thought cheeky again, except I'd learned so much and could see the improvement in my own kids. I'm allowed to care for **three children under five**. The money's not great. But I enjoy the job and the status which goes with it. When my two start school, I'm going to learn how to train new child minders.'

Day-care nurseries

Day-care nurseries cater for babies from about six weeks old to children up to five years old. They are run by the local authority, by private or voluntary schemes and by companies as a workplace creche for their staff. Babies under one year are usually cared for in a separate room because they have different needs. This also reduces the higher risk of infection from the older children.

Day-care nurseries may be adapted rooms or may be purpose-built. They should be staffed by trained nursery nurses. Parents should check for this. Those run by the local authorities often have long waiting lists. They give priority to single parents who must work, to children with special health problems and those at risk of abuse. Their fees are based on the parent's income. Like the fees for child minders and home helps, these can be met by the social services department if the parents are on a low income.

The social worker

'I am a social worker concerned with **child welfare**. My job is to help families in difficulties. Some tasks are practical like arranging a home help for a mother after the birth of her baby. Others are major tasks to prevent a family splitting up. My priorities are the child's welfare and well-being. I have a duty to investigate reports of child abuse.

'I am empowered by the local authority to take into care children who:
- are orphans
- fail to attend school
- are beyond parental control
- commit a crime punishable by prison for adults.

I have a statutory duty to return a child to its family as soon as possible. Most children come into care at the request of their parents who later take them back. While in care, I try to place them with **foster parents** rather than in a **local authority residential home**. I may help to arrange for a child's **adoption**.

'Before a child is taken into care, a **case conference** is held to investigate the facts. A **multi-disciplinary** group which includes the police, family doctor and health visitor analyses the evidence. A family case conference helps us get a clearer picture of the risk. Before a child is put on the **"at risk" register**, the group must be satisfied that there is a risk of significant harm.

'This morning, Joy requests my help urgently. She has a violent husband, a teenager in care, a three year old and a baby. Before leaving the office, I check what cash, housing and child services are immediately available. When I arrive, Joy is in the street with bruises on her face, a bundle of clothing and her two infants in her arms.

'Joy beams on hearing that I have found her working teenager a place in a local authority **hostel**. We take the baby to a day-care nursery and the youngster to a child minder. **Housing** is available so we go there at once. Later, her

Joy and her family need immediate help

husband turns up, full of apologies and wanting her back.

'I place Joy's children on the "at risk" register. Both parents need to work on their relationship before the family re-unites and they have agreed to **counselling**. I hope this family can solve its problems without taking the young ones into care. I met Joy and her husband soon after they married. They seemed so happy. It's hard to know what goes so wrong in relationships.'

━ Questions ━

1 Suggest reasons why the careers of home help and child minder may be particularly suitable for parents of young children.

2 Give four conditions which a child minder must meet.

3 Explain
   a why Joy's children are put on the 'at risk' register?
   b the range of services available to Joy
   c some conditions for taking a child into care
   d whether you agree with each, and why.

4 Some people believe family life is private, and the community should not interfere. Write an essay, stating your opinion.

The attachment theory

Adults can write stories of perfect mothering. In reality, no mother is perfect, no home is perfect, no child is perfect. Mothers are people, and people generally try to do their best. The attachment theory is said to 'threaten' women because of its message that the child's whole future can be damaged by imperfect mothering in the first year of life. They say that:

◆ where the child–mother relationship is less than good, other relationships with long-term carers may protect the child
◆ children benefit from the greater variety of social contacts
◆ they can and do become attached to other carers
◆ other carers can be extra sources of comfort and security.

Adoption

Adoption used to be the answer to two social problems. In 1968, one in ten British couples was **infertile**, unable to have a child. And women who had babies outside marriage were often unable to support them. By 1996, these problems were different. One in six British couples have problems of fertility. But new careers for women and changing attitudes to birth outside marriage encourage more single mothers to keep their babies. An unwanted pregnancy can be legally terminated by abortion too.

In 1992 there were 8000 adoptions in the UK compared with 27,000 in the peak year of 1968. Today, the lifestyle of couples wanting to adopt is examined. **Home study reports** by social workers take a long time and are costly. And while couples wait, thousands of children in care desperately need homes. Some have special needs. This group includes teenagers, children who are disabled, of black or mixed parentage, siblings who do not want to be split up and victims of child abuse.

On adoption, the child becomes a full member of the new family. The **biological** (natural) parents give up all rights and responsibilities. The adoptive parents become responsible in law for the child's health and well-being. Many children in care

■ Parent me!

dream of being adopted by a family they can call their own.

The Children Act (1975) allowed adults, who were adopted as children, access to their original birth record from the Registrar General. Before then, adoption was a private affair. Adults are now advised to first seek the help and guidance of a **counsellor**. This is because their emotions may be in a terrible turmoil and their expectations may be too high.

Fostering

When children are first taken into care, most of them are placed in foster homes. The reason is that family life is seen as better than life in an institution. Some children have to stay in **residential homes** while the problems of their families are being sorted out. Other children may be very disturbed and need psychiatric care for their behaviour problems. Residential homes may be run by the local authority or by voluntary agencies.

Preparing children for **placement** is a skilled task. The children have to be 'matched' to their new families, not the other way around, and this takes a long time. The matching process includes a team of social workers, natural families, previous carers, new families and the children themselves.

When the matching is successful, **foster parents** (and step-parents) can apply for **custodianship** or adoption. The child must have been in their care for some time. The child is not left out of this process – her or his wishes are taken into account.

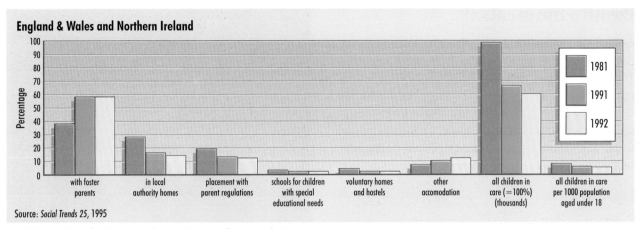

England & Wales and Northern Ireland

Legend: 1981, 1991, 1992

Categories (x-axis): with foster parents | in local authority homes | placement with parent regulations | schools for children with special educational needs | voluntary homes and hostels | other accomodation | all children in care (=100%) (thousands) | all children in care per 1000 population aged under 18

Source: *Social Trends 25*, 1995

■ Children looked after by local authorities: by type of accommodation

The most recent study (Beveridge and Cleaver, 1987) suggests that between 20 and 46 per cent of foster placements break down. Many children have 10 or 15 placements before they become adults. Their emotional lives can be deeply damaged. If they were taken into care because they were beyond parental control or committed crimes, they may not even want to attach to their new families.

Children in transition

Children who are moved from placement to placement are children in transition (see unit 64). One reason why they find it difficult to attach to new carers is because they are suffering loss. No matter how inadequate the home they have lost, it was *theirs*. Although social workers, residential social workers and foster parents do their best, the outlook for children in care is bleak.

- Twenty-five per cent miss at least one year of school, partly because they are excluded for disruptive behaviour.
- Nine per cent stay on in education after age sixteen, compared to a national average of 80 per cent.
- Seventy-five per cent have no qualifications, compared to a national average of 8 per cent.
- Disturbed and under-educated girls tend to damage themselves by having children whom they cannot support while boys tend to commit crimes against other people and society.

Dysfunctional families

A family is **dysfunctional** if its members live in constant misery. Parents who feel 'bad' about themselves **unconsciously** pass on these feelings to the child. Research finds that babies and children before the age of three can suffer **depression**. They are emotionally **withdrawn** and racked with **tension**. Early help can prevent later problems and produce well-adjusted children who grow into healthy happy adults. The study concluded that child care services should provide help for all families, not just ones which are obviously dysfunctional.

▬ *Questions* ▬

1 Give your opinion of the statement: 'Where the child–mother relationship is less than good, other relationships with long-term carers may protect the child.'

2 What does 'matching' mean? List the people who take part in the matching process.

3 Discuss the following statements:
   a 'My adoptive parents are great. Who cares for real ones!'
   b 'I can't wait to find out who my real parents are!'
   c 'I still miss the baby girl I gave away.'
   d 'I just hope my child doesn't turn up and ruin my life again.'

4 Do you agree with the statement: 'Somebody's gotta be crazy about that kid!'? Give reasons for your answer.

5 Investigate fostering and adoption.

141

Positive life events

A study in the USA asked 100,000 people to list the events in life which made them most happy. These are named **positive life events**. The findings were presented on a scale of 0 to 100.

Winning a lot of money and gaining a new job scored lower than love, marriage, children and friendship. It seems that human relationships are valued more highly than material resources.

Positive life events	Score			
	Women		Men	
	under 21	21+	under 21	21+
Falling in love	87.0	73.1	75.7	72.9
Gaining a friend	75.6	73.4	63.0	58.3
Getting married or engaged	71.3	71.4	47.0	73.5
Birth of a child	60.5	70.1	41.4	57.8

Negative life events

A study in the UK found that the most stressful life events on a scale of 0 to 100 are:

Negative life events	Score
Death of a child	97.5
Death of a spouse	95.5
Sent to prison	89
Serious money problems	88
Spouse unfaithful	86.5
Criminal court case	84.5
Getting divorced	81.5
Losing a job	79.5

Death rips apart an established loving relationship. Birth is the beginning of a new relationship.

Marriage

The vows of commitment, the promise to be faithful, the pleasures of a new home, the birth of a child – these events help create long-term bonds between the couple. They become more intimate than lovers. They become best friends.

■ 'For better, for worse
For richer, for poorer
In sickness and in health...
Till death us do part.'

Marriage today is seen as an equal relationship based on love and compatibility. Each spouse provides:
- an equal sharing of the work and responsibilities
- satisfaction of the sexual needs of the partner
- tender loving care in raising the children
- help in creating a secure stable home
- support in times of trouble and distress
- personal autonomy *within* the vows of marriage
- an equal sharing in decision-making for family life.

Cohabitation is living together outside marriage. Over 50 per cent of all women now live with their partners before they marry for the first time, compared with just 3 per cent in 1969. One in three children are born outside marriage. Of these, 55 per cent are born to couples cohabiting.

Monogamy The law states that a woman and man may be married to only one partner at a time. But monogamy also means a couple's decision to be sexually faithful. Married couples and cohabitees usually choose to be monogamous. Some do not always manage this.

People marry with the goal of staying together for life. The **honeymoon** period lasts about a year and can be a difficult time. Pre-marriage dreams and false expectations have to be dropped. Each spouse has to change parts of her/his behaviour to fit the new relationship. These changes involve **personal growth**, and some spouses are unwilling to grow.

Couples who cohabit intending to marry want to identify any problems before they take their vows. They try to learn if they are really **compatible**, suited to each other. Compatibility is more than just falling in love. Love is such a powerful emotion that people can see the other person through 'rose-coloured spectacles'. They can suffer intensely when they find out that the beloved cannot meet all their needs.

■ Being in love is not enough. Couples need to be compatible, too

Research into relationships

Relationships have a chance to work better if the couple are not too different in: age, weight, height, looks, values, attitudes, interests and intelligence. For example, if a couple in different age groups prefer different music, this can cause conflict. Most people feel more comfortable (less threatened) with partners of equal physical, intellectual, emotional and social attributes.

Other research finds that these statements are generally true.

◆ People in close loving relationships are happier, healthier and live longer than people on their own.
◆ Having many friends is not the same as having one person who supports you through thick and thin. It is the *quality* of the relationship which counts, not the *quantity* of friends.
◆ People in their teens are still unsure of their identity and may choose unsuitable friends.
◆ Lonely people can feel unhappy, depressed and worthless. They are ill more often than people in committed relationships.
◆ People with children tend to live longer, though children can be a source of stress.
◆ One study concluded: 'The most effective way to have a happy and healthy life is to *get married and stay married.*'

■ *Questions*

1 List some events which make you most happy. Place them in the order of priority for you. What conclusions can you draw about the value you place on your relationships?

2 List the negative life events which involve the family.

3 Give the meanings of
  a monogamy
  b cohabitation
  c personal growth
  d compatibility.

4 In class, brainstorm some reasons for the age and gender differences in the chart of positive life events.

5 'Marriage depends upon two people with the same goals being committed to helping each other achieve them.' Discuss.

Divorce

Divorce rips apart the rewards and satisfactions of married life. It is the legal death of a relationship. The pain this brings starts long before the divorce and some couples look for blame. They may have been incompatible before they married and took their vows in denial of this truth. The younger the couple, the more likely they are to do this.

Denial

People are not happy 'living a lie'. Denial is damaging for both the person and the spouse. It is a major factor in marriage breakdown. When divorce seems likely, one spouse may have worked through much of their pain. The partner, more often the woman with children, may still value the relationship. They are left emotionally attached to an ex-spouse, which causes on-going pain.

Children of divorce

Spouses are related by law. Their children are related by law and blood (genes). Spouses can divorce but children remain part of each parent. Some studies find that children of divorce are more unhappy than children of parents who stay in an unhappy marriage. Other studies disagree. One factor is clear: the children of divorce suffer a major loss. They lose one parent in the home.

The Children Act (1989) put 'the best interests of the children first'. When awarding a **residency** order, the judge takes the child's welfare as 'paramount' (top priority). If the mother has custody, the law requires the father to pay **child support**. If she is a full-time home-maker, she can claim **maintenance** for herself too. The father must be allowed **reasonable access** to the children. Custody goes to the father if the mother wishes it, or she is proved an unfit parent, or has abandoned the child.

Child abduction

This is the crime of snatching a child from the parent who was awarded custody. The other parent is advised to lodge a complaint at the Passport Office in case the child is taken abroad. The Hague Convention on International Child Abduction provides for the return of children snatched by one parent and taken abroad. The Children's Legal Centre helps fight this crime at home. Child abduction is on the increase.

Mothers and divorce

The National Family Conciliation Council was set up to help divorcing couples avoid battles over money, access and custody. **Joint custody** is now more common. The guiding rule is that children have a **right** to see the other parent.

■ 'Things will get better when we're married,' Ami fixes her veil with shaking hands. 'I can't call it off now. What will people think?'

■ 'I trapped myself by proposing,' Ali tells a friend. 'Still, we both want a home of our own and we both like kids.'

Mothers have more cause to be nervous of the consequences of divorce than fathers. Family resources have to cover two homes instead of one. Some fathers start a new family and have less time, energy and money to support their first family. A few fathers disappear and cannot be traced. In 1984, the Matrimonial and Family Proceedings Act required the courts to 'place greater emphasis on the desirability of both parties becoming economically self-sufficient'. This usually means a full-time home-maker must find work outside the home.

Attitudes to working mothers

From 1985 to 1995, the proportion of working wives rose from 55 per cent to 71 per cent. Whether married or single, women still earn less than men. If their job is non-manual, they hold less senior posts. They do more manual work than men. The bar chart shows that women disapprove of mothers working when they have children, and 63 per cent believe mothers should only work part-time when their children are at school. Yet 50 per cent of mothers with young children are in full or part-time work. The Working Mothers Association and Institute of Personnel Management state 'the provision of state creches or state-aided nurseries is vital if women are to have the same career opportunities as men.'

Who is providing the care?

Unsupported mothers and their children tend to be less healthy than supported mothers. Many

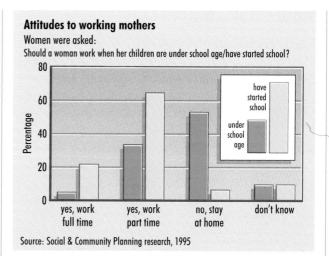

Attitudes to working mothers
Women were asked:
Should a woman work when her children are under school age/have started school?

Source: Social & Community Planning research, 1995

mothers would like to work outside the home and be self-supporting. But child care costs more than they can earn. About £9 billion is paid every year in family benefits.

▬ *Questions* ▬

1 Give your opinions of **a** Ami and **b** Ali's priorities.
2 Plan and prepare a class talk on one of the following issues. Each is complex and many-sided.
   a Do babies really need full-time mothers?
   b Do people really want their taxes spent on state nurseries?
   c Are women the only nurturing gender?
   d Working mothers have two jobs – parent and worker – are they losing out?
   e Mothers are always in the wrong.
   f Single mothers and their children are the new disadvantaged.

Day care places for children under five						
United Kingdom			*Thousands*			
	1971	*1981*	*1986*	*1991*	*1992*	*1993*
Local authority day nurseries	23	32	33	33	30	28
Local authority playgroups		5	5	3	5	3
Registered day nurseries	296	23	29	88	105	127
Registered playgroups		433	473	502	496	475
Registered child minders	90	110	157	273	297	352
Total	409	603	698	899	932	985

Source: *Social Trends 25,* 1995

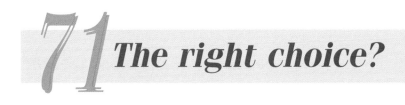

Values and choices

Values are the ideas or beliefs by which people live. They are the standards judged to be important in life. Some values run deep: love of truth, keeping promises, fair play, family loyalty. Other values are opinions which have not been analysed.

— Investigation

Copy and complete the list below to analyse some of your values. They are related to child care tasks (see unit 2). You may keep your work private if you wish. If you disagree with a value, write 'I do not value... because ...'. Once you have completed the list tick the values which are likely to help you make more *effective* choices. Put a star by those values which might change as you get older.

I do/do not value fair play because ...

I do/do not value family loyalty because ...

I do/do not value compassion because ...

I do/do not value a sense of humour because ...

I do/do not value housework because ...

I do/do not value working without supervision because ...

I do/do not value hard work because ...

I do/do not value decision-making because ...

I do/do not value goals because ...

I do/do not value food studies because ...

I do/do not value consumer awareness because ...

I do/do not value exercise because ...

I do/do not value good health because ...

146 ■ Parents can value their baby beyond their own life

— Investigation

Values and choices
You will need:

diced apple and crisps (sufficient portions of both are necessary so that each student can choose freely)

Your values are basic to the choices you make. They affect your behaviour and the way you expect other people to behave. Fact-find on these statements using food as the choice you are making.

a Choose one of the two foods and eat it.

b List the values on which your choice was based: taste? dental health? nutritional content? satisfying hunger? weight concern? copying a friend? pleasing the teacher? other? don't know?

c Re-write the above choices putting the health values first.

d In an earlier study, ten students said they would have chosen differently if they had been on their own. From this evidence alone, what conclusions can you draw about the possible effect of other people on (i) choices of behaviour and (ii) values?

Conflicting values

When making choices, one value can conflict with another. **Peer pressure** (the opinion of friends) can be hard to resist. Suzy values fair play but she chooses to join in teasing the new student. What else does Suzy value? Describe how she is likely to feel later as a consequence of her choice.

Keval, age twelve, nags his parents, 'Everyone in my class stays out late at night.' Who is putting pressure on whom? Suggest two likely values of the parents who resist this pressure. Describe two likely consequences of letting Keval stay out late. What other information might help Keval's parents to make an *informed* choice?

Peer pressure

Parents and carers can suffer from peer pressure too. Flora, aged three, and her babysitter, aged eighteen, enjoy a stroll in the park. They meet a

■ Flora's babysitter gives in to peer pressure

friend who says kids don't really need fresh air and exercise. Flora's babysitter gives in to this peer pressure and agrees to play billiards. Flora tries to amuse herself under the table in the dark, smoke-filled hall. When they get home, Flora's mother is cross. 'Young people! You're all the same. Like sheep!'

a Suggest some likely consequences for Flora as a result of her babysitter's choice.

b Suggest some choices for the babysitter rather than give in to peer pressure and some likely consequences of these choices.

c Explain, with reasons, why Flora's mother is cross.

d Anger can lead people to forget that they value truth. Is it a fact or an opinion that young people are all the same, like sheep? Give reasons for your answer.

Values and choices have important consequences

Imagine two students began the list opposite: 'I do not value fair play because nobody plays fair with me.' What are the likely consequences for these students? Will they find it easy to make friends or become more lonely? In short, will their value help them become more *effective* in their work, play and relationships?

— Investigation —

Test some consequences of values and choices.

For each of the values listed opposite, suggest some likely consequences for the children of parents who disagree with it. This task is not easy. Take your time. Perhaps have a class discussion first.

For example,

The likely consequences of not valuing family loyalty include: ...

— Questions —

1 Turn back to unit 8 and re-read about decision-making. Explain what the following terms mean.
  a values
  b goals
  c peer pressure

2 'Values and choices have important consequences.' Give your opinion of this statement in essay form.

72 *The self*

'Who am I?'
'Where am I going?'
'What does my life really mean?'

The teens are *the* decision-making years. Choices have to be made about school and career, what kind of person to become, when to start serious dating. These decisions can be difficult because they have long-term consequences. The changes to your physical shape which started at puberty are not complete (unit 77). Worry over one or more of these **identity** problems is fairly usual.

Turn back to unit 61, and re-read about autonomy. Learning to make effective choices is not easy. Teenagers may turn to same-sex groups for support. These can be **gangs** with a leader who rules, and a strict **hierarchy** (order of importance). Loyalty to the group is essential. If members have different values, they are cast out. Using age mates to find your identity can have problems. When you give away your autonomy, you **empower** others to be in control. Some people abuse this power. They use it to control others.

Friendship groups are more **democratic**. Friends listen, share, swop, empathize – interact. The rules are not laid down by one person. Peer groups can give valuable support in the teens but check they are not abusive.

Examine your goals

'I aim to be a dancer/musician/athlete/Nobel Prize winner.'
'I aim to be famous but I'm hopeless at everything.'

Are your goals realistic? Do they match your abilities? Can you identify with the work? Are you aiming too low or too high? Is your career goal mainly to help you feel 'good' about yourself?

The purpose of a goal is to keep your focus on what you intend to achieve. Some teenagers choose to be school drop-outs before finding their identity. Others choose to be sexually active before they can support a family. These are short-term goals. Their long-term consequences can be sad. Before there is a chance to enjoy an independent life with a satisfactory job, choices and options are closed off.

'Sex is my affair. It's my body, and my business.' Do you agree with this sixth former, speaking at a Manchester conference? Why?

148   ■ A friendship group discussing what do to next

Examine your values

It is thought that values underlie much of human behaviour. And that goals, choices and decision-making are directly related to values. Most people's goals are to lead a more *effective* life; to be happier and healthier in their work, play and relationships. Will your values help you reach your goals?

People can hold values they never examine. They simply feel they are right. Ed values risk-taking. He says, 'I'm a fun guy. I enjoy taking risks. I like drinking too much, taking drugs and girls. If I fancy a girl, no way will I use a condom.'

Ed examines his value for risk-taking. He realizes he chose it because he wants to be very different from his brother. 'He's so sensible,' Ed sneers. 'It's easy for him. He got all the love.' Does Ed's value come from feeling good or bad about himself? List the emotions which you think rule his value: hurt feelings? jealousy? spite? revenge? respect? admiration? happiness? other?

Ed thinks he is getting revenge on his brother but who is he really damaging? List some likely consequences for the girls who fall for Ed. Values which are chosen from negative emotions are very damaging to the self. They lead to wrong moral choices. They stop people having the free choice to lead happy and healthy lives.

Investigation

Choose one of your values and analyse it more closely by working through the following checklist.

- Is it a value you hold from free choice?
- Do you fully accept all the consequences of your value?
- What other options are available within your value?
- Are you aware of the consequences of those options?
- Do you feel really comfortable with your value?
- Are you ready and willing to debate it in public?
- Is it a powerful and important part of your life?
- Are you happy knowing that your value controls your behaviour and your choices – perhaps for the rest of your life?

Questions

1. Choose another value you hold strongly and work down the checklist, trying to answer each question in more detail.

2. Explain, with reasons, if an unwanted teen pregnancy is more likely to be the consequence of
   a negative feelings
   b poor teachers
   c bad luck
   d short-term goals?

3. List some likely consequences of allowing peer group pressure to empower the following personal choices.
   a Sally chooses a subject which does not interest her because her friends choose it.
   b To gain peer approval, Brenda argues in class with a teacher she really respects.
   c Anwar turns down a good job offer when his friends jeer at it.

4. Do you empower others to control your choices? Write examples of teen empowerment with
   a happy and   b unhappy consequences.

5. 'The unexamined life isn't worth living.' Give your opinion of this statement in relation to Ed's value and lifestyle.

6. Lee and Don both come from dysfunctional families. Both want children. Lee hopes not to damage them in the way he was damaged. Don insists his childhood was happy. Suggest, with reasons, which man is more likely to become an effective father.

7. Find out the age of majority. Who is legally responsible for your choices and behaviours before then?

8. Discuss the differences between autonomy and independence.

9. Describe any peer group you know.

10. 'Short-term goals can have long-term consequences.' Discuss.

73 Rules for relationships

A great deal of human behaviour is governed by **rules**. The rules of law are punishable by the State if they are broken. The rules of relationships can be **flexible**, but they hold almost the same power. Check the tasks in this unit with your friendships.

Fair shares

Some psychiatrists say there is no such thing as **selfless** love. A relationship is a **bargain** made between two people. They **trade** in company, security, affection, status, looks, money, lifestyle and self-esteem. If both people feel they are getting a fair deal, the relationship works. If one person 'takes' more than 'gives', the relationship is unsatisfactory. This is because the **rewards** do not equal the **costs.**

The rewards of relationships are often non-material things. 'It's not fair,' says Mr Blue, as he sees Mr Green wheeling his disabled wife to the shops. 'That man has a miserable life. I don't know why he looks so happy.'

a Name some non-material rewards Mr Green might be getting from caring for his wife.

b Name some of his costs (things he is giving up).

c Name four rewards you would expect to take from a friend.

d Name four costs you are prepared to give in return.

e In your experience, do relationships always involve costs?

f Name four costs you might be reluctant to pay, and say why.

The following are some major rules of relationships.
◆ Keep a confidence – avoid **betrayal**.
◆ Wait to be given a confidence – avoid prying.
◆ Share happy experiences as well as problems.
◆ Be loyal and defend the person in public.
◆ Show loving support, especially at failure.
◆ Ask for support – share your weaknesses.
◆ Offer help – avoid waiting to be asked.
◆ Respect ownership – return borrowed things.
◆ Make eye contact when you speak.
◆ Avoid cruel jokes about a friend's weaknesses.
◆ Avoid jealousy of a friend's other relationships.

▬ Investigation ▬

Analyse the value of relationship rules.

a Working in pairs, devise a scene that is the opposite of one rule.

b Role-play the scene together or in front of the class.

c Record the feelings and responses the scene produced.

d Put the rules listed above in their order of priority for you.

e Explain which two you think are (i) most and (ii) least valuable.

f Suggest one other rule and analyse its value by role-play.

Self-disclosure

'A trouble kept is a trouble doubled
A trouble shared is a trouble halved.'

Are you loyal? Do you trust others? Can you talk about yourself, disclose your real feelings? Self-disclosure is a valuable skill in relationships. Empathy is another. Brainstorm ways in which each might help a relationship work.

Boys find self-disclosure more difficult than girls. They tend to be more effective at keeping secrets and standing up for friends. Empathy in same-gender groups is less of a problem than in opposite-gender ones. Suggest some reasons why.

Breaking the rules of friendship

Is the following scene familiar?
A: 'What's wrong?'
B: 'Nothing.'
A: 'Why are you sulking?'
B: 'I'm not.'
A: 'Is it something I said?'
B: 'I don't want to discuss it.'

Kevin, a student and Clive, a builder, are friends. When they go out, Clive willingly pays for Kevin who lives on a grant. Each time Clive asks for shopping favours because he works late, Kevin forgets. Clive says nothing, but begins to dislike

■ Young love

paying for Kevin. Their friendship soon ends.
a Name which rule of friendship Kevin broke.
b Name which rule of friendship Clive broke.
c Suggest reasons why Clive did not disclose his hurt feelings.
d How did this prevent Kevin having a chance to put things right?
e What did Clive's silence cost the relationship?
f From your findings, give your opinion of the value of saying your feelings are hurt.

Romantic love

'Love seeketh not itself to please
Nor for itself hath any care
But for another gives its ease
And builds a Heaven in Hell's Despair.'
William Blake

For most people, Hell's Despair is feeling totally unloved and unwanted. Compare Blake's beautiful and romantic poem with the following cold text: 'To be effective at relationships, keep the rules, provide a high level of rewards, and avoid inflicting costs.' Are they saying the same or different things?

Young people often feel lonely, girls more than boys. If they marry mainly to escape loneliness, it returns more strongly soon afterwards. Support from a friend can relieve the pains of:
◆ anxiety, which is fear of future pain
◆ hurt, which is present pain in an on-going relationship
◆ anger, which is pain from the past that has not been expressed.

— Questions

1 Do you agree that people drift apart without rewards? Why?
2 Do you think people consciously trade attributes? Why?
3 What values, if any, is a close friend?
4 How might this unit help you become a more effective friend?
5 List some costs to parents of raising children. List some rewards you think they get in return.
6 Suggest three ways these rules might apply to dating.
7 'Men tend to find marriage more rewarding than women.' Discuss some reasons why this might be.

74 *Choosing to negotiate*

The family is an autonomous group in society. Families work best when each member **co-operates**. After infanthood, each person has to fit in their needs with the needs of other family members. A teenager's natural wish for more independence and autonomy can conflict with the parents' natural concern for their health and happiness.

— Investigation —

Analyse the data in the graph below.

a What is the highest stage of married happiness? Is this stage happy all the time? Give reasons for your answer.

b Name three different kinds of stress you think a baby brings.

c Name the highest stage of married happiness with children at home. In class brainstorm some reasons for this.

d What is the lowest stage of married happiness? Suggest some reasons for this.

e Are couples very happy having grown-up children at home? Again, brainstorm in class some reasons for this.

f Couples with children live longer than those without. Try to think of some emotional reasons for this.

g What conclusions, if any, can you draw about the effect of children on married happiness? It might be interesting to conduct a survey on this topic with adults you know well.

The wicked step-mother theme?

All families have conflicts. When they happen in step-families, the step-parent can be blamed. Children's stories with a 'wicked step-parent' theme are partly responsible for this. But the wicked step-parent in children's stories symbolizes **all** parents, not just step ones.

It is also normal for children to imagine they are adopted when they are cross with their parents. They invent comfort stories about being the lost offspring of royalty. In 1995, one in twelve of all families were 'steps', with a total of 2.5 million children.

Winners and losers

Conflicts can end in one of four situations.
'I win – you lose!'
'You win – I lose!'
'I lose – you lose!'
'I win – you win!'

Though conflict feels painful, learning to manage it can be fun. Lovers quarrel and have fun making up. Conflict does not have to be any of the first three situations. There is a choice. If you choose the 'win–win' situation, be willing to **negotiate**. Plan what you must *give* in order to *take*.

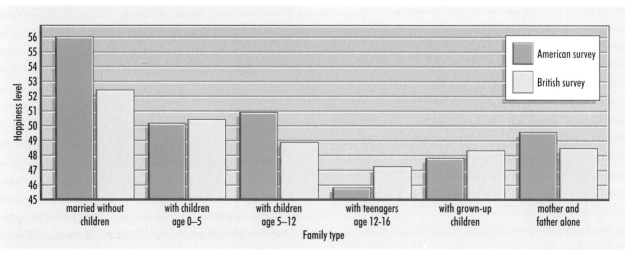

Investigation

Consider these situations and then answer the questions below.

1

Student: 'There's no point asking. You never let me go out.'

Parent: 'You haven't asked. And you went out last weekend.'

Student: (mutters) 'I'm a prisoner. I can't wait to leave home.'

Parent: (cross) 'That does it! You certainly can't go out now.'

2

Student: 'If I promise to be back early, may I go out?'

Parent: 'Let me think. Didn't you go out at the weekend?'

Student: 'If I do my homework first, and stay out a short while?'

Parent: 'I don't know. You're out so often. O.K. But be back soon. '

a Identify which situation is 'win–win' and which 'lose–lose'.

Explain clearly what is going on in each case.

b Choose, with reasons, the following words which suit student A and student B: brave, martyr, victim, coward, sulker, friend.

c Which of the words above do you think suit (i) winners and (ii) losers?

d Which student is sensitive to the relationship, and which only to the self?

e Using role-play, analyse what happens to negotiations if:
   (i) one person begins by accusing or blaming the other
   (ii) one person keeps side-tracking to other issues or past hurts
   (iii) one person refuses to give and just wants to take.

f From your findings, say which is more effective: **confrontation** or **negotiation**? Give reasons for your answer.

Body language

Children can be taught to negotiate. But their feelings show in their body language. This can be deliberate: hunched shoulders means they are not listening. Or it may be unconscious – they are unaware that their body language is giving them away.

Practise facial expressions in the mirror. Record how you feel when: **a** you smile and **b** you scowl. How might this information help you appear more friendly? Suggest, with reasons, certain situations where you might choose to smile rather than scowl.

One survey of teenagers found:

88 per cent respect their parents as people
75 per cent hold the same values as parents
57 per cent enjoy their parents' company
33 per cent find communication difficult
25 per cent believe there is a wide generation gap
4 per cent do not enjoy their parents' company.

These findings suggest that major battles between teenagers and parents are rare. Minor arguments over clothes and hairstyles are more usual. In fact, serious issues of moral behaviour and attitudes to sex are rarely a problem.

Questions

1 It is said body language never lies. Do you agree? Why?

2 Create two rules to improve your negotiating skills.

3 Suggest ways to apply your rules to
   a friendships
   b work
   c when babysitting a child.

4 Do you think being married stops conflict? Explain your reply.

5 Find fairy tales with a 'wicked step-parent' theme. Do you think these help or hinder a child in conflict with parents?

6 Do some teenagers try to take control too early? Do some parents 'let go' too late? Discuss this in class.

75 *Parent yourself*

'Effective parents are those who can parent themselves.'

Ask parents what blessing they most wish for their baby (apart from health) and the answer is happiness. 'I want her to have a happy life.' 'As long as he's happy, that's the main thing.' Parents interact with their baby to encourage happy feelings. 'Look! The first smile!' they cry in delight. They set about encouraging more happy smiles.

Happy feelings come and go. They are not a permanent state. People feel happy in between feeling bored, lonely, anxious, angry. The blessing that parents really wish for their baby is **containment**. This is the ability when adult to:
◆ manage their own emotions
◆ not to feel 'devoured' by 'bad' feelings
◆ know that bad feelings will pass
◆ focus on 'good' feelings and the positive sides of life
◆ know that good feelings will pass.

Problems

At sixteen, Ephra thinks life is full of unfair pressures. Her parents want her to succeed at school. Her friends ask her to parties with drugs and opportunities for sex. She feels pressures from not knowing her identity or her goals, and from the changes in her shape at puberty. Ephra stops eating. She refuses to interact socially, and isolates herself from her family and friends.

Ed, aged sixteen, had an unhappy childhood. He is now so angry he thinks only of revenge. He joins a gang and takes up drinking because the alcohol makes him feel powerful. He has been arrested once for violence. Next time, it will be a detention centre.

Counselling

Ephra and Ed go for counselling. They are taught to 'parent themselves'. Some of the goals of effective parenting are to:
◆ seek the best for their children, at all times
◆ protect them from people or objects which are damaging
◆ teach them the difference between right and wrong

◆ comfort them when they are sad and cheer them up when they are miserable
◆ help them deal with angry or anxious feelings
◆ show them how to focus on the good sides of life
◆ encourage and praise each new stage in their development
◆ love them, and help them build up a good self-image.

Parent yourself

Are you too slow? dull? shy? sensitive? tall? short? worthless? – really a terrible person! If you *choose* to think of yourself like that, other people are likely to think the same. Decide on two 'bad' things about yourself and write the opposite two 'good' things. Can you be those things? Yes, if you *choose* to think of yourself like that! (Height cannot be changed, but you can change the way you feel about it.)

Some people *choose* to criticize themselves all the time. They *choose* to let an inner voice keep saying they are too shy, dull, and so on. Is this an effective way to be happy? The only important things to criticize are those which involve wrong moral choices. One of the major problems in the teens is the longing for the community, the family and the self to be perfect, which they are not.

— Investigation

Examine the values of parenting the self by answering these questions.
a Is Ephra seeking the best for herself by not eating?
b Is Ed protecting himself from damage?
c Who are Ephra and Ed really damaging, and why?
d How is each managing their anxious and angry feelings?
e If you were Ephra, what advice would you give yourself? Why?
f If you were Ed, would you stay in your gang, and why?

These statements summarize important aspects of parenting.

- Happy stable parents tend to produce happy stable children.
- Children from stable secure homes tend to do better than children from homes where conflicts remain unresolved.
- Adults who cannot 'parent themselves' often find it difficult to parent their children.
- Children learn about relationships from their parents and tend to repeat the same patterns of behaviour when they become parents.
- Divorce is always distressing for children but they are not damaged if the parents show emotional maturity.
- Conflict at home does not damage children when parents are willing to find solutions to their problems.

Tasks and goals

No-one escapes unhappy feelings. Everyone needs to learn how to manage them. A baby's task is to construct a *realistic* view of the world. At some stage, children have to understand that their parents are neither very good nor very bad. They also have to construct a realistic view of other people as they really are.

Today's goals are to raise happy children, who feel 'good' about themselves and the world they are in. The task of parents is to meet the baby's needs as soon as possible. They cannot do this 100 per cent of the time. No situation is perfect. No parent is perfect. No baby is perfect – except in the parents' eyes! Most parents try very hard to be **good enough**. Good enough parents usually raise good enough children.

■ Learning to manage unhappy feelings

Questions

1 Think of a problem which makes you anxious. 'Parent yourself' by working through the list opposite. Change is a slow process, it does not happen overnight. Do you think you might need to 'parent yourself' fairly often? Adults do. From the graph of married happiness on page 152, try to suggest some reasons for this.

2 'Autonomy includes not depending on others to boost your self-esteem.' Discuss.

3 'Perfect marriages, perfect parents and perfect children do not exist. Trying hard to be "good enough" is a good enough goal.' Write an essay giving your opinions of these statements.

The woman

A woman's egg is named an **ovum**. At birth, she has about 100,000 undeveloped eggs in her **ovaries**. Each ovary grows to the size and shape of an almond at puberty. Each month, one egg is ripened and bursts out of the ovary at **ovulation**.

The ripe egg is no bigger than a pin dot. After ovulation, it is drawn into the openings of the **fallopian tubes** (oviducts). The egg is moved along the tubes by feathery fronds. It takes five to seven days for the egg to reach the **uterus** (womb).

The uterus is a strong stretchy organ which looks like an upside-down pear. It is about 10 cm long, and 6.5 cm wide at its top. It has thick walls of muscle, which contract strongly when the woman is giving birth. The tissue which lines the uterus is named the **endometrium**. It has its own special blood supply. Each month, the endometrium swells and thickens to make a 'nest' for a new baby. If the egg is not fertilized the lining breaks down and is shed at **menstruation**.

At the 'neck of the womb' is a thick ring of fibrous tissue named the **cervix**. It has a tiny opening, the **os**, to allow menstrual blood out and sperm in. The **vagina** is a strong muscular tube

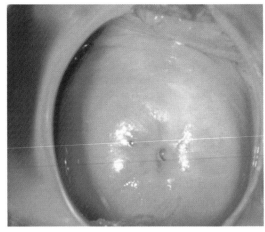

■ A healthy cervix. Notice the os in the centre

which leads to the outside. The **clitoris** is the main organ of sexual pleasure. It fills with blood and **erects** when the woman is sexually aroused.

The man

A man starts to produce **sperm** (spermatozoa) at puberty. He makes millions of sperm every day. A single sperm is so tiny that if all the sperm which created all the people who have ever lived and

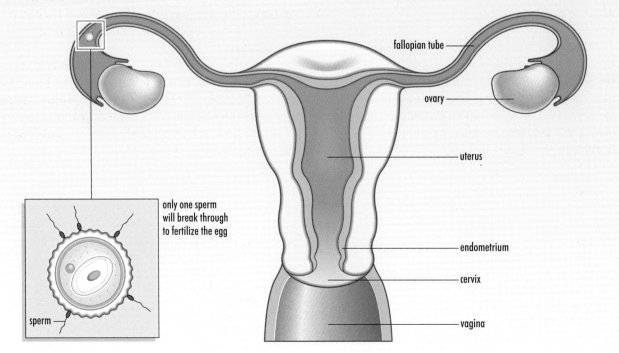

fallopian tube

ovary

uterus

only one sperm
will break through
to fertilize the egg

endometrium

cervix

sperm

vagina

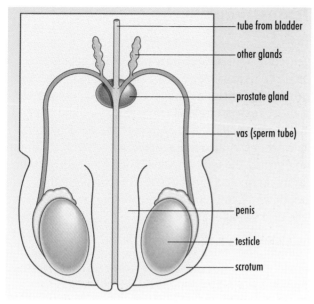

■ The male reproductive system

those living now were put together, they would just about fit into a thimble.

Sperm are made in the **testicles**, which hang outside the man's body in a pouch named the **scrotum**. When the man is aroused, sperm leave the testicles and travel along narrow **vas** tubes to the **prostate** and other glands. These glands pour fluid onto the sperm as they pass. The mixture, which is 95 per cent to 97 per cent fluid, is named semen.

The **penis** is a soft, stretchy organ containing thousands of tiny blood vessels. When the man is sexually aroused, blood pumps into the penis, making it hard and firm. This **erection** is essential for sexual intercourse, when the man's penis enters the woman's vagina. Semen is pumped out of the penis at **ejaculation**.

The sex drive

The sex drive is the instinct to reproduce. At a basic level, it is the primitive urge of all animals for sex. At a more evolved level for humans, it is the wish for physical pleasure through **sexual intercourse**. At its highest level, it is the desire to express love through genital intimacy. The **genitals** are the organs of sexual intercourse.

The sex drive of both genders is triggered at puberty and lasts until very old age. But the desire for sex is controlled by many factors. People are more evolved than animals. They control their basic drives. They choose their partners. People without partners can gain sexual release and pleasure by **masturbation**. Factors which also affect the choice of partners are those which meet the emotional, intellectual and social needs of the couple.

Fertilization

During intercourse when the man ejaculates, some 300 million sperm are released into the vagina. They swim through the os of the cervix into the uterus. The sperm then swim towards whichever fallopian tube holds the egg. It is a long journey and only about 200 sperms survive the course. When a sperm penetrates the egg and their two centres fuse, this is named **conception** or **fertilization**.

When the fertilized egg arrives in the uterus, it develops tiny fronds which burrow into the tissue of the endometrium. This is named **implantation**. Once the egg is safely implanted, **pregnancy** begins. The miracle of life which then develops is discussed in units 84 to 92.

Questions

1 Copy the diagrams and label the parts from memory.
2 On your copy of the female reproductive system, mark the place
   a where conception occurs
   b where implantation occurs.
3 Give the meanings of
   a ovulation
   b fallopian tubes
   c endometrium
   d cervix
   e testicles
   f semen
   g conception

157

Puberty is the maturing stage from childhood to adulthood. It starts with a sudden increase in height which can be as much as 3 cm in eight weeks. The head, feet and hands grow first, then the limbs and lastly the trunk. This uneven growth can cause awkward movements for a while. On average, puberty takes three years at the end of which people become capable of **reproducing** themselves, having children.

Size reached as percentage of total growth after birth		
Age in years	Brain and head	Sex organs
6	85	12
8	90	12
10	95	12
12	98	12
14	99	20
16	100	40
18	100	80
20	100	100

The sex hormones

Hormones are chemicals made in the **endocrine** glands. They act as triggers for many body processes. Endocrine glands have no ducts. They release their hormones directly into the bloodstream. This transports them around the body to where they are needed.

Testosterone

The sex drive is triggered by a group of hormones generally named **testosterone**. Both genders produce testosterone: women in their ovaries and **adrenal glands**; men in the testicles and adrenal glands. Testosterone is responsible for the increased level of skin and genital oils at puberty. It triggers the **apocrine** sweat glands in the armpit and groin. These changes can lead to body odour, spots, acne and greasy hair. There is a greater need for hygiene in the teens to remove the stale oils and sweat.

Men produce ten times more testosterone than women. This extra testosterone is required to develop their **secondary sexual characteristics**. These include facial and body hair, broader shoulders, deeper voice, greater muscle mass, lung size and red blood cells. Testosterone is also needed for sperm to be produced.

Oestrogen

Both genders produce **oestrogen**; women in their ovaries and men in their testicles. Women produce ten times more oestrogen than men. The extra oestrogen is required to develop their secondary sexual characteristics: breasts, wider hips and a layer of fat under the skin which gives women their rounder shape. Oestrogen also causes eggs to ripen.

Women
- breasts develop
- layer of fat builds under skin
- hip area widens
- menstruation begins

- pituary gland in brain sends hormones to ovaries and testicles
- ovaries and testicles produce oestrogen and testosterone
- underarm and pubic hair develops
- genitals enlarge and start to function
- apocrine glands in armpit and groin produce sweat

Men
- facial and body hair develops
- larynx enlarges so voice deepens
- chest area widens
- sperm is produced

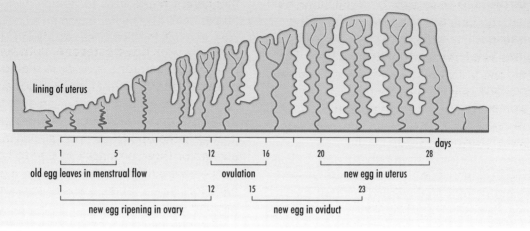

lining of uterus

days

1   5   12   16   20   28

old egg leaves in menstrual flow   ovulation   new egg in uterus

1   12   15   23

new egg ripening in ovary   new egg in oviduct

■ The menstrual cycle

The monthly cycle

An average **menstrual** cycle is 28 days, though any time from 22 to 35 days is normal. The menstrual cycle is controlled by oestrogen and another hormone, **progesterone**.

If the egg is unfertilized, the muscles of the uterus contract to shed the endometrium. One in three women feel these contractions as **menstrual cramps** (period pains). Before a period, some women suffer **pre-menstrual tension**, PMT. This is felt as mood swings, and a slight increase in body tension.

Many people dislike taking medication. They believe in the power of the mind to control the body's pain. Exercise is the natural way to avoid or at least reduce menstrual cramps and PMT.

The **pituitary gland** produces two hormones, FSH and LH, which 'master-mind' puberty. In rare cases, the pituitary does not make enough FSH or LH. If there are no signs of sexual development by age fifteen, *and weight is average for age*, a visit to the doctor is necessary. Usually, there is a history of 'late' development on one or both sides of the family. But if something is wrong, then early therapy avoids fertility problems in adulthood.

▬ *Questions* ▬

1 Plot and draw a graph of the size increase in organ growth.
  a Give the ages at which growth of the sex organs is most rapid.
  b Give the age at which the sex organs are fully mature.
  c Give the age at which growth of the brain and head stop.

2 What is puberty and how long does it generally last?

3 What is made in the endocrine glands? Name two functions of
  a oestrogen
  b testosterone.

4 A fifteen-year-old shows no signs of puberty. Suggest what actions she can take.

5 Suggest some hygiene tips for a fourteen-year-old who is concerned with greasy hair and body odour.

6 From the menstrual charts, copy and complete the following:

The uterus	*The ovary*
Day 1 Bleeding begins	Egg starts to ripen
Day 5 Bleeding ends	Egg still ....
Days ? Endometrium starts to thicken	Egg released into .....
Days ? Endometrium is ripe	Egg travels to .....
Day 28 Endometrium broken down	New egg starts to ...

7 The body temperature rises slightly at ovulation. When is this?

8 Investigate sanitary protection and hygiene.

78 Fertility

To be **fertile** is to be capable of producing a child. A woman may be fertile from puberty until the **menopause** when her periods stop. But early pregnancy, before the age of fifteen, has an increased risk of disability as the egg may not be fully ripe. Between 31 and 35, fertility drops in some women. From 35, ovulation slows down and, in some months, no eggs are ripened. Menopause occurs when the ovaries stop making oestrogen.

A man may be fertile from puberty until old age. But the sperm of an elderly man are not so well-formed and there is an increased risk that the baby may have some disability. Sperm, unlike eggs, are not present at birth. About 50,000 are made each minute from puberty onwards. Healthy sperm need a temperature slightly below body heat. They are damaged or misshapen at a higher heat. The scrotum, outside the body, provides a cooler place.

Home ovulation predictor tests provide a relatively accurate way of predicting when a woman is most likely to conceive. They measure a surge of LH hormones which appears in the urine at ovulation. The kits can be bought at a chemist, but they are expensive for the average young couple to use every month. The instructions differ so must be read and followed with care.

Eggs and sperm have a very short lifespan. If the egg is not fertilized after about 36 hours, it becomes overripe and dies soon after. The average times for the survival rates of sperm inside the woman's body are estimated as follows:

- the vagina   2.5 hours
- the cervix   48.0 hours
- the uterus   24.0 hours
- the fallopian tube 48.0 hours

But people are very different and so are their reproductive cells. In spite of the above estimates, eggs and sperm have been known to meet and fertilize up to five days after sexual intercourse.

Fertility trends

The trend today is for women to delay starting a family. They wait until they have work experience and become independent. The UK Office of Population Censuses and Surveys (OPCS) reported that, from 1984 to 1994, fewer women in their 20s had babies while births to women over 40 rose by 50 per cent. The higher a woman's social class, the later she has her first birth. As a *health* and *social* priority, some doctors suggest age 26 is ideal for a first baby.

A second trend is for women to choose not to have a family. The OPCS forecasts that 20 per cent of women born in the 1960s, 1970s and 1980s may never have children. The reasons for these new trends include: more freedom for women in their choice of career, more changes in lifestyles and goals, more marriage breakdown and divorce, more knowledge of children as a drain on personal and money resources, more acceptance of the choice to be child-free.

Close parity

Close parity is the birth of a second baby within two years of the first baby. The World Fertility Survey found a short birth interval between two children leads to a higher risk of death for both children in infancy or early childhood. If births less than two years apart were postponed for two years, a child's risk of dying before age five would be halved. In developed countries, maternal and infant mortality are low. But the woman tends to have a healthier pregnancy when births are spaced out. Some couples prefer the great changes demanded by a family to happen all at once.

To plan a family is to take control of your sexual life. Not to plan a family can lead to:
- hasty marriages in which the couple may not be compatible
- unwanted babies who are rejected by their parents
- single parents who break down under the stress
- married couples who cannot afford another child.

Fertility control

Some couples use *natural* methods to plan their families. They make love on the days in a woman's menstrual cycle when she is unlikely to conceive. Turn back to page 156 and re-read about fertilization. The os produces a fluid named **cervical mucus**. From day one to day ten of the

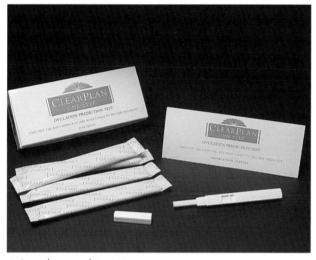

■ An ovulation predictor test

menstrual cycle and from day sixteen to day twenty-eight, this mucus is thick and sticky. Sperm cannot swim easily through it. These days are named the **safe period** for couples who choose this method to plan their family.

From day ten to day sixteen of each menstrual cycle, the mucus becomes thin and watery. Sperm can easily swim through it. Day ten to day sixteen are the same days that the egg ripens, bursts out of the ovary and begins to travel along the fallopian tube. These are the days during which a woman is likely to conceive following sexual intercourse.

The 'safe' period can be *unsafe* without special teaching. Some women do not have regular menstrual cycles. Even for those who do, a change in the diet or stress can upset the cycle. Other names for the safe period include the **cervical mucus method**, the **rhythm method**, the **calendar method** and the **ovulation method**.

▬ *Investigation* ▬

Read the following goals to find out those you intend to reach before planning a family. Complete the list with as many details as you wish.

I will/will not want good career prospects because ...

I will/will not seek a loving partner because ...

I will/will not expect to be married ...

I will/will not need a home of my own ...

I will/will not need some savings ...

I will/will not expect to change my lifestyle ...

I will/will not expect to work harder ...

I will/will not need to be happier ...

I will/will not need to be more patient ...

I will/will not need to be healthy ...

I will/will not expect to improve my diet ...

I will/will not want to be much older ...

I will/will not expect to plan my family ...

▬ *Questions* ▬

1 A woman with a regular monthly cycle of 28 days has a period on the first day of March. Estimate the days of her safe period.

2 Explain why the safe period is not at all safe for a woman whose periods are not regular.

3 Give the age trend in motherhood. 'The higher a woman's social class, the later her first birth.' For such a woman, suggest some of her likely long-term goals.

4 What is meant by close parity? Suggest some advantages and some drawbacks of spacing a family.

5 Some people say child-free. Others say childless. Give your opinion of the choice of words in as much detail as you wish.

Family planning – also called **contraception**, **birth control** and **fertility control** – involves choosing from a variety of methods in order to avoid an unwanted pregnancy.

Perfect use conditions

Contraception can be highly effective under perfect use conditions. For example, when the man learns how to use a condom before he first has sexual intercourse. The failure rate for the condom, under perfect use conditions during the first year of use resulting in unsought pregnancy, is 2 per cent. From average use conditions (perfect and imperfect use), the failure rate is 16 per cent.

Methods

The **male condom** is a sheath of thin rubber which is rolled over the erect penis. Sperm is trapped in the small bulge at the tip. Condoms are disposable and cannot be reused.

The **female condom** is a larger sheath put into the vagina and covering the vulva. This is a recent method and early reports suggest that it lacks aesthetic appeal. There are no data yet on its failure rate.

The **diaphragm** (cap) is a sheath of rubber which fits over the cervix. Sperm enters the vagina but the individual sperms are blocked from swimming through the os. **Spermicides** (foams, tablets or creams containing substances which kill sperm) are used with the diaphragm in case it splits or is placed incorrectly. Without spermicides, the diaphragm has a failure rate of between 12 and 38.9 per cent. With spermicides, the failure rate for the diaphragm under perfect and average use conditions is 6 and 18 per cent respectively. Unlike the condom, the diaphragm can be reused.

Intra-uterine devices (IUD) are plastic devices implanted in the uterus. They seem to work by setting up an irritation so the egg cannot implant. IUD methods have a failure rate of between 2.5 and 4.5 per cent.

Hormone **pills** contain synthetic oestrogen and/or progesterone. They work by one or more of the following methods: **a** the egg is not ripened, **b** its progress along the fallopian tube is slowed,

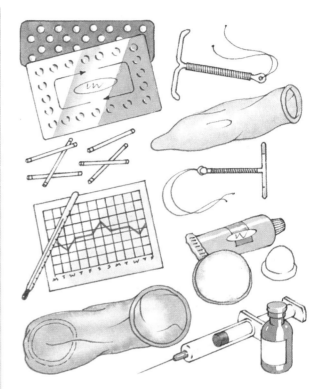

■ Identify each contraceptive method

c the mucus is changed so that sperms cannot swim through the os, **d** the endometrium is changed so the egg cannot implant in the uterus. Hormonal methods can be taken orally, injected or implanted under the skin. Their failure rate is between 3.8 and 8.7 per cent.

The **intra-uterine system** (IUS) combines the IUD and hormonal methods. AN IUD is implanted in the uterus which contains the hormone progesterone and works in much the same way as the pill.

Safe period (or rhythm method) is based on the woman's monthly cycle (see unit 78). The couple can make love without any contraceptive device at her low fertility times. Using the safe period has a failure rate of between 13.8 and 19.2 per cent.

Sterilization is invasive surgery. The egg or sperm-carrying tubes are cut and tied back. All surgery involves a slight risk. This method is not easy to reverse. Sterilization has a failure rate of between 0.2 and 0.5 per cent.

Withdrawal is the method in which the penis is withdrawn from the vagina before the man ejaculates. However, sperm can leak from the penis into the vagina even before the man fully ejaculates, which makes this a very unreliable method of contraception. Withdrawal has a failure rate of between 14.7 and 27.8 per cent and is *not* advised for couples who want to avoid pregnancy.

If protection fails or no protection is used the **morning-after pill**, PC4, can be used for up to two days after unprotected sex to prevent pregnancy. But its failure rate is high, about 33 per cent. The new RU486 pill blocks the hormones needed to sustain pregnancy and is more reliable than PC4. Both PC4 and RU486 have side effects.

The only method of birth control which is completely reliable is **abstinence**. This is avoiding sexual intercourse until you wish to start your family. Like all the other methods, abstinence is a matter of personal choice and of respecting this choice in a partner.

A question of choice

No method of family planning is perfect. The IUD causes heavier bleeding, with longer and/or more painful periods. Women who change partners increase their risk of sexual disease because the threads of the IUD leave a small passageway open through the os into the uterus. The hormonal methods, including the IUS, are not suitable for some women due to their side effects.

The success of the safe period depends upon the woman having a very regular menstrual cycle. Withdrawal is not a reliable method of contraception even when the man has very good control over his ejaculation. Sterilization is not

Contraception: by method used				
Great Britain		*Percentages*		
	1976	*1986*	*1991*	*1993*
Pill	29	23	23	25
Male condom	14	13	16	17
Hysterectomy	7	12	12	12
Vasectomy	6	11	13	12
IUD	6	7	5	5
Withdrawal	5	4	3	3
Safe period	1	1	1	1
Cap/Diaphragm	2	2	1	1
Other	1	1	1	1
At least one method	68	71	70	72

Source: *Social Trends 25, 1995*

suitable for couples who hope to have a family at some future date. (In the table, male sterilization is given its medical name, **vasectomy**. The table has no data for female sterilization. A **hysterectomy** is the surgical removal of the uterus.)

The condom and diaphragm are named **barrier methods** because the rubber acts as a barrier to trap the sperm. The rubber *can* split, though this is not usual. The male condom can also slip off. The diaphragm may not be placed correctly. A few people are allergic to the rubber in barrier methods. They can now buy non-allergy ones.

When choosing a method of family planning, the factors to be considered include: the age of the couple, their health and religious beliefs; the reliability of the method, its costs, ease of use, aesthetic appeal, and if it can be easily reversed. Another very important factor is whether or not the method offers any protection from sexually transmitted diseases (see unit 80).

■ *Questions* ■

1 What is contraception and why is it used?
2 List the contraceptive methods:
   a used by women
   b used by men
   c which allow sperm to enter the vagina.
3 What does abstinence mean?
4 The safe period is sometimes called **periodic abstinence**. Brainstorm in the class the reason for this.

4 Explain the following methods of contraception:
   a intra-uterine device
   b intra-uterine system
   c hormone pill
   d the condom
   e the rhythm method.
5 Collect advertisements for family planning and put them in your folder. Design a poster to promote fertility control.

Unprotected sex

A case study

Zoe and Zac, both seventeen, spend hours planning their wonderful future together. When they first make love, Zac uses the **withdrawal** method. When they marry four months later, Zoe is four months pregnant. After the birth, the health visitor explains the **barrier methods** of contraception. Zac tries the **condom**. Zoe tries the **diaphragm**. Sometimes they forget, or choose to take a risk. Zoe is pregnant when their first child is three months old.

After the second birth, Zoe asks for **sterilization**. She is advised against this and opts for the **pill**. When she reads of the health risks of the pill, she stops taking it and thinks of having an **IUD** fitted. Meanwhile the couple use the **safe period** but neither likes waiting for Zoe to be at her low fertile time. When she finally goes to the clinic for the IUD, she is pregnant again. The couple's third child is born when their first is two years old.

It is crowded in their tiny flat. There is no privacy and the couple stop making love. Neither discusses this choice. Both are terrified of their high fertility. **Abstinence** seems to be their only choice. Zac starts coming home late. Zoe feels trapped. At night they lie silently together, yet miserably apart, wondering what happened to their plans for a wonderful future. The couple believe that their lives are out of control.

Risk-taking and fertility

The younger the couple, the more risks they take. Though no family planning method is perfect, each is more effective than the 'no method' practice of unprotected sex. Pregnancy occurs within one year for 92 per cent of young couples using no method of family planning. This can happen the first time (or at almost any other time) they have unprotected sex.

The figures in the table alarmed the nation. The Department of Health set up a target to halve the number of conceptions to girls under sixteen by the year 2000. Another survey found that nearly

■ This is *not* the wonderful future Zoe and Zac had planned for

Teenage conceptions in England and Wales		
Age of girl	*Conception rate per 1000 sexually-active girls*	
	1981	*1991*
Under 14	1.1	1.3
14	4.6	6.6
15	15.8	19.9
16	37.7	43.4
17	56.8	65.5
18	76.2	84.9
19	94.0	96.0

half the babies born to girls age fifteen to nineteen were unwanted. These new mothers said they were reluctant to use birth control.

Family planning and women

Family planning is *critical* in a woman's life. It involves the most serious choices she has to make. Yet Britain has the worst record on teenage pregnancies in the European Union. Of the 100,000 conceptions each year among teenage girls, about a third end in abortion.

Though family planning is critical in a man's life, he does not face the same long-term risks to his health. Complications in pregnancy or childbirth resulted in the deaths of 238 UK women between 1987 and 1990. Though the pill and sterilization have health risks (see unit 79), even they, as well as all other methods, are safer than using no method and having a birth.

— *Investigation* —

Analyse some factors in the case study

a When planning their wonderful future together what did Zoe and Zac forget as a top priority in their plan?

b How do we know that they did not want children at age seventeen?

c State your opinion of withdrawal as a birth control choice for young couples.

d Name the methods the couple chose before the second pregnancy, and why each failed.

e Zoe was nineteen when she asked for sterilization. Give reasons why she was advised against the surgery.

f What extra information could Zoe have sought about the pill before she stopped taking it?

g State how the safe period works, and why this method failed.

h Identify some advantages for the couple of choosing an IUD.

i Suggest why communication between the couple broke down and some likely consequences if this continues.

j Do you agree abstinence was their only choice? State some other conclusions the couple might have drawn.

k 'No one method of birth control is perfect but each has value, and requires proper management.' Explain how this statement ties in with Zoe and Zac's attitude to family planning. Identify ways in which they can gain control over their fertility.

— *Questions* —

1 It is unlawful for people under age sixteen to have sex. Give your opinion of this law.

2 Suggest reasons why the girls age fifteen to nineteen were reluctant to use birth control. Prepare to discuss these reasons in class.

3 'All's fair in love and war.' Is this more likely to be a male or a female saying, and why?

4 'Family planning is critical in a woman's life.' Give your opinion of this statement.

5 Research shows that becoming pregnant may be an **unconscious** choice for a girl with low status and/or low self-esteem. Getting a girl pregnant may be an unconscious choice for a boy with low status and/or self esteem to prove his manhood. Discuss.

6 Prepare a talk on family planning methods to include: where it can be obtained, instructions for use, safety and health factors, problems of use, acceptability (culture/religious objections), cost, other.

Genito-urinary diseases

The condom is now promoted as having two functions. It not only protects against unwanted pregnancy, it also gives some protection against **sexually transmitted disease**, and the HIV infection which leads to AIDS. People have a far higher risk of catching a sexually transmitted disease than HIV; over half a million new cases occur each year. Doctors now name them genito-urinary (GU) diseases. Some can infect the urine passages as well as the genitals. GU diseases are treated at GUM (genito-urinary medicine) clinics attached to most hospitals.

These are the special points to note about the germs of genito-urinary disease.

♦ They can cause severe damage to the foetus or infect the baby at birth.
♦ They can cause infertility if the germs travel up the vagina and penis to the egg and sperm-carrying tubes, forming hardened scar tissue which blocks the tubes.
♦ They can infect a woman's whole reproductive system causing painful and long-term **pelvic inflammatory disease** (PID).
♦ They can breed on a woman's cervix causing pre-cancer cells to form which can lead to **cancer of the cervix**.
♦ As with unwanted pregnancy, women tend to suffer more serious and long-term health problems from a GU infection than men.

GUM CLINIC WAITING ROOM

See? Everyone's perfectly ordinary, just like you

The symptoms of GU disease

The symptoms of GU disease can be: an itchy or smelly discharge; burning and frequency on urinating; sores or warts on the mouth, throat, genitals or anus. But often there are no symptoms, so people cannot tell if they have GU disease. This is more usual for women as their organs are internal. Sexually-active women age 17 to 25 are at greatest risk of becoming 'silent reservoirs' of GU disease, unknowingly passing them to their partners while the germs are causing great damage in their reproductive system.

Types of GU disease

There are at least 25 different types of genito-uninary disease. One disease which is spreading rapidly through the UK is **chlamydia**. Up to 30 per cent of men and 70 per cent of women with chlamydia have no symptoms. The disease can cause a baby to be born prematurely. Half of all pregnant women with chlamydia pass it to their babies at birth. Chlamydia is the most common cause of eye disease in newborns and the leading cause of pneumonia in young babies. Chlamydia can lead to PID in women and infertility in both genders.

Herpes is a virus infection which forms painful cold sores on the genitals. The disease is cancer-related, and can cause women to miscarry. If present at birth, one in two babies will be infected. Of these, two out of three will die and half the rest will have brain damage or sight defects. Herpes can be treated, but not cured. The disease flares up at intervals through life.

Apart from herpes, GU diseases can be easily cured. *But only if they are treated early, at the first symptoms*. Since so many people have no symptoms, protection is essential. Condoms protect the genitals from contact. The packets have instructions which must be followed with great care before, during and after sex. The diaphragm (cap) protects the cervix but not genital contact. Passing urine and washing the genitals after sex reduces the risk of herpes.

Condoms are the only birth control devices which offer protection against both unwanted pregnancy and GU

QUESTION: Which of these people is most likely to have a sexually transmitted disease?

ANSWER: All of them . . . (or none)

disease. A woman is twice as vulnerable as a man to serious long-term problems from each. This double vulnerability places men under a double duty and moral obligation to protect women from these greater risks. While most men understand and accept this responsibility, a few threaten to leave their partner if they cannot have unprotected sex. Other men pay prostitutes twice the going rate for sex without a condom.

GUM clinics are listed in the telephone book under Venereal or Sexually Transmitted Disease Clinic. Therapy is secret. The names of sexual contacts are requested so they can be treated too. This is named **contact tracing**. The community's health depends upon the success of contact tracing to reduce the high rate of, and great misery caused by, GU disease.

AIDS

The HIV infection which leads to AIDS is passed in bodily fluids: mainly semen, blood and vaginal fluids. Homosexual men have been its main victims, to date. Drug abusers can get AIDS if they share infected needles. An infected woman can pass HIV to her unborn baby, and in her breast milk. Haemophiliacs and people needing blood transfusions have also been its victims.

One major problem is the time between HIV infection and the onset of AIDS. After ten years, only half of those infected will have developed AIDS, though many will have symptoms of a breakdown in the immune system. A woman has 20 times the risk of being infected by a man than he has of being infected by her. For AIDS, protected sex means the man protecting the woman from contact with his bodily fluids. However, if she abuses drugs or has unprotected sex with other men, it is the woman's duty and moral obligation to protect the man from her bodily fluids.

Though highly effective, condoms can rip or slip off. They do not provide 100 *per cent protection* against AIDS, GU disease, infertility, pregnancy, damaged babies or anything else. At present, the best protection against AIDS appears to be sexual fidelity with one faithful partner.

▬ *Questions* ▬

1 List some likely consequences for a girl who has unprotected sex with a boy she hardly knows. Explain why she should not wait until she has symptoms before going to her GP or GUM clinic.

2 Name the birth control methods which do not prevent the exchange of bodily fluids. Suggest, with reasons, a suitable contraceptive method for a person who is non-monogamous.

3 A careful consumer decides against buying cut-price condoms. Suggest a reason for his decision.

4 Study the instructions on the proper use of condoms, and give reasons for each instruction.

Causes of infertility

To be infertile is to be incapable of producing a child. The rate of fertility problems is increasing for many reasons, some of which are not understood. One in 6 couples have problems. In 10 to 15 of cases, the problem involves both partners. In 30 per cent of cases, the man is involved. In up to 20 per cent of cases, no medical reason for infertility in either partner is found.

Sperm need to be high in number, well-shaped, fast swimmers and nourished in plenty of semen. Over-heating may be a major cause of the recent drop in sperm count. (Bathing the testicles in hot water is a primitive method of birth control.) Tight clothing raises the temperature; a US study found that men who wear boxer shorts have a higher sperm count than those who wear jockey briefs. Being overweight can keep the area hot. Over-exercise can lower the production of testosterone, and certain chemicals are being checked for their effects in reducing male fertility.

Eggs need to be ripe and the fallopian tubes and ovaries healthy. Problems include under or overripe eggs, and a too fast or slow progress along the tubes to the uterus. (The timing is important because the endometrium needs to be thick and lush ready for the egg, neither shedding nor yet ripe.)

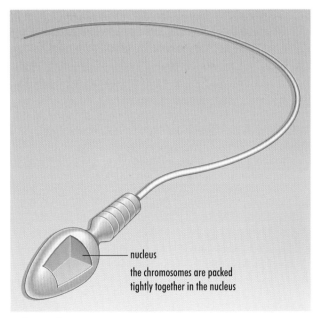
nucleus
the chromosomes are packed
tightly together in the nucleus

Blocked tubes in either gender may be due to scarring after surgery or a GU disease. Blocked tubes in women can be due to **endometriosis**, a condition in which fragments of the tissue break away. They travel through the fallopian tubes and grow near the ovaries. The growth blocks the opening to the tubes so the egg cannot enter.

Radiation from X-rays can be damaging. Both genders should ask **a** if an X-ray is strictly necessary and **b** if their ovaries or testicles are properly protected from the radiation. They should keep the dates of their X-rays (since medical records are often lost), and ask their doctors if they are using the Royal College of Radiologists guidelines.

Both genders can have hormone problems and these can be treated with fertility drugs. Before seeking fertility therapy, young couples are advised to wait until after one full year of trying for a baby. During this time, they can improve their general health (unit 86).

Fertility treatments

The inability to have children can be shattering. Adoption or fostering is a solution, but cannot remove the pain. Couples who fail to become **biological** (natural) parents may suffer lasting sorrow. Others endure painful and costly tests to identify the cause of their fertility problems.

Advances in reproductive technology mean that many types of fertility treatment are now available. Not all of them work for all couples. The following are four of the possible therapies.

In-vitro fertilization (IVF)

A fertility drug stimulates the ovaries to ripen many eggs. Just before ovulation, the ripe eggs are removed through the abdomen wall by syringe. They are placed in a Petri dish with a specimen of the husband's semen and fertilized. When the embryos are a few days old, they are placed in the uterus through the cervix.

Gamete intra-fallopian transfer (GIFT)

GIFT begins like IVF, then the eggs and semen are put in the fallopian tubes to be fertilized. A general anaesthetic is required as the tubes can be

■ A normal sperm

■ Louise Joy Brown was the first person to be conceived by IVF

reached only by surgery. When GIFT or IVF are successful, **multiple births** are common because the fertility drugs increase the number of eggs which are ripened.

Sperm-washing

This is a high-tech procedure which improves the strength of poor quality sperm. It may be used in combination with IVF or GIFT.

Donations

Egg donation: the egg of another woman is fertilized in vitro and the embryo is placed in the uterus.

Sperm donation: the semen of another man is used in vitro or is placed by syringe near the cervix so that the sperm can swim up to the egg.

Embryo donation: the egg and sperm of another woman and man are fertilized in vitro and placed in the uterus.

Surrogacy donation: the uterus of another woman is used to develop the egg which has been fertilized in vitro.

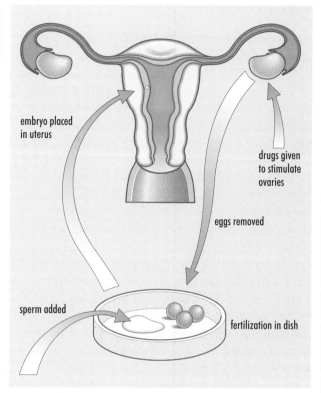

■ In-vitro fertilization

Questions

1 How long should young couples wait before seeking the help of a fertility doctor?

2 Sami's tubes are blocked and her husband's are clear. Explain why she chooses IVF and not GIFT.

3 Give one reason for the increase in multiple births.

4 'Infertility can damage a couple's relationship.' Discuss this statement from the feelings of
   a the partner who is infertile
   b the partner without the problem
   c when no medical cause in either partner is found.

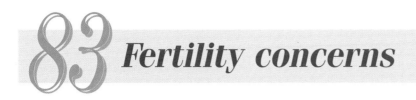

Fertility ethics

Some people believe that the basic distinction between right and wrong comes from a moral sense, not from reason: 'it *feels* wrong'. Others believe that an act is right if it benefits more people than it harms. The new technologies are causing great debate. For example, eggs, semen and embryos can be frozen and thawed for use at a later date, but if the couple no longer need them, should scientists be allowed to use them for learning more about genetic diseases? Or should they be destroyed? There is less debate over destroying eggs and semen than there is over destroying an embryo.

Some people believe that, apart from IVF and GIFT, the other procedures for infertile couples are morally wrong. The Warnock Committee on reproductive ethics stated: 'Because embryos have the potential to become human persons, neither the relief of infertility, nor the advance of knowledge, justifies their deliberate destruction.'

Fertility guidelines

In 1990, the government passed the Human Fertilization and Embryology Act. It listed the following conditions:

- Complete anonymity for the couple and for the donors of eggs, semen and embryos.
- Both partners should give written consent to the treatment.
- A limit of ten children born from one donor's services.
- A woman giving birth by egg or embryo donation is the child's legal mother. The donor has no rights over, or duties to, the child.
- Frozen embryos can be stored for a maximum of ten years.

Termination of pregnancy

A termination of pregnancy used to be thought of as an easy option for couples who took risks with their fertility. Research shows that it is not an easy option at all. The decision to terminate a pregnancy causes great anxiety and distress. Not only single but married couples seek terminations. The major reason is a failure of contraception.

The 1990 Act stated that a termination of pregnancy is legal if two doctors agreed on one of the following conditions:

- that the pregnancy is not more than 24 weeks
- that to continue the pregnancy would be of

■ The right to choose a termination of pregnancy arouses strong feelings on both sides of the debate

greater risk to the woman's physical or psychological health than to terminate it
- that to continue the pregnancy would be of greater risk to the health of the woman's existing children than to terminate it
- that there is a strong likelihood of severe handicap in the foetus.

Before termination of pregnancy was made legal, many women became infertile after having 'back-street' abortions, and some died. Today, having a pregnancy terminated in hospital should have no effect on a woman's fertility, according to a joint study by the Royal Colleges of General Practitioners and Surgeons. In a ten-year trial involving almost 1500 pregnant woman, researchers found no significant difference in the time it took to conceive again.

■ *Questions* ■

1 Do you think donors should be anonymous? Why?

2 If you had donated an egg or sperm, might this affect the way you feel about yourself? Why?

3 Do the conditions for a termination of pregnancy include a foetus which is the result of rape?

4 If you were a Member of Parliament, how would you vote on the abortion issue, and why? Which, if any, of the conditions that allow termination of pregnancy would you change, and why?

5 How might the health of a woman's existing children be at risk if the mother is forced to continue with an unwanted pregnancy?

6 'Court gives go ahead for abortion on handicapped woman'

A British court authorized doctors to terminate the pregnancy of a Down's woman aged 25. Her mother requested the abortion because her daughter had a mental age of three and a half years. Discuss.

7 'Divorcing father seeks parental rights'

A husband, separated from his pregnant wife, asked the courts to prevent her aborting his child. Discuss the father's rights.

8 After taking a fertility drug, Pam conceived sextuplets. It was possible to abort four foetuses leaving two with a better chance. Pam and her husband refused, 'We cannot choose between babies. That is dreadful.' Sadly, none of the six babies survived. Pam said, 'Without modern technology, I could not conceive. Although it brings great help, it brings difficult and painful choices too.' Discuss.

9 In countries which undervalue women, 99 per cent of abortions are of baby girls. Discuss some implications of this.

10 'Adoption, not abortion.' Do you agree with this slogan? Why?

11 Describe fertility trends in the Western world and place them in their order of priority in your life.
- Improved methods of birth control
- Changes in people's goals and lifestyles
- An increase in fertility problems
- More men involved in the parental role
- Advances in home technology
- The desire for two-income households
- Lack of child-care nurseries
- Changes in the abortion laws
- Rising costs of raising a child
- Reduced risk of infant mortality
- Improvement in the mother and child's health
- Increase in the divorce rate
- Wanting to avoid close parity
- Improved understanding of children's needs
- Other

A baby's gender

There are 23 pairs of **chromosomes** inside each human cell, except for the egg and sperm cells. These have 23 *single* chromosomes. At fertilization, the baby inherits 23 single chromosomes from each parent. These make up the 23 pairs.

Sperm have either an X or a Y chromosome. Eggs have only an X. When sperm X fertilizes egg X, the baby is a girl. When sperm Y fertilizes egg X, the baby is a boy. The father's chromosomes 'determine' the gender of the baby.

Genes carry information

Each chromosome contains a strand of **DNA** (deoxyribonucleic acid). There are three billion pieces of information on one DNA strand, the same number of heartbeats in a lifetime. **Genes** are segments of DNA. They work mostly in pairs and make proteins which control development. The effects of some genes hide the effects of others. These genes are named **dominant**. The others are named **recessive**.

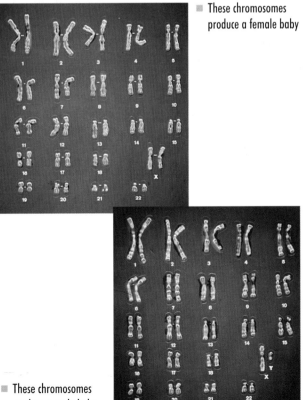

■ These chromosomes produce a female baby

■ These chromosomes produce a male baby

── Investigation ──

Analyse how sex determination works.
You will need:

150 pulses of one colour (X chromosomes) and 50 pulses of a different colour (Y chromosomes). These will be the sex chromosomes.

a Put 100 X pulses in one jar to represent the eggs.

b Put 50 Y pulses (for male) and 50 X pulses (for female) in a second jar. Mix. This jar represents the sperm.

c Without looking, remove one pulse from each jar.

d Lay this pair under the column for females or males.

e Repeat c and d until the jars are empty.

f Record the evidence of your findings.

Brown eyes are dominant over grey eyes. The effects of recessive genes can show through in the grandchildren because the baby inherits single chromosomes from each parent to make up the 23 pairs. Parents with brown eyes have a one in four chance of having a grey-eyed child if one parent inherited the recessive gene for grey eyes. If both parents inherited the grey-eyed gene, they have a one in two chance of a grey-eyed child.

Genes and disease

Most inherited diseases are carried on recessive genes. If two healthy people have the recessive gene for cystic fibrosis, there is a one in two chance their baby will suffer from cystic fibrosis.

A **mutation** is a sudden change in a gene or chromosome. Some mutations are the result of heavy exposure to X-rays, certain chemicals, radiation leaks from nuclear power stations and unsafe dumping of radioactive waste. Others are *random*; they just happen and nobody knows why. There is no cure because every cell in the body carries the mutation. Serious mutations tend to die out because the baby rarely develops past puberty.

Down's syndrome is caused by an extra chromosome. It is **not** an inherited condition but a random mutation. However, it can be related to

■ A Down's child having fun on the beach

Mother's age	Chance of Down's syndrome
20–24	1 in 2000
25–29	1 in 1500
30–34	1 in 1000
36–39	1 in 300
40–44	1 in 100
45+	1 in 50

the age of the parents. Down's babies tend to have similar features, are mentally handicapped, slow to develop physically, and some stay dependent for life.

Men also increase their chance of fathering a Down's baby as they get older. A man over 39 is three times as likely to father a Down's syndrome child as a man under 35.

Sex-linked characteristics on the X chromosome show through in men because they have no back-up X to hide the defect. Two million British men have red-green colour blindness. This colour defect is more serious with the increases in technology. Colour coding is essential in many jobs: pharmacy, printing and textile industries, food processing, cartography, air and road traffic control.

Haemophilia is a sex-linked characteristic which upsets normal blood clotting. Bleeding, even from a minor cut, does not stop. It is difficult to protect a small boy from hurting himself while encouraging him to be active. Not only must cuts be avoided. Bumps and falls can cause internal bleeding. Therapy is by injections of **clotting factor 8** taken from the blood of **donors** and most of the 5000 haemophiliacs in the UK can lead healthy lives.

■ Testing for colour blindness

Questions

1 A couple with two girls long to have a boy. Explain the chances that their next baby will be a boy.

2 If healthy parents both have a recessive gene for disease, give the chances of a baby suffering from it.

3 A couple aged 23 worry because the man's mother had a Down's baby at age 42. Explain their chances of avoiding this.

4 Design, with reasons, a play space for a haemophiliac child.

5 Investigate Down's syndrome.

6 Investigate blood donation and social interdependence.

7 'Nature gets the balance of the genders right.' From your findings, explain whether this statement is a fact or an opinion.

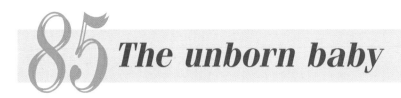

85 The unborn baby

The embryo

The first three months in the uterus is the **embryo** stage. The cells divide and grow most rapidly during this time. They change their shape for different functions. One cell changes to become part of an eye or a hand. Another cell changes to become heart, bone or muscle tissue. It is all very magical and mysterious.

The **placenta** is a soft spongy organ which grows from the uterus wall. It contains blood vessels of the mother and of the embryo. But the blood of the mother and embryo *do not mix*. They remain separate systems. All the substances which the embryo needs: oxygen, food and hormones, are filtered through fine membranes in the placenta from the mother's blood to the embryo.

The **umbilical** cord is a thick rope of blood vessels which takes the substances from the placenta to the embryo. They travel to the tiny heart which pumps them around the body. The waste products of metabolism are collected up and taken back to the placenta through the umbilical cord. The embryo is protected in a bag of waters named the **amniotic sac**. These three structures begin to develop in the first weeks of life.

At about three weeks, the embryo is 4 mm long and the tiny heart begins to beat. By six weeks, the shapes of arms, feet and eyes are forming. By eight weeks, the embryo is 3 to 4 cm long and weighs 1 g. The lungs, liver, kidneys and brain are developing. The face can be seen more clearly; foot and palm prints appear; even the nails are growing.

The foetus

From three months to birth, the new life is named a **foetus**, which means a 'young one'. By four months, the teeth are forming, the heart beat can be heard and many reflexes are present. From five to six months, the foetus sucks its thumb, yawns, hiccups, turns over, swallows a little amniotic fluid and may urinate into it. The mother feels strong kicking movements as the foetus stretches its limbs. The father can see and feel these movements. In the last weeks, the foetus grows plumper and lies head downwards in preparation for birth.

As the foetus grows larger, so does the placenta and cord. At birth the placenta weighs 450 g and measures 20 cm across, the size of a large dinner plate. The umbilical cord is 50 cm long.

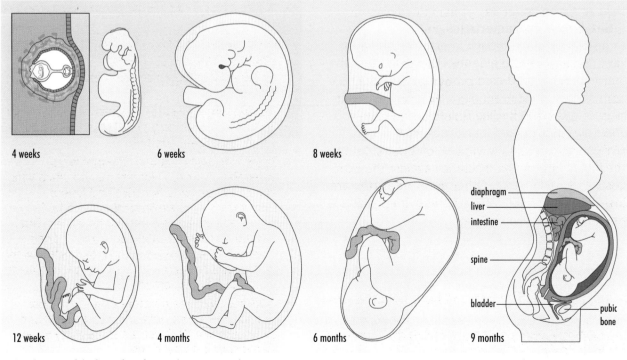

4 weeks   6 weeks   8 weeks

12 weeks   4 months   6 months   9 months

diaphragm
liver
intestine
spine
bladder
pubic bone

■ Development of the foetus from four weeks to nine months

▬ *Investigation* ▬

Carry out the following investigation to gain some idea of uterine weight.

You will need:

a tape measure, weight scales.

a Identify some objects which weigh 1 g.

b Identify objects weighing the same as a full term placenta.

c Identify items which measure 50 cm in length.

d Package an item which weighs the same as a foetus at birth.

Twins

If two eggs ripen in one month, each can be fertilized by two different sperm. The two embryos inherit two different sets of genes. When they implant in the uterus, each forms a separate placenta and cord. The babies are **fraternal** twins, and can be two sisters, two brothers, or a sister and brother.

One egg fertilized by one sperm can suddenly divide into two. The two embryos have the same genes and so are **identical** twins. When they implant in the uterus, they share one placenta. Identical twins have the same gender.

Another name for identical twins is **uniovular** twins because they come from the same egg. Fraternal twins are called **binovular** because they come from two different eggs. Twins occur about once in every 100 births, triplets once in every 7569 births; sextuplets once in every 5 million births. Some parents with twins on both sides of the family take out an insurance against the extra cost of multiple births. Other **multiple births** are increasing as a result of the fertility drugs which ripen many eggs.

▬ *Child observation* ▬

Record any twins or other multiple births in the child's family.

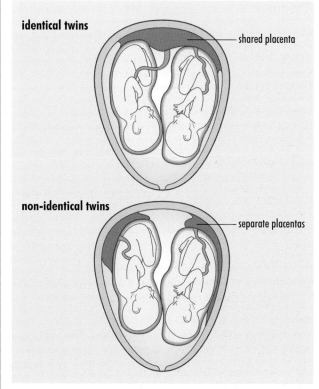

■ The contents of the uterus for identical and fraternal twins

▬ *Questions* ▬

1 Describe how the new life develops during the first four months of pregnancy.

2 Explain clearly how the foetus gains its nourishment.

3 Describe the contents of the uterus for fraternal twins and explain why such twins can be the same or different genders.

4 Twins Jim Lewis and Jim Springer were separated at birth. They first met 40 years later. They had the same hairstyle and type of moustache, wore similar clothes and had similar social attitudes and moral values. Both worked as fitters of safety equipment. Their wives had the same first name, their sons were named James Allan and James Alan, and each family had a dog named Toy.

   Fraternal twins are no more alike than other siblings. Give your opinion as to whether Jim Lewis and Jim Springer are more likely to be identical or fraternal twins.

'The health of a nation depends upon the health of its women.'

D. Baldwin

Pre-conceptual care

Most babies are born perfectly healthy. But **birth defects** do occur, and the time of greatest risk is during the embryo stage. Some birth defects are **genetic**. Others are *preventable*, they can be avoided. For example, new research is finding a link between prolonged heat for the mother (saunas, jacuzzis, long hot baths) and birth defects.

The adult body can tolerate many poisons that the delicate new life cannot. A woman may have no idea she has substances in her blood which can harm her baby. Though the placenta is a splendid filter, it cannot keep back all harmful substances. The toxins in alcohol, nicotine, drugs and medicines; the germs of rubella and chicken pox; environmental pollutants such as lead, certain chemicals and radiation (including X-rays); all these can damage the delicate new life.

A woman visits her doctor to have her pregnancy confirmed an average six weeks after a missed period. But this is half way through an embryo's life. So a couple planning their family need to plan for a healthy lifestyle before the woman conceives. This is called **pre-conceptual care**.

Health authorities suggest that pre-conceptual care begins three months *before trying for a baby*. This allows time for any problems which might be found to be sorted out. If the couple are using the birth control pill, the woman stops taking it, and this allows time for her own hormone cycle to settle down.

Screening tests

A couple with a family history of inherited disease can visit the **genetic counselling clinic**. The chances of passing on the disease are analysed by computer and the results enable the couple to make decisions about starting a family.

The **rubella** virus can pass through the placenta. A **blood test** screens for antibodies to rubella. If there are no antibodies, the vaccination must be given three months before trying to conceive. Immunizations against measles, mumps and hepatitis may be advised.

The role of the father

A father begins supporting his child by supporting his partner at the pre-conception stage. The stress of an unplanned pregnancy, the lack of emotional or economic support, can lower the health of mother and child. This is not always the case, but unsupported mothers have a higher rate of sickness in pregnancy. They suffer more miscarriages and terminations of pregnancy. Their babies have a higher rate of premature birth and infant death. Their children have a greater risk of accidents and ill-health.

The father can improve his health and so improve the health of his sperm. If he and his partner work together, planning for a healthy baby becomes a happy activity, a shared goal.

A healthy lifestyle

A healthy lifestyle avoids the use of illegal substances. Cocaine and heroin increase the chance of miscarriage, premature labour, stillbirth and infant death. Other illegal drugs are linked with low birthweight and birth defects.

Drinking

A unit of alcohol is 8 g of pure alcohol. This is equivalent to a half pint of ordinary strength beer, a pub measure of spirits or a glass of wine. The recommended maximum amounts per day are 3 units for women and 4 units for men. Above these sensible limits alcohol may be related to stress, social problems and or ill health.

In the last weeks before birth, the foetus develops its lung muscles by 'breathing' movements. A Hammersmith Hospital study monitored this 'breathing' in six foetuses. When the mother drank orange juice, the foetus 'breathed' 46 per cent of the time. When vodka was added to the juice, the foetus 'breathed' 14 per cent of the time.

Smoking

Heavy smoking is defined as 20 or more cigarettes per day. Smoking can lead to lung cancer, respiratory disease and heart disease. Nicotine speeds up the foetal heart rate. Carbon monoxide reduces the volume of oxygen in the blood. There is a:

- greater risk of complications during the birth
- higher risk of a premature baby
- higher risk of low birthweight. Infants of women who smoke are, on average, 200 g lighter than they should be.

Caffeine

During pregnancy, the liver takes longer to break down the drug **caffeine** in coffee, tea or cola drinks. It can stay in the body and cause a sensitive reaction. Reducing caffeine intake at pre-conception helps reduce any craving for it in pregnancy.

Exercise

Regular exercise is part of a healthy lifestyle. It improves the working of all body systems, keeps body weight in proportion to height and builds and tones the muscles. Walking and swimming are excellent ways to strengthen the muscles of the abdomen, lower back and legs for a more comfortable pregnancy.

Posture

Posture is the way people carry themselves. A pregnant woman has to carry a baby as well. The increasing weight of the foetus is carried more easily if the woman stands and sits with her weight evenly balanced. If she slouches, an extra strain is

■ Swimming is an excellent way to exercise at any time. It also helps with menstrual cramps and PMS

placed on the muscles of support. Good or poor posture is a *habit*. Poor posture is common during puberty while people are adjusting to their new height and body shape.

The goals of pre-conceptual care

Pre-conceptual care is carried out in order to:

- build up the couple's general health
- check the woman's diet, exercise, rest and sleep patterns
- analyse risk factors such as infections and inherited defects
- identify issues such as health medication or drug abuse
- promote a healthy pregnancy and reduce the risk of complications at birth
- enable the arrival of a healthy baby at full term.

Questions

1. Name three toxic substances which can pass through the placenta and the stage of greatest risk for the unborn baby.
2. Suggest a contraceptive method during pre-conceptual care.
3. Write about
   a. the placenta's ability to filter out alcohol
   b. the effects of smoking on the foetus
   c. a woman's choice to improve her health pre-pregnancy.

Eating well before pregnancy is as important as eating well during it. A deficiency of one food may be noticed only after the embryo stage. **Pica** is a craving for unusual foods or strange substances. For example, a craving for chalk may mean a shortage of calcium and/or vitamin D. A craving for soil may mean a deficiency of other essential minerals.

Vitamin supplements may reduce the risk of major birth defects, such as cleft palate, limb deficiencies and heart malformations. A study from Hungary of more than 4000 pregnancies found that the rate of major (and minor) birth defects was lower among women taking a multi-vitamin supplement. Too much vitamin A can harm the foetus. Checking the diet for foods high in vitamins and minerals at pre-conception is the natural way to boost health before pregnancy.

Folate is essential for cell division. Cells divide most rapidly during the embryo stage. Because not all pregnancies are planned, women of child-bearing age are advised to take 0.4 mg (milligrams) of folate daily, even if the diet is balanced. This reduces the risk of spina bifida and other nervous system defects. Folate and vitamin B12 interact. A deficiency of one can lead to a deficiency of both.

Good sources of folate are fresh or frozen vegetables, especially green leafy ones, yeast extract, citrus and other fruits, chick peas, nuts, eggs and wholemeal bread.

■ Why is this woman eating coal?

Fatty acids help the baby's nervous system develop normally. The World Health Organization (WHO) found that pregnant or breast-feeding women need at least 2 g of fatty acids daily. A diet rich in milk and cheese provides enough fatty acids and calcium for both mother and child.

Iron pills may be advised to supplement a pregnant woman's diet. The unborn baby builds up a store of iron in its blood, liver, spleen and muscles. If the mother does not eat enough iron-rich foods, the baby's supply will still be stored, but the woman will become anaemic. *Nature makes sure the baby's needs come first!*

Hygiene in food preparation is especially important. **Listeria** are deadly food-poisoning bacteria which can cause miscarriages and stillbirths. The bacteria are more common in some soft cheeses, cook-chill foods, chickens and pates. Newborns can die from listeria. Others suffer serious effects, including brain-damage.

Dental care

The two hormones, oestrogen and progesterone, play different roles in pregnancy. Their balance is also different and expectant mothers are more at risk of developing gum disease (gingivitis). This shows as streaks of blood on the toothbrush or as reddened puffy gums. Oral hygiene is always important, but more so in pregnancy. The dentist or dental hygienist will clear any infection and give advice on future care.

Work and rest

A woman who works outside the home can begin to make plans for **maternity leave**. Some women have less energy and cut down their work to part-time because they need more rest. Others continue in full-time employment until a few weeks before the estimated date of the birth.

Weight gain

A pregnant woman needs 15 per cent more calories in her daily diet. Her healthy weight gain over the 40 weeks of pregnancy is 10 to 12.5 kg. This gain is due to her increased breast size, the

Start each day the healthy way

Birth defects by weight (number per 1000 live births, in the UK)	
Weight of baby (grams)	*Number of babies with defects per 1000 live births*
Under 1500	16
1500–2000	13
2000–2500	6
2500–4000	3

Although the baby's nutritional needs come first, they cannot be fully met if Irma is not eating well. The lower the birthweight of her baby, the greater the risk of birth defect.

Low birthweight

Fifty per cent of low birthweight babies have some mental slowness, and three times the chance of epilepsy, cerebral palsy, and learning or behaviour problems. In general, doctors do not try to save babies under 500 g. But a baby weighing 283 g at birth has been saved and is mentally normal. She is 'a miracle of nursing skills and reproductive technology'.

layer of fat which builds for making milk and the weight of the foetus, placenta, cord and amniotic fluid. After the first three months, appetite often increases. This increase remains up to the birth and during breast-feeding.

Reasons for low weight gain include poor diet, stress, over-exercise, smoking, drinking and problems of foetal development. The woman's attitude may be involved. Irma is 1.6 m tall, weighs 44.5 kg and likes being thin. She reduces her diet further because she thinks a small baby will reduce the risk of a painful birth.

In fact, Irma is increasing her risk of a difficult birth. A malnourished uterus may not work well and her labour could be prolonged or even stop.

— Child observation

Ask about any pica the child's mother may have had. Pool the class findings to find out if a lack of one particular nutrient can be identified.

— Questions

1 Obtain the booklet 'Babies and benefits' (see page 190). Investigate the help and benefits available to women. Make notes on the special benefits available to families on low incomes and those with disabilities. You can extend this investigation by conducting a survey into women's opinions of these benefits.

2 Explain why weight gain is checked throughout pregnancy.

3 Diane is 1.5 m and weighs 73 kg when her baby is conceived. At full term, she weighs 91 kg. What was her weight gain? List some likely reasons for it. Name foods which satisfy hunger, are high in nutritional value, yet should avoid excess weight gain.

4 Plan a diet and exercise programme for Diane to avoid excess weight gain in pregnancy.

5 Explain the meaning of 'Nature makes sure the baby's needs come first'.

The signs of pregnancy

The first signs of pregnancy include some or all of the following:

- menstruation stops; no more periods until after the birth
- tingling and swelling of breasts; nipples darken
- feeling and/or being sick; metal taste in the mouth
- needing to urinate more often; being constipated
- feeling tired; needing more rest and sleep.

── Investigation ──

Investigate information leaflets about pregnancy testing kits.

You will need:

various leaflets about brands of DIY testing kits.

- a Compare brand names, packaging, labelling, quantity, prices.
- b Identify which hormone in urine is measured and why.
- c Note the instructions for proper urine collection.
- d How long after a missed period should the test be done?
- e State the degree of reliability the manufacturers promise.
- f Not all women have regular periods. Should the test be done once? more often? Why?

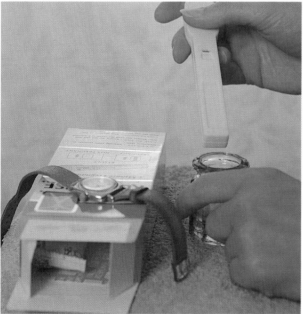

■ When a period is missed, a woman can test her urine at home

The family doctor

The woman visits her family doctor to have her pregnancy confirmed. An appointment is then made for her to visit the ante-natal clinic. The name for a birth is **delivery**. The delivery date is estimated (EDD) by adding 40 weeks to the first day of the woman's last period. The family doctor keeps in contact with the progress of her pregnancy and checks her health records from the ante-natal clinic.

At the ante-natal clinic

Pregnancy is a time of being well, not ill. The expectant mother is a client of the clinic staff, not a patient. She meets the **midwife**, a nurse with specialist training in pregnancy, birth and after care. Together they make plans for the birth (unit 90).

The midwife needs detailed information on the following:

- Medical history – to identify any allergies, epilepsy, asthma, diabetes, drug therapy, heart problems and so on.
- Family history – to identify any of the above in the family and any risk of a serious genetic disease.
- Present history – to identify any problems such as blood loss, pain, unexpected vomiting.
- Cultural and social history – to identify any special needs of the family-to-be (unit 89).

The Rhesus factor

There are four main blood groups: A, B, O and AB. There is also a factor in blood which is either **Rhesus positive** (Rh+) or **Rhesus negative** (Rh−). These two factors are not compatible. Only about 15 per cent of people are Rh−. A woman who is Rh− may have a baby who is Rh+. First babies are not affected since the mother's and baby's blood do not mix. But the two bloods can mix during a birth and the mother's blood may build up antibodies which damage any later babies. After the first birth, the mother may need an injection of Anti–D (anti-Rhesus factor). In cases where the Rh− factor is not detected, the baby can have mild anaemia or be so ill that a complete change of blood by transfusion is essential.

Screening tests

A **blood sample** identifies the woman's blood group and Rhesus factor. The blood sample is also screened for:

a anaemia – in which case iron supplements are required

b antibodies to rubella

c sickle-cell anaemia and beta-thalassemia

d syphilis – a GU disease

e hepatitis B – a liver disease which can affect the foetus

f alpha fetoprotein – which is linked to spina bifida (a disorder of the backbone) and Down's syndrome

g Down's syndrome. The Bart's (Triple) test calculates the risk of this condition. This test is offered to women over 35.

A urine sample checks the sugar level for diabetes. The woman's diet is changed or she may need medication. A healthy placenta produces hormones, and these are checked in the urine sample.

An **ultrasound scan** beams sound waves of high intensity through the abdomen wall into the uterus, The sound waves form an image of the foetus on a monitor. The ultrasound scan is done at sixteen to eighteen weeks. It measures the size of the foetus and its position in the uterus; detects twins or more; checks the foetal organs for any defects; and records the position of the placenta.

Record keeping

The **CliniCard** is the new high-tech way to keep all this information together. It looks like a credit card but acts like a computer disk. At each visit the CliniCard data is displayed on a television monitor. The woman's weight increase, **fundal height** (the size of the uterus related to foetal growth) and test results are updated and plotted against graphs of expected health. Reminders to test for anaemia are displayed at 26 and 34 weeks. Any risk factors found at the first visit are displayed at each new visit and can be checked. A print-out is made of the updated CliniCard data for the couple to examine at home (see unit 92).

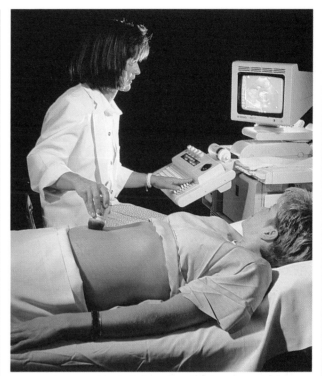

■ An ultrasound scan is usually done around sixteen weeks

Classes

Couples are offered **parenthood education** organized by the local health authority and run by the midwife or health visitor. The classes teach relaxation and breathing skills to help at birth, and information on breast-feeding, hygiene, safety and child development.

═ *Questions* ═

1 Name which tests in this unit can be done at pre-pregnancy.

2 'The most reliable sign of pregnancy is a missed period.' Give reasons why you agree or disagree with this statement.

3 Why is the Bart's (Triple) test offered to women over 35?

4 Suggest three ways in which parenthood education is important for parents.

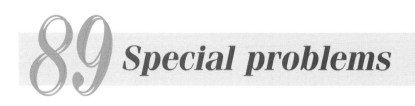

Miscarriage and ectopic pregnancy

The medical name for a miscarriage is a **spontaneous abortion**. When this happens the foetus is expelled from the uterus and the pregnancy ends. Up to 60 per cent of miscarriages are due to serious defects in the foetus. An **ectopic pregnancy** is one where the embryo grows inside the fallopian tube. This can happen when there is a blockage in the tube and the fertilized egg is trapped and begins to grow there. As the embryo gets larger, the walls of the tube burst. The symptoms are bleeding from the vagina and severe pain on one side of the lower abdomen. Medical help is needed urgently to stop the bleeding and remove the embryo. After the surgery, there is a 50 per cent chance the damaged tube is permanently blocked. The woman remains fertile if her other tube is healthy. Ectopic pregnancies are on the increase, partly due to the increase in GU diseases which cause scarring.

Screening for women at risk of birth defects

1 Amniocentesis removes a sample of amniotic fluid for screening. A needle is put through the

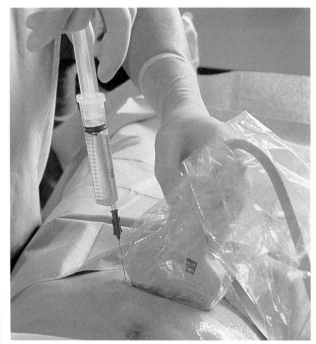

■ Amniocentisis test in progress

abdomen into the uterus and a little fluid is drawn out to be tested for Down's syndrome, haemophilia, spina bifida and muscular dystrophy. Amniocentesis is done at 16–20 weeks. Not all defects can be detected and it can cause miscarriage.

2 Chorionic villus sampling (CVS) removes tissue from the implantation site for screening. A tube is put through the cervix and tissue is cut from the site. CVS is offered in early pregnancy, at eight to ten weeks, and can detect more defects than other screening. But it has a higher risk of miscarriage than amniocentesis.

Both these tests are offered only to women over 35, to those with a partner or family history of genetic disease or to those with an abnormal result in another test.

Eclampsia (toxaemia)

At each visit to the ante-natal clinic **blood pressure** is checked for **pre-eclampsia**, a serious condition of later pregnancy. The symptoms are high blood pressure, headaches and vision upset. **Eclampsia** (or toxaemia) affects all organs and can lead to kidney failure. In the UK ten mothers and 1000 babies die each year, but many more are saved by ante-natal care.

Late booking

'Booking' means having the pregnancy confirmed by the doctor and making firm plans with the midwife about where the baby is to be born. The death rate of babies is five times higher when mothers are late in booking. During pregnancy, women should visit the clinic at first every four weeks, then every two weeks and, in the last month, every week. The reasons for late booking include:
- not understanding the need for ante-natal care
- being unable to afford travelling time or expense
- being a young single girl terrified of her parents finding out
- being too confused and unhappy over an unwanted pregnancy to care what happens
- being a mother already and thinking one pregnancy is much like another.

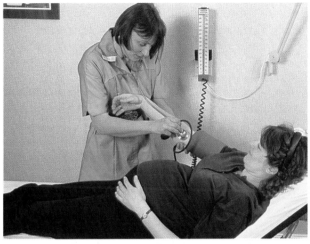

■ An appointment at the ante-natal clinic

The whole person

A healthy pregnancy and birth involves more than just physical care. The woman's emotional and social care are important. At the clinic, she meets other women in the same condition and this may help her accept the idea of becoming a mother. The midwife's concern may also switch on the mother's concern. If there are problems at home, the different people working in health and social welfare can help.

The whole family

'The more involved an expectant father, the more involved he will be when the baby is born.'

Zeta is thrilled to be pregnant. She rings her own and Karim's parents with the exciting news.

Karim only hears he is to be a father when his father rings to congratulate him. On the way home, he buys Zeta flowers and a book on pregnancy. She says, 'Don't waste money. Sell the car so I can buy smart baby things. Do more overtime. Otherwise, I don't need your help. Pregnancy is a woman's business.' Suggest some likely consequences of Zeta's attitude.

Support in pregnancy

The **family doctor** or GP (general practitioner) confirms the pregnancy, and writes a certificate of expected confinement (birth).

The **midwife** specializes in hospital and home childbirth. She sees the mother before, during and for a few days after the birth.

The **health visitor** specializes in child and family health. She visits the home regularly after the birth.

The **social worker** specializes in family rights and welfare. She provides practical and legal help to families in difficulties.

The **home help** shops and cleans the home for the new mother if she is sick or disabled.

The **obstetrician** is a doctor who specializes in pregnancy and childbirth in ante-natal clinics and operating theatres.

The **gynaecologist** is a doctor specializing in the reproductive health of women. Maternity units in hospitals are part of OB/GYN departments.

The **paediatrician** is a doctor specializing in child health who helps if there is something wrong with the baby at birth.

▬ *Questions* ▬

1 Try to invite one of the above people to give a talk on her/his work. Prepare questions about what she or he does.

2 Create and role-play a scene in which the father of a three year old prepares his child for the new baby.

3 If a woman of child-bearing age has pain and bleeding, what should she suspect? State what life-saving steps she must take.

4 Explain why a miscarriage can be a 'blessing in disguise'?

5 Give five reasons why ante-natal care is valuable.

6 Visit a maternity shop or use mail-order catalogues. Choose, with reasons, a maternity outfit suitable for a working mother.

Labour is the process of giving birth. The couple can draw up a birth plan long before labour begins.

- The father makes sure he can be contacted at all times.
- They keep the numbers of other family members by the telephone.
- They plan the quickest route to the hospital or clinic.
- They check the taxi firm or keep the car topped up with petrol!
- They put new film in the camera and collect plenty of small change for phone calls.

Home or hospital birth?

In 1987 the National Perinatal Epidemiology Unit studied hospital and home births. It found no scientific support for the belief that hospital is the safest place to give birth. One in ten people contracts an infection while in hospital. The newborn and elderly are particularly at risk. However, lives are undoubtedly saved when things go wrong.

Some women feel safer surrounded by friendly hospital staff and the new birth technologies. For them, a home birth could be frightening. Other women find hospitals cold, impersonal places. They dislike foetal monitoring (see unit 91), and fear loss of control. These negative feelings can start or add to problems in labour. For these women, more complications can happen in hospital than at home.

Water births can be in the hospital birthing pool or at home in a large rubber pool. The woman relaxes in the warm water and finds this soothing. Home births are not advised for a first baby, in case of complications.

First signs of labour

There are three signs of labour, they usually happen in the following order.

1 Contractions These are squeezing waves of muscles of the uterus. Contractions can begin a few weeks before the real event. They do not become regular for longer than an hour. If the woman relaxes and has a warm bath they are likely

■ Some women find giving birth in water is more soothing

to stop and she knows this is a false alarm. Labour is under way (established) when the contractions come regularly at ten to fifteen minutes, or when they become strong and painful.

2 A show The placenta separates from the uterus wall, and the plug of mucus which blocked the cervix passes down the vagina as a small 'show' of blood. The foetus is no longer protected from germs.

3 Waters breaking The bag of waters breaks and the amniotic fluid flows or trickles out. Again, the foetus is no longer protected.

The three stages of labour

The first stage is the longest, especially for a first baby, it often takes more than twelve hours from the onset of established labour. The cervix has to 'ripen'. It must soften and thin before it can stretch to the 10 cm necessary for the baby to enter the birth canal (vagina). This is named **dilation**.

As the contractions speed up in time and intensity, the woman can feel slightly alarmed. The father's presence can provide practical help as well as emotional support. He can help the mother breathe properly through each contraction. He boosts her confidence by holding her hand, giving back rubs, sips of water or juice, or, just by being there.

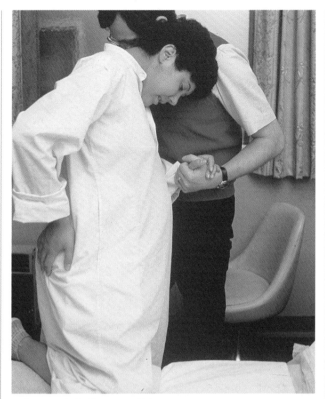

■ A woman in the first stage of labour

The second stage of labour is the **birth** itself. This is the quickest yet hardest part because the baby must be pushed out. The midwife works with the mother, checking the infant's progress and telling the mother when to push. The baby's head appears first, and the shoulders and body follow quickly after.

The third stage is the **afterbirth**. The placenta, umbilical cord and amniotic sac are expelled about 20 minutes later. Many hospitals speed up this process by injection to reduce the risk of post-natal haemorrhage. The shot is given at the time of birth and causes a rapid and prolonged contraction of the uterus. Women who plan a natural childbirth can discuss this with their midwife and exclude it from their birth plan. The afterbirth is checked to make sure that all the contents have come away.

Pain relief

A woman may plan to avoid using **pain relief** because the drugs pass through the placenta and affect the foetus. Newborns can be 'floppy', sleepy and limp, with low or unsteady **vital signs** (blood pressure, heart and breathing rate). Very few births are completely pain-free. When pain relief is required, women need to understand that they have not failed some test of courage or endurance. This mistaken idea can add emotional distress to a labour which has begun to cause physical distress.

Gas is the first choice of pain relief as the woman remains in control. It is a mixture of oxygen and nitrous oxide breathed in through a hand-held mask. The woman decides when she needs the gas and when she can manage on her own. Other choices of pain-relief include injection of a painkiller into a muscle and **epidural block**. An epidural is an injection of local anaesthetic into the fluid around the spinal cord. The nerves below that point are blocked and the local anaesthetic allows the woman to experience birth.

— *Child observation*

Record which choice of pain-relief or other details of the child's birth the parents may wish to discuss.

■ *Questions*

1 Sue's waters break at 9 p.m. She telephones the hospital and is told to come in. Identify the material resources she needs for her comfort and hygiene during a three-day stay in hospital.

2 Explain why the midwife or hospital must be informed when any one of the signs of labour begins.

3 It is thought fathers bond more strongly with their babies when they witness the miracle of birth. Give your opinion of the father being in the delivery room.

4 Investigate natural childbirth and breathing techniques. You may wish to survey the opinions of mothers too.

Foetal monitoring

The stages of labour can be monitored by bands strapped around the mother's abdomen. One band is pressure sensitive and records the strength and frequency of the contractions. Another records the responses of the foetus on ultrasound. Foetal monitoring gives useful information, but it prevents the woman moving freely. If she had planned to be mobile, she may feel she has lost control of her birth plan.

Possible complications

Induction If the baby is very late, or there is risk to the woman or child's health, labour can be induced (started). This is done by breaking the waters, by putting a hormone pessary of oxytocin in the vagina or a hormone drip in the arm.

Episiotomy If the opening of the vagina cannot widen enough to let the baby's head through, it can tear in uneven edges. An episiotomy is a surgical cut to stop the vagina tearing in ragged edges, and is stitched up after the birth.

Forceps delivery If the baby is distressed (short of oxygen), it can be pulled out by forceps placed on the head. Another method is by **ventouse extraction**. This is a suction cap which fits on the baby's head to pull it out. Forceps can also be used if the birth is **breech**, (the bottom comes first) or the contractions are too weak to push the baby out.

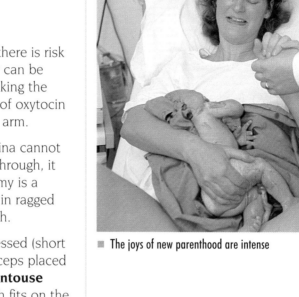
■ The joys of new parenthood are intense

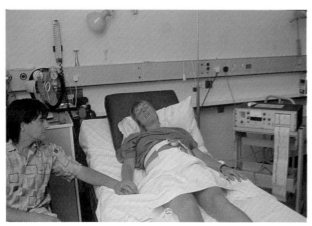
■ The baby's heartbeat is recorded on the foetal monitor

Caesarean section If there are serious health reasons for a quick delivery, the baby is removed by surgery. The woman's abdomen wall and uterus are opened and the baby is lifted out. Caesarean sections are major operations and women need a longer stay in hospital to heal and recover their strength.

All surgery carries a risk of complications. In 1988 in the UK, the Maternity Alliance found 'An all-time high of caesarean births, some 75,000 yearly or 11.3 per cent. This rose to over 13 per cent by 1994.' The concern is whether or not this increase is really necessary.

However a baby is born, the joys of new parenthood are intense. Fathers tend to weep. Mothers laugh and cry at the same time. The medical staff beam with delight and offer their congratulations. The delivery room is a very happy place.

Baby blues

The joys of seeing the new baby are intense, yet during the week after birth up to 80 per cent of mothers feel miserable. The baby blues can make a woman anxious, tense, confused. She may sleep less well, lose concentration, forget things, burst into tears for no obvious reason. She may even say she hates the baby. Yet she holds her child close and nurtures it with tender loving care. In turn, her partner's support can be of great help during this unsettled time.

The baby blues are a mild depression lasting a few hours or a few days. But if a woman is not prepared for them, she can suffer guilty feelings too. She is ashamed of her behaviour. She thinks she is 'unnatural' as a mother because she expected to be blissfully happy once her baby was in her arms. The baby blues can slow down the process of bonding if the mother does not know that they will soon pass.

Post-natal depression

One in ten women suffers post-natal depression. This is a serious illness and the woman may hide her feelings for as long as she can. Unlike the baby blues, post-natal depression starts slowly in the weeks or even months after the birth. But in a few cases, it is caused by the normal baby blues which do not go away but become worse as time goes by.

It is terrible for a woman to feel she cannot love her baby. But depressed people are too ill to help themselves. They live in a world of dark confused pain. On better days, they understand how much the baby needs their love, their warmth, their comfort and protection. This adds to the pain and makes the condition worse. If help is not available, the infants of these mothers tend to become very withdrawn.

A woman's health

It can be seen that the health of women – both physical and psychological – is of critical importance to the health of future generations. Mothers are at their most dependent with a new baby. The sense of responsibility which occurs at bonding can feel overwhelming. Pregnancy and birth are events of tense excitement, high expectations and real-life drama. No amount of preparation can prepare a woman for these actual experiences. Many women stay calm during pregnancy, partly due to changes in their hormone levels. But labour and birth, and the fact that life will never be the same again, are events which have a profound impact on women.

Role-play the following scenes, each of which can have a deep emotional impact on a woman.
- A woman first tells her partner she is pregnant.
- She tells her mother, family and close friend.
- She finds her skirt size no longer fits.
- She waits in a hospital queue for a screening test.
- She begins 'comparison shopping' for baby equipment.
- She changes her hairstyle to draw attention away from her size.
- She says farewell to her colleagues at work.
- She prepares her personal things to take to hospital.
- She experiences her first contractions.
- She realizes that she needs pain-relief.
- She and her partner gaze at their new baby.

▬ *Questions* ▬

1 Find out the number of students in the class who were born in hospital.
2 Give the meanings of
  a foetal monitoring
  b induction
  c breech birth
  d post-natal depression.

3 Most mothers recover quickly from the baby blues. Name three factors which are likely to help.
4 Suggest, with reasons, why an unplanned pregnancy and/or birth complications might make the baby blues worse.

Happy ever after

Post-natal checks

The new baby is examined soon after the birth to make sure all is well (see unit 48). The mother's post-natal check-up is performed four to six weeks after the birth. Her blood pressure, urine and weight are checked to make sure all is well. The uterus is measured to check it is returning to its normal size and the muscles are recovering their strength.

Post-natal exercises help a woman regain her figure and her strength more quickly. As she becomes fitter, she feels more confident of tackling her new role as a mother.

Advice on birth control is provided either before the mother leaves hospital, or during her post-natal check-up. The Pill is not recommended during breast-feeding. It reduces the milk supply and the hormones can pass into the baby's system. A safer choice is the low dose progesterone-only 'mini-pill'.

Breast-feeding reduces the risk of becoming pregnant again. The hormone prolactin may be responsible for this. A woman must fully breast-feed and avoid giving supplements of formula milk. But the risk of pregnancy is only reduced. It is not completely removed. The reasons for this are not well understood.

During nursing, women are advised to avoid any medication not prescribed by the doctor. There is always a risk of even mild drugs being passed to the baby in breast milk. The mother must follow the same diet regime as during her pregnancy. If her baby cries between feeds, this may be a sign that she needs to boost her nutritional intake, particularly at the evening meal. She must also continue to take care of her general health.

The new family

The health visitor cares for the new family and offers advice on any feeding problems, hygiene concerns, crying and so on. At the same time, she notes the home interaction, how each member of the family responds to the new baby. Parenthood involves a great change in lifestyle because the baby's needs come first. Mother and father have to learn new management and coping skills. Their parents have to learn new grandparenting skills.

Older siblings have to learn new sharing skills. The health visitor can offer advice if some family members feel unhappy during these changes.

The CliniCard

The baby's progress is reviewed at 10 to 14 days, at 6 weeks, at 3 to 4 months, at 6 to 9 months and at 18 to 24 months. These reviews may take place at the Well-baby clinic or at the doctor's surgery. The baby receives its immunizations. The sensory system is checked for any sight, hearing, speech or other impairments. The child's progress chart is updated. The family doctor plays an important role in the new family's health and, in these ways, a child's physical, intellectual, emotional and social history is slowly built up. At school entry, the child's health is checked again. In the near future, the foetal history from the CliniCard will form the start of the person's health history throughout life and may all be kept on the same computer card.

Attitudes to parenthood

A group of mothers were asked to read and discuss the following two quotes.

'For centuries, men have been taught that child care is woman's work. Much of this teaching came from women themselves. Mothers jealously guard their role as sole carer by building a mystique

■ A high-tech way of keeping records up-to-date

surrounding "the womb". Today's man is slowly learning to change his attitude and become involved in family life. This is not made easy by a new mother who snatches back her baby, or jeers at his attempts at nursing the child.'

(Record your immediate feelings about this quote.)

'Men still rule the roost! Today's mothers complain that modern men have become "the great experts" in baby care. Fathers give strict instructions to their partners on proper child-rearing methods. They then blame the mother when the baby cries. This undermines a new mother's confidence in handling her baby.'

(Record your immediate responses to this quote.)

The women were very divided in their responses. One group found both quotes typical of the way new parents behave. They wanted all couples planning to have a baby to be forced to read them. Then both partners could know exactly what to expect.

The other group said that they did not know any parents who behaved like that nowadays. They found both quotes insensitive, sexist and deeply offensive. They thought both were likely to do more harm than good and neither had any place in building a happy family life.

Comment on the responses of each group. Compare them with your own. If yours are different and original, you may wish to share them in class. Prepare a full debate for later on.

■ Dad changes the nappy

Fathers

Recent studies into fatherhood have found that many men become anxious for their partners during pregnancy and birth. This anxiety often increases when the mother and baby arrive home. The anxiety was the result of the men feeling helpless. They could share their partner's joys, but not her worry or pain. They hid their feelings because they believed a man's job is to be the 'rock' of support in his woman's life. Do you agree with this view? Explain the reasons for your opinion.

— Questions

1 Name four checks on a **a** baby's health and **b** a woman's health during their post-natal care.

2 Select, with reasons, one method of contraception suitable for a couple with a six-week-old baby.

3 Suggest ways in which a father can become involved in the new family at each of the following times:
   a during the mother's pregnancy
   b during the birth
   c during the early weeks of a baby's life
   d during the child's second and third year
   e when the child reaches school age.

4 What does the 'battle of the sexes' mean? Do you think it has a place in family life? Give reasons for your answer.

5 Describe the roles of the midwife and health visitor.

6 Explain in as much detail as you can the value to the parent and child of regular attendance at Well-baby clinics.

List of resources

1 **Health Education Authority** publishes free leaflets on a wide range of health issues and child-care topics. You can get copies from your local **Health Education Unit**. Find the address in your local phone book.

2 **Ministry of Agriculture, Fisheries and Food** (MAFF) has free booklets on 'Food Safety', 'Healthy Eating', 'Eight Guidelines for a Healthy Diet', 'Understanding Food Labels', 'About Food Additives', 'The New Microwave Labels'. They are all available free from Food Sense, MAFF Publications, London SE99, London SE99 7TT. Tel: 0181 694 8862

3 **Department of Health** has a free booklet 'While you are Pregnant: safe eating and how to avoid infection from food and animals' which you can get from your local Health Education Unit.

4 **Department of Social Security** (DSS) has free leaflets on the rights of parents and children. 'Babies and benefits: A guide for expectant and new mothers' is particularly useful.

5 Your local **Post Office** has the free DSS and other leaflets.

6 Your **local authority** has the DSS and other leaflets. It also provides free speakers on Home Safety and many other topics.

7 **St John Ambulance Service** may provide free speakers and training courses in First Aid.

8 Your **local library** has sections on child health, nutrition, early learning and emotional development, pregnancy and birth.

9 **The Consumers Association** produces a monthly magazine *Which*? with information on child-care products and services. Your local library stocks *Which*? and may stock some parenthood magazines.

10 **Commercial companies** such as Nestlé, Cow and Gate, Clarks shoes, Kiddicraft Toys, Creda and many more, may provide free speakers, videos and/or leaflets of their products and services.

11 **Office of Fair Trading** has free leaflets on consumer issues.

12 **Department of Trade and Industry** has a free leaflet 'Keep your baby safe' (nursery equipment) from DTI Promotions, Measham Handling Centre, PO Box 100, Swadlincote, Derbyshire DE12 7DR.
The staff and parents at Well Baby Clinics, Mother and Toddler Groups, Pre-School Playgroups and Nursery Schools may help with your **observations** and **surveys**. Ask when they might be available. Prepare your questions fully before keeping your appointment.

Support groups

Some support groups are voluntary. They may or may not have free leaflets and speakers. If the address is in your phone book, there is a local branch. If not, ask directory enquiries.

Association for Shared Parenting
Association of British Adoption and Fostering
    Agencies
Attachment Disorder Parents Network
British Diabetic Association
British Pregnancy Advisory Service
Brook Advisory Centres: Sex counselling for young
    people
Child Accident Prevention Trust
Cystic Fibrosis Research Trust
Disablement Information and Advice
Down's Babies Association
Families Need Fathers
Family Planning Association: Free advice on sex and
    sexual health issues, including contraception
Haemophilia Society
Hyperactive Children's Support Group
La Leche League: breast-feeding support group
National Asthma Campaign
National Campaign for Nursery Education
National Childbirth Trust: pregnancy and birth issues
National Childminders' Association
National Council for One Parent Families
National Eczema Society
National Society for Epilepsy
National Society for the Prevention of Cruelty to
    Children (NSPCC)
National Step-Family Association
Pre-School Playgroups Association
Relate: help with marriage or relationship problems
RoSPA (Royal Society for the Prevention of Accidents)
    Birmingham
RoSPA Scotland, Edinburgh
Samaritans: help with depressed feelings
Sickle Cell Anaemia Relief
Shelter: free information pack on leaving home
Youth Access

Index